T0184934

The Definitive Guide to MongoDB

A Complete Guide to Dealing with Big Data Using MongoDB

Second Edition

David Hows

Peter Membrey

Eelco Plugge

Tim Hawkins

The Definitive Guide to MongoDB: A Complete Guide to Dealing with Big Data Using MongoDB

Copyright © 2013 by David Hows, Peter Membrey, Eelco Plugge, Tim Hawkins

This work is subject to copyright. All rights are reserved by the Publisher, whether the whole or part of the material is concerned, specifically the rights of translation, reprinting, reuse of illustrations, recitation, broadcasting, reproduction on microfilms or in any other physical way, and transmission or information storage and retrieval, electronic adaptation, computer software, or by similar or dissimilar methodology now known or hereafter developed. Exempted from this legal reservation are brief excerpts in connection with reviews or scholarly analysis or material supplied specifically for the purpose of being entered and executed on a computer system, for exclusive use by the purchaser of the work. Duplication of this publication or parts thereof is permitted only under the provisions of the Copyright Law of the Publisher's location, in its current version, and permission for use must always be obtained from Springer. Permissions for use may be obtained through RightsLink at the Copyright Clearance Center. Violations are liable to prosecution under the respective Copyright Law.

ISBN-13 (pbk): 978-1-4302-5821-6

ISBN-13 (electronic): 978-1-4302-5822-3

Trademarked names, logos, and images may appear in this book. Rather than use a trademark symbol with every occurrence of a trademarked name, logo, or image we use the names, logos, and images only in an editorial fashion and to the benefit of the trademark owner, with no intention of infringement of the trademark.

The use in this publication of trade names, trademarks, service marks, and similar terms, even if they are not identified as such, is not to be taken as an expression of opinion as to whether or not they are subject to proprietary rights.

While the advice and information in this book are believed to be true and accurate at the date of publication, neither the authors nor the editors nor the publisher can accept any legal responsibility for any errors or omissions that may be made. The publisher makes no warranty, express or implied, with respect to the material contained herein.

President and Publisher: Paul Manning
Lead Editor: Michelle Lowman
Development Editor: James Markham
Technical Reviewers: Alexandre Beaulne and Stephen Steneker
Editorial Board: Steve Anglin, Mark Beckner, Ewan Buckingham, Gary Cornell, Louise Corrigan, Jim DeWolf, Jonathan Gennick, Jonathan Hassell, Robert Hutchinson, Michelle Lowman, James Markham, Matthew Moodie, Jeff Olson, Jeffrey Pepper, Douglas Pundick, Ben Renow-Clarke, Dominic Shakeshaft, Gwenan Spearing, Matt Wade, Steve Weiss, Tom Welsh
Coordinating Editor: Jill Balzano
Copy Editor: James Compton
Compositor: SPi Global
Indexer: SPi Global
Artist: SPi Global
Cover Designer: Anna Ishchenko

Distributed to the book trade worldwide by Springer Science+Business Media New York, 233 Spring Street, 6th Floor, New York, NY 10013. Phone 1-800-SPRINGER, fax (201) 348-4505, e-mail orders-ny@springer-sbm.com, or visit www.springeronline.com. Apress Media, LLC is a California LLC and the sole member (owner) is Springer Science + Business Media Finance Inc (SSBM Finance Inc). SSBM Finance Inc is a Delaware corporation.

For information on translations, please e-mail rights@apress.com, or visit www.apress.com.

Apress and friends of ED books may be purchased in bulk for academic, corporate, or promotional use. eBook versions and licenses are also available for most titles. For more information, reference our Special Bulk Sales–eBook Licensing web page at www.apress.com/bulk-sales.

Any source code or other supplementary materials referenced by the author in this text is available to readers at www.apress.com. For detailed information about how to locate your book's source code, go to www.apress.com/source-code/.

We would all like to dedicate this book to the same person, someone who only one of us has ever actually met but someone who has had a significant impact on all of our lives. 15 years ago Dave Uden took something of a risk to support one of us and helped us achieve our potential. That support changed everything and profoundly affected how that person saw the world. In the coming years, that person extended the same support openly to others, two of whom he now considers two of his closest friends. All of us feel that our lives would have been very different without that initial support.

To Dave Uden, then, we extend our sincerest thanks. We owe you more than words can say.

Contents at a Glance

Contents

About the Authors

David Hows is an Honors graduate from the University of Woolongong in NSW, Australia. He got his start in computing trying to drive more performance out of his family PC without spending a fortune. This led to a career in IT, where David has worked as a Systems Administrator, Performance Engineer, Software Developer, Solutions Architect, and Database Engineer. David has tried in vain for many years to play soccer well, and his coffee mug reads "Grumble Bum."

Peter Membrey is a Chartered IT Fellow with nearly 15 years of experience using Linux and open source solutions to solve problems in the real world. An RHCE since the age of 17, he has also had the honor of working for Red Hat and writing several books covering open source solutions. He holds a master's degree in IT (Information Security) from the University of Liverpool and is currently a PhD candidate at the Hong Kong Polytechnic University, where his research interests include cloud computing, big data, science, and security. He lives in Hong Kong with his wonderful wife Sarah and son Kaydyn. His Cantonese continues to regress, though his Esperanto is coming along nicely.

Eelco Plugge is a young IET/BSC Professional showing a great interest in the field of IT security. He started working as an encryption specialist at the tender age of 21, and is currently involved in the Mobile Device Management industry while sporadically writing a book. Eelco has recently completed his MSc in Computer Security at the University of Liverpool, holds several professional certifications, and has a passion for Linux, network security, and encryption technologies. Eelco lives in the Netherlands with his young family. Loves sushi, hates overcomplicating matters.

Tim Hawkins produced one of the world's first online classifieds portals in 1993, `loot.com`, before moving on to run engineering for many of Yahoo EU's non-media-based properties, such as search, local search, mail, messenger, and its social networking products. He is currently managing a large offshore team for a major US eTailer, developing and deploying next-gen eCommerce applications. Loves hats, hates complexity.

About the Technical Reviewers

Originally from Canada's great north, **Alexandre Beaulne** pursued a bachelor degree in systems neuroscience at McGill University in Montreal, followed by a master's degree in financial engineering at HEC Montreal. His studies, however, culminated in his attendance at Hacker School in New York City. He has repeatedly made the unsupported claim that he "gets" Haskell's monads.

Stephen Steneker (aka Stennie) is an experienced full stack software developer, consultant, and instructor. Stephen has a long history working for Australian technology startups including founding technical roles at Yahoo! Australia & NZ, HomeScreen Entertainment, and Grox. He holds a BSc (Computer Science) from the University of British Columbia.

In his current role as a Technical Services Engineer for MongoDB, Inc., Stephen provides support, consulting, and training for MongoDB. He frequently speaks at user groups and conferences, and is the founder and wrangler for the Sydney MongoDB User Group (http://www.meetup.com/SydneyMUG/).

You can find him on Twitter, StackOverflow, or Github as @stennie.

Acknowledgments

My thanks to all members of the MongoDB team, past and present. Without them we would not be here, and the way people think about the storage of data would be radically different. I would like to pay extra special thanks to my colleagues at the MongoDB team in Sydney, as without them I would not be here today.

—David Hows

Writing a book is always a team effort. Even when there is just a single author, there are many people working behind the scenes to pull everything together. With that in mind I want to thank everyone in the MongoDB community and everyone at Apress for all their hard work, patience, and support. Special thanks go to Dave and Eelco for really driving the Second Edition home.

I'd also like to thank Chuck Smith, a friend (and founder of the Esperanto language version of Wikipedia) who got me hooked on Esperanto and kept my motivation nice and high. It coincided with my work on the Second Edition, and I am positive that the excitement from learning Esperanto spilled over into this rewrite. Thanks must also go to Dr. L. L. Zamenhof, the man who created Esperanto. A man way ahead of his time, and I hope to carry that dream forward.

Lastly, thanks to my wife Sarah for being patient and supportive as always.

—Peter Membrey

To the 9gag community, without whom this book would have been finished months ago.

—Eelco Plugge

I would like to acknowledge the members of the mongodb-user and mongodb-dev maillists for putting up with my endless questions.

—Tim Hawkins

Introduction

I am a relative latecomer to the world of databases, starting with MySQL in 2006. This followed the logical course for any computer science undergraduate, leading me to develop on a full LAMP stack backed by rudimentary tables. At the time I thought little about the complexities of what went into SQL table management. However, as time has gone on, I have seen the need to store more and more heterogenous data and how a simple schema can grow and morph over time as life takes its toll on systems.

My first introduction to MongoDB was in 2011, when Peter Membrey suggested that instead of a 0 context table of 30 key and 30 value rows, I simply use a MongoDB instance to store data. And like all developers faced with a new technology I scoffed and did what I had originally planned. It wasn't until I was halfway through writing the code to use my horrible monstrosity that Peter insisted I try MongoDB, and I haven't looked back since. Like all newcomers from SQL-land, I was awed by the ability of this system to simply accept whatever data I threw at it and then return it based on whatever criteria I asked. I am still hooked.

—David Hows

Our Approach

And now, in this book, Peter, Eelco Plugge, Tim Hawkins, and I have the goal of presenting you with the same experiences we had in learning the product: teaching you how you can put MongoDB to use for yourself, while keeping things simple and clear. Each chapter presents an individual sample database, so you can read the book in a modular or linear fashion; it's entirely your choice. This means you can skip a certain chapter if you like, without breaking your example databases.

Throughout the book, you will find example commands followed by their output. Both appear in a fixed-width "code" font, with the commands also in boldface to distinguish them from the resulting output. In most chapters, you will also come across tips, warnings, and notes that contain useful, and sometimes vital, information.

—David Hows

## PART 1

MongoDB Basics

CHAPTER 1

■ ■ ■

Introduction to MongoDB

Imagine a world where using a database is so simple that you soon forget you're even using it. Imagine a world where speed and scalability *just work*, and there's no need for complicated configuration or setup. Imagine being able to focus only on the task at hand, get things done, and then—just for a change—leave work on time. That might sound a bit fanciful, but MongoDB promises to help you accomplish all these things (and more).

MongoDB (derived from the word *humongous*) is a relatively new breed of database that has no concept of tables, schemas, SQL, or rows. It doesn't have transactions, ACID compliance, joins, foreign keys, or many of the other features that tend to cause headaches in the early hours of the morning. In short, MongoDB is a very different database than you're probably used to, especially if you've used a relational database management system (RDBMS) in the past. In fact, you might even be shaking your head in wonder at the lack of so-called "standard" features.

Fear not! In the following pages, you will learn about MongoDB's background and guiding principles, and why the MongoDB team made the design decisions that it did. We'll also take a whistle-stop tour of MongoDB's feature list, providing just enough detail to ensure that you'll be completely hooked on this topic for the rest of the book.

We'll start by looking at the philosophy and ideas behind the creation of MongoDB, as well as some of the interesting and somewhat controversial design decisions. We'll explore the concept of document-oriented databases, how they fit together, and what their strengths and weaknesses are. We'll also explore JSON and examine how it applies to MongoDB. To wrap things up, we'll step through some of the notable features of MongoDB.

Reviewing the MongoDB Philosophy

Like all projects, MongoDB has a set of design philosophies that help guide its development. In this section, we'll review some of the database's founding principles.

Using the Right Tool for the Right Job

The most important of the philosophies that underpin MongoDB is the notion that *one size does not fit all*. For many years, traditional relational (SQL) databases (MongoDB is a document-oriented database) have been used for storing content of all types. It didn't matter whether the data was a good fit for the relational model (which is used in all RDBMS databases, such as MySQL, PostgresSQL, SQLite, Oracle, MS SQL Server, and so on); the data was stuffed in there, anyway. Part of the reason for this is that, generally speaking, it's much easier (and more secure) to read and write to a database than it is to write to a file system. If you pick up any book that teaches PHP, such as *PHP for Absolute Beginners,* by Jason Lengstorf (Apress, 2009), you'll probably find that almost right away the database is used to store information, not the file system. It's just so much easier to do things that way. And while using a database as a storage bin works, developers always have to work against the flow. It's usually obvious when we're not using the database the way it was intended; anyone who has ever tried to store information with even slightly complex data, had to set up five tables, and then tried to pull it all together knows what we're talking about!

The MongoDB team decided that it wasn't going to create another database that tries to do everything for everyone. Instead, the team wanted to create a database that worked with documents rather than rows and that was blindingly fast, massively scalable, and easy to use. To do this, the team had to leave some features behind, which means that MongoDB is not an ideal candidate for certain situations. For example, its lack of transaction support means that you wouldn't want to use MongoDB to write an accounting application. That said, MongoDB might be perfect for part of the aforementioned application (such as storing complex data). That's not a problem, though, because there is no reason why you can't use a traditional RDBMS for the accounting components and MongoDB for the document storage. Such hybrid solutions are quite common, and you can see them in production apps such as the New York Times website.

Once you're comfortable with the idea that MongoDB may not solve all your problems, you will discover that there are certain problems that MongoDB is a perfect fit for resolving, such as analytics (think a real-time Google Analytics for your website) and complex data structures (for example, blog posts and comments). If you're still not convinced that MongoDB is a serious database tool, feel free to skip ahead to the "Reviewing the Feature List" section, where you will find an impressive list of features for MongoDB.

■ **Note** The lack of transactions and other traditional database features doesn't mean that MongoDB is unstable or that it cannot be used for managing important data.

Another key concept behind MongoDB's design is that there should always be more than one copy of the database. If a single database should fail, then it can simply be restored from the other servers. Because MongoDB aims to be as fast as possible, it takes some shortcuts that make it more difficult to recover from a crash. The developers believe that most serious crashes are likely to remove an entire computer from service anyway; this means that even if the database were perfectly restored, it would still not be usable. Remember: MongoDB does not try to be everything to everyone. But for many purposes (such as building a web application), MongoDB can be an awesome tool for implementing your solution.

So now you know where MongoDB is coming from. It's not trying to be the best at everything, and it readily acknowledges that it's not for everyone. However, for those who do choose to use it, MongoDB provides a rich document-oriented database that's optimized for speed and scalability. It can also run nearly anywhere you might want to run it. MongoDB's website includes downloads for Linux, Mac OS, Windows, and Solaris.

MongoDB succeeds at all these goals, and this is why using MongoDB (at least for us) is somewhat dream-like. You don't have to worry about squeezing your data into a table—just put the data together, and then pass it to MongoDB for handling.Consider this real-world example. A recent application co-author Peter Membrey worked on needed to store a set of eBay search results. There could be any number of results (up to 100 of them), and he needed an easy way to associate the results with the users in his database.

Had Peter been using MySQL, he would have had to design a table to store the data, write the code to store his results, and then write more code to piece it all back together again. This is a fairly common scenario and one most developers face on a regular basis. Normally, we just get on with it; however, for this project, he was using MongoDB, and so things went a bit differently.

Specifically, he added this line of code:

```
request['ebay_results'] = ebay_results_array
collection.save(request)
```

In this example, request is Peter's document, ebay_results is the key, and ebay_result_array contains the results from eBay. The second line saves the changes. When he accesses this document in the future, he will have the eBay results in exactly the same format as before. He doesn't need any SQL; he doesn't need to perform any conversions; nor does he need to create any new tables or write any special code—MongoDB just worked. It got out of the way, he finished his work early, and he got to go home on time.

Lacking Innate Support for Transactions

Here's another important design decision by MongoDB developers: The database does not include transactional semantics (the element that offers guarantees about data consistency and storage). This is a solid tradeoff based on MongoDB's goal of being simple, fast, and scalable. Once you leave those heavyweight features at the door, it becomes much easier to scale horizontally.

Normally with a traditional RDBMS, you improve performance by buying a bigger, more powerful machine. This is scaling vertically, but you can only take it so far. With horizontal scaling, rather than having one big machine, you have lots of less powerful small machines. Historically, clusters of servers like this were excellent for load-balancing websites, but databases had always been a problem because of internal design limitations.

You might think this missing support constitutes a deal-breaker; however, many people forget that one of the most popular table types in MySQL (MYISAM—which also happens to be the default) doesn't support transactions, either. This fact hasn't stopped MySQL from becoming and remaining the dominant open source database for well over a decade. As with most choices when developing solutions, using MongoDB is going to be a matter of personal preference and whether the tradeoffs fit your project.

■ **Note**   MongoDB offers durability when used in tandem with at least two servers, which is the recommended minimum for production deployments. It is possible to make the master server wait for the replica to confirm receipt of the data before the master server itself confirms that the data has been accepted.

Although single-server durability is not guaranteed, this may change in the future and is currently an area of active interest.

JSON and MongoDB

JSON (Java Script Object Notation) is more than a great way to exchange data; it's also a nice way to store data. An RDBMS is highly structured, with multiple files (tables) that store the individual pieces. MongoDB, on the other hand, stores everything together in a single document. MongoDB is like JSON in this way, and this model provides a rich and expressive way of storing data. Moreover, JSON effectively describes all the content in a given document, so there is no need to specify the structure of the document in advance. JSON is effectively *schemaless* (that is, it doesn't require a schema), because documents can be updated individually or changed independently of any other documents. As an added bonus, JSON also provides excellent performance by keeping all of the related data in one place.

MongoDB doesn't actually use JSON to store the data; rather, it uses an open data format developed by the MongoDB team called *BSON* (pronounced Bee-Son), which is short for binary JSON. For the most part, using BSON instead of JSON won't change how you work with your data. BSON makes MongoDB even faster by making it much easier for a computer to process and search documents. BSON also adds a couple of features that aren't available in standard JSON, including the ability to add types for handling binary data. We'll look at BSON in more depth in "Using Document-Oriented Storage (BSON)," later in this chapter.

The original specification for JSON can be found in RFC 4627, and it was written by Douglas Crockford. JSON allows complex data structures to be represented in a simple, human-readable text format that is generally considered to be much easier to read and understand than XML. Like XML, JSON was envisaged as a way to exchange data between a web client (such as a browser) and web applications. When combined with the rich way that it can describe objects, its simplicity has made it the exchange format of choice for the majority of developers.

You might wonder what is meant here by *complex data structures*. Historically, data was exchanged using the comma-separated values (CSV) format (indeed, this approach remains very common today). CSV is a simple text format that separates rows with a new line and fields with a comma. For example, a CSV file might look like this:

```
Membrey, Peter, +852 1234 5678
Thielen, Wouter, +81 1234 5678
```

A human can look at this information and see quite quickly what information is being communicated. Or maybe not—is that number in the third column a phone number or a fax number? It might even be the number for a pager. To avoid this ambiguity, CSV files often have a header field, in which the first row defines what comes in the file. The following snippet takes the previous example one step further:

```
Lastname, Firstname, Phone Number
Membrey, Peter, +852 1234 5678
Thielen, Wouter, +81 1234 5678
```

Okay, that's a bit better. But now assume some people in the CSV file have more than one phone number. You could add another field for an office phone number, but you face a new set of issues if you want several office phone numbers. And you face yet another set of issues if you also want to incorporate multiple e-mail addresses. Most people have more than one, and these addresses can't usually be neatly defined as either home or work. Suddenly, CSV starts to show its limitations. CSV files are only good for storing data that is flat and doesn't have repeating values. Similarly, it's not uncommon for several CSV files to be provided, each with the separate bits of information. These files are then combined (usually in an RDBMS) to create the whole picture. As an example, a large retail company may receive sales data in the form of CSV files from each of its stores at the end of each day. These files must be combined before the company can see how it performed on a given day. This process is not exactly straightforward, and it certainly increases chances of a mistake as the number of required files grows.

XML largely solves this problem, but using XML for most things is a bit like using a sledgehammer to crack a nut: it works, but it feels like overkill. The reason for this is that XML is highly extensible. Rather than define a particular data format, XML defines how you define a data format. This can be useful when you need to exchange complex and highly structured data; however, for simple data exchange, it often results in too much work. Indeed, this scenario is the source of the phrase "XML hell."

JSON provides a happy medium. Unlike CSV, it can store structured content; but unlike XML, JSON makes the content easy to understand and simple to use. Let's revisit the previous example; however, this time you will use JSON rather than CSV:

```
{
    "firstname": "Peter",
    "lastname": "Membrey",
    "phone_numbers": [
        "+852 1234 5678",
        "+44 1234 565 555"
    ]
}
```

In this version of the example, each JSON object (or document) contains all the information needed to understand it. If you look at phone_numbers, you can see that it contains a list of different numbers. This list can be as large as you want. You could also be more specific about the type of number being recorded, as in this example:

```
{
    "firstname": "Peter",
    "lastname": "Membrey",
    "numbers": [
        {
            "phone": "+852 1234 5678"
        },
        {
            "fax": "+44 1234 565 555"
        }
    ]
}
```

This version of the example improves on things a bit more. Now you can clearly see what each number is for. JSON is extremely expressive, and, although it's quite easy to write JSON by hand, it is usually generated automatically in software. For example, Python includes a module called (somewhat predictably) `json` that takes existing Python objects and automatically converts them to JSON. Because JSON is supported and used on so many platforms, it is an ideal choice for exchanging data.

When you add items such as the list of phone numbers, you are actually creating what is known as an *embedded document*. This happens whenever you add complex content such as a list (or *array*, to use the term favored in JSON). Generally speaking, there is also a logical distinction. For example, a `Person` document might have several `Address` documents embedded inside it. Similarly, an `Invoice` document might have numerous `LineItem` documents embedded inside it. Of course, the embedded `Address` document could also have its own embedded document that contains phone numbers, for example.

Whether you choose to embed a particular document is determined when you decide how to store your information. This is usually referred to as *schema design*. It might seem odd to refer to schema design when MongoDB is considered a schemaless database. However, while MongoDB doesn't force you to create a schema or enforce one that you create, you do still need to think about how your data fits together. We'll look at this in more depth in Chapter 3.

Adopting a Nonrelational Approach

Improving performance with a relational database is usually straightforward: you buy a bigger, faster server. And this works great until you reach the point where there isn't a bigger server available to buy. At that point, the only option is to spread out to two servers. This might sound easy, but it is a stumbling block for most databases. For example, neither MySQL nor PostgresSQL can run a single database on two servers, where both servers can both read and write data (often referred to as an *active/active cluster*). And although Oracle can do this with its impressive Real Application Clusters (RAC) architecture, you can expect to take out a mortgage if you want to use that solution—implementing a RAC-based solution requires multiple servers, shared storage, and several software licenses.

You might wonder why having an active/active cluster on two databases is so difficult. When you query your database, the database has to find all the relevant data and link it all together. RDBMS solutions feature many ingenious ways to improve performance, but they all rely on having a complete picture of the data available. And this is where you hit a wall: this approach simply doesn't work when half the data is on another server.

Of course, you might have a small database that simply gets lots of requests, so you just need to share the workload. Unfortunately, here you hit another wall. You need to ensure that data written to the first server is available to the second server. And you face additional issues if updates are made on two separate masters simultaneously. For example, you need to determine which update is the correct one. Another problem you can encounter: someone might query the second server for information that has just been written to the first server, but that information hasn't been updated yet on the second server. When you consider all these issues, it becomes easy to see why the Oracle solution is so expensive—these problems are extremely hard to address.

MongoDB solves the active/active cluster problems in a very clever way—it avoids them completely. Recall that MongoDB stores data in BSON documents, so the data is self-contained. That is, although similar documents are stored together, individual documents aren't made up of relationships. This means that everything you need is all in one place. Because queries in MongoDB look for specific keys and values in a document, this information can be easily spread across as many servers as you have available. Each server checks the content it has and returns the result. This effectively allows almost linear scalability and performance. As an added bonus, it doesn't even require that you take out a new mortgage to pay for this functionality.

Admittedly, MongoDB does not offer *master/master replication*, in which two separate servers can both accept write requests. However, it does have *sharding*, which allows data to split across multiple machines, with each machine responsible for updating different parts of the dataset. The benefit of this design is that, while some solutions allow two master databases, MongoDB can potentially scale to hundreds of machines as easily as it can run on two.

Opting for Performance vs. Features

Performance is important, but MongoDB also provides a large feature set. We've already discussed some of the features MongoDB doesn't implement, and you might be somewhat skeptical of the claim that MongoDB achieves its impressive performance partly by judiciously excising certain features common to other databases. However, there are analogous database systems available that are extremely fast, but also extremely limited, such as those that implement a key/value store.

A perfect example is *memcached*. This application was written to provide high-speed data caching, and it is mind-numbingly fast. When used to cache website content, it can speed up an application many times over. This application is used by extremely large websites, such as Facebook and LiveJournal.

The catch is that this application has two significant shortcomings. First, it is a memory-only database. If the power goes out, then all the data is lost. Second, you can't actually search for data using memcached; you can only request specific keys.

These might sound like serious limitations; however, you must remember the problems that memcached is designed to solve. First and foremost, memcached is a data cache. That is, it's not supposed to be a permanent data store, but only to provide a caching layer for your existing database. When you build a dynamic web page, you generally request very specific data (such as the current top ten articles). This means you can specifically ask memcached for that data—there is no need to perform a search. If the cache is out-of-date or empty, you would query your database as normal, build up the data, and then store it in memcached for future use.

Once you accept these limitations, you can see how memcached offers superb performance by implementing a very limited feature set. This performance, by the way, is unmatched by that of a traditional database. That said, memcached certainly can't replace an RDBMS. The important thing to keep in mind is that it's not supposed to.

Compared to memcached, MongoDB is itself feature-rich. To be useful, MongoDB must offer a strong set of features, such as the ability to search for specific documents. It must also be able to store those documents on disk, so that they can survive a reboot. Fortunately, MongoDB provides enough features to be a strong contender for most web applications and many other types of applications as well.

Like memcached, MongoDB is not a one-size-fits-all database. As is usually the case in computing, tradeoffs must be made to achieve the intended goals of the application.

Running the Database Anywhere

MongoDB is written in C++, which makes it relatively easy to port and/or run the application practically anywhere. Currently, binaries can be downloaded from the MongoDB website for Linux, Mac OS, Windows, and Solaris. There are also various official versions available for Fedora and CentOS, among other platforms. You can even download the source code and build your own MongoDB, although it is recommended that you use the provided binaries wherever possible. All the binaries are available in both 32-bit and 64-bit versions.

■ **Caution** The 32-bit version of MongoDB is limited to databases of 2GB or less. This is because MongoDB uses memory-mapped files internally to achieve high performance. Anything larger than 2GB on a 32-bit system would require some fancy footwork that wouldn't be fast and would also complicate the application's code. The official stance on this limitation is that 64-bit environments are easily available; therefore, increasing code complexity is not a good tradeoff. The 64-bit version for all intents and purposes has no such restriction.

MongoDB's modest requirements allow it to run on high-powered servers or virtual machines, and even to power cloud-based applications. By keeping things simple and focusing on speed and efficiency, MongoDB provides solid performance wherever you choose to deploy it.

Fitting Everything Together

Before we look at MongoDB's feature list, we need to review a few basic terms. MongoDB doesn't require much in the way of specialized knowledge to get started, and many of the terms specific to MongoDB can be loosely translated to RDBMS equivalents that you are probably already familiar with. Don't worry, though; we'll explain each term fully. Even if you're not familiar with standard database terminology, you will still be able to follow along easily.

Generating or Creating a Key

A document represents the unit of storage in MongoDB. In an RDBMS, this would be called a row. However, documents are much more than rows because they can store complex information such as lists, dictionaries, and even lists of dictionaries. In contrast to a traditional database where a row is fixed, a document in MongoDB can be made up of any number of keys and values (you'll learn more about this in the next section). Ultimately, a *key* is nothing more than a label; it is roughly equivalent to the name you might give to a column in an RDBMS. You use a key to reference pieces of data inside your document.

In a relational database, there should always be some way to uniquely identify a given record; otherwise it becomes impossible to refer to a specific row. To that end, you are supposed to include a field that holds a unique value (called a *primary key*) or a collection of fields that can uniquely identify the given row (called a *compound primary key*).

MongoDB requires that each document have a unique identifier for much the same reason; in MongoDB, this identifier is called _id. Unless you specify a value for this field, MongoDB will generate a unique value for you. Even in the well-established world of RDBMS databases, opinion is divided as to whether you should use a unique key provided by the database or generate a unique key yourself. Recently, it has become more popular to allow the database to create the key for you.

The reason for this is that human-created unique numbers such as car registration numbers have a nasty habit of changing. For example, in 2001, the United Kingdom implemented a new number plate scheme that was completely different from the previous system. It happens that MongoDB can cope with this type of change perfectly well; however, chances are that you would need to do some careful thinking if you used the registration plate as your primary key. A similar scenario may have occurred when the ISBN (International Standard Book Number) scheme was upgraded from 10 digits to 13.

Previously, most developers who used MongoDB seemed to prefer creating their own unique keys, taking it upon themselves to ensure that the number would remain unique. Today, though, general consensus seems to point at using the default ID value that MongoDB creates for you. However, as is the case when working with RDBMS databases, the approach you choose mostly comes down to personal preference. We prefer to use a database-provided value because it means we can be sure the key is unique and independent of anything else. Others, as noted, prefer to provide their own keys.

Ultimately, you must decide what works best for you. If you are confident that your key is unique (and likely to remain unchanged), then you should probably feel free to use it. If you're unsure about your key's uniqueness or you don't want to worry about it, then you can simply use the default key provided by MongoDB.

Using Keys and Values

Documents are made up of keys and values. Let's take another look at the example discussed previously in this chapter:

```
{
    "firstname": "Peter",
    "lastname": "Membrey",
    "phone_numbers": [
        "+852 1234 5678",
        "+44 1234 565 555"
    ]
}
```

Keys and values always come in pairs. Unlike an RDBMS, where every field must have a value, even if it's NULL (somewhat paradoxically, this means *unknown*), MongoDB doesn't require that a document have a particular value. For example, if you don't know the phone number for a particular person on your list, you simply leave it out. A popular analogy for this sort of thing is a business card. If you have a fax number, you usually put it on your business card; however, if you don't have one, you don't write: "Fax number: none." Instead, you simply leave the information out. If the key/value pair isn't included in a MongoDB document, it is assumed not to exist.

Implementing Collections

Collections are somewhat analogous to tables, but they are far less rigid. A collection is a lot like a box with a label on it. You might have a box at home labeled "DVDs" into which you put, well, your DVDs. This makes sense, but there is nothing stopping you from putting CDs or even tapes into this box if you wanted to. In an RDBMS, tables are strictly defined, and you can only put designated items into the table. In MongoDB, a collection is simply that: a collection of similar items. The items don't have to be similar (MongoDB is inherently flexible); however, once we start looking at indexing and more advanced queries, you'll soon see the benefits of placing similar items in a collection.

While you could mix various items together in a collection, there's little need to do so. Had the collection been called media, then all of the DVDs, CDs, and tapes would be at home there. After all, these items all have things in common, such as an artist name, a release date, and content. In other words, it really does depend on your application whether certain documents should be stored in the same collection. Performance-wise, having multiple collections is no slower than having only one collection. Remember: MongoDB is about making your life easier, so you should do whatever feels right to you.

Last but not least, collections are effectively created on demand. Specifically, a collection is created when you first attempt to save a document that references it. This means that you could create collections on demand (not that you necessarily should). Because MongoDB also lets you create indexes and perform other database-level commands dynamically, you can leverage this behavior to build some very dynamic applications.

Understanding Databases

Perhaps the easiest way to think of a database in MongoDB is as a collection of collections. Like collections, databases can be created on demand. This means that it's easy to create a database for each customer—your application code can even do it for you. You can do this with databases other than MongoDB, as well; however, creating databases in this manner with MongoDB is a very natural process. That said, just because you can create a database in this manner doesn't mean you have to or even that you should. All the same, you have that power if you want to exercise it.

Reviewing the Feature List

Now that you understand what MongoDB is and what it offers, it's time to run through its feature list. You can find a complete list of MongoDB's features on the database's website at www.mongodb.org/; be sure to visit this site for an up-to-date list of them. The feature list in this chapter covers a fair bit of material that goes on behind the scenes, but you don't need to be familiar with every feature listed to use MongoDB itself. In other words, if you feel your eyes beginning to close as you review this list, feel free to jump to the end of the section!

Using Document-Oriented Storage (BSON)

We've already discussed MongoDB's document-oriented design. We've also briefly touched on BSON. As you learned, JSON makes it much easier to store and retrieve documents in their real form, effectively removing the need for any sort of mapper or special conversion code. The fact that this feature also makes it much easier for MongoDB to scale up is icing on the cake.

BSON is an open standard; you can find its specification at `http://bsonspec.org/`. When people hear that BSON is a binary form of JSON, they expect it to take up much less room than text-based JSON. However, that isn't necessarily the case; indeed, there are many cases where the BSON version takes up more space than its JSON equivalent.

You might wonder why you should use BSON at all. After all, CouchDB (another powerful document-oriented database) uses pure JSON, and it's reasonable to wonder whether it's worth the trouble of converting documents back and forth between BSON and JSON.

First, we must remember that MongoDB is designed to be fast, rather than space-efficient. This doesn't mean that MongoDB wastes space (it doesn't); however, a small bit of overhead in storing a document is perfectly acceptable if that makes it faster to process the data (which it does). In short, BSON is much easier to *traverse* (that is, to look through) and index very quickly. Although BSON requires slightly more disk space than JSON, this extra space is unlikely to be a problem, because disks are cheap, and MongoDB can scale across machines. The tradeoff in this case is quite reasonable: you exchange a bit of extra disk space for better query and indexing performance.

The second key benefit to using BSON is that it is easy and quick to convert BSON to a programming language's native data format. If the data were stored in pure JSON, a relatively high-level conversion would need to take place. There are MongoDB drivers for a large number of programming languages (such as Python, Ruby, PHP, C, C++, and C#), and each works slightly differently. Using a simple binary format, native data structures can be quickly built for each language, without requiring that you first process JSON. This makes the code simpler and faster, both of which are in keeping with MongoDB's stated goals.

BSON also provides some extensions to JSON. For example, it enables you to store binary data and to incorporate a specific datatype. Thus, while BSON can store any JSON document, a valid BSON document may not be valid JSON. This doesn't matter, because each language has its own driver that converts data to and from BSON without needing to use JSON as an intermediary language.

At the end of the day, BSON is not likely to be a big factor in how you use MongoDB. Like all great tools, MongoDB will quietly sit in the background and do what it needs to do. Apart from possibly using a graphical tool to look at your data, you will generally work in your native language and let the driver worry about persisting to MongoDB.

Supporting Dynamic Queries

MongoDB's support for dynamic queries means that you can run a query without planning for it in advance. This is similar to being able to run SQL queries against an RDBMS. You might wonder why this is listed as a feature; surely it is something that every database supports—right?

Actually, no. For example, CouchDB (which is generally considered MongoDB's biggest "competitor") doesn't support dynamic queries. This is because CouchDB has come up with a completely new (and admittedly exciting) way of thinking about data. A traditional RDBMS has static data and dynamic queries. This means that the structure of the data is fixed in advance—tables must be defined, and each row has to fit into that structure. Because the database knows in advance how the data is structured, it can make certain assumptions and optimizations that enable fast dynamic queries.

CouchDB has turned this on its head. As a document-oriented database, CouchDB is schemaless, so the data is dynamic. However, the new idea here is that queries are static. That is, you define them in advance, before you can use them.

This isn't as bad as it might sound, because many queries can be easily defined in advance. For example, a system that lets you search for a book will probably let you search by ISBN. In CouchDB, you would create an index that builds a list of all the ISBNs for all the documents. When you punch in an ISBN, the query is very fast because it doesn't actually need to search for any data. Whenever new data is added to the system, CouchDB will automatically update its index.

Technically, you can run a query against CouchDB without generating an index; in that case, however, CouchDB will have to create the index itself before it can process your query. This won't be a problem if you only have a hundred books; however, it will result in poor performance if you're filing hundreds of thousands of books, because each query will generate the index again (and again). For this reason, the CouchDB team does not recommend dynamic queries—that is, queries that haven't been predefined—in production.

CouchDB also lets you write your queries as map and reduce functions. If that sounds like a lot of effort, then you're in good company; CouchDB has a somewhat severe learning curve. In fairness to CouchDB, an experienced programmer can probably pick it up quite quickly; for most people, however, the learning curve is probably steep enough that they won't bother with the tool.

Fortunately for us mere mortals, MongoDB is much easier to use. We'll cover how to use MongoDB in more detail throughout the book, but here's the short version: in MongoDB, you simply provide the parts of the document you want to match against, and MongoDB does the rest. MongoDB can do much more, however. For example, you won't find MongoDB lacking if you want to use map or reduce functions. At the same time, you can ease into using MongoDB; you don't have to know all of the tool's advanced features up front.

Indexing Your Documents

MongoDB includes extensive support for indexing your documents, a feature that really comes in handy when you're dealing with tens of thousands of documents. Without an index, MongoDB will have to look at each individual document in turn to see whether it is something that you want to see. This is like asking a librarian for a particular book and watching as he works his way around the library looking at each and every book. With an indexing system (libraries tend to use the Dewey Decimal system), he can find the area where the book you are looking for lives and very quickly determine if it is there.

Unlike a library book, all documents in MongoDB are automatically indexed on the _id key. This key is considered a special case because you cannot delete it; the index is what ensures that each value is unique. One of the benefits of this key is that you can be assured that each document is uniquely identifiable, something that isn't guaranteed by an RDBMS.

When you create your own indexes, you can decide whether you want them to enforce uniqueness. If you do decide to create a unique index, you can tell MongoDB to drop all the duplicates. This may or may not be what you want, so you should think carefully before using this option because you might accidentally delete half your data. By default, an error will be returned if you try to create a unique index on a key that has duplicate values.

There are many occasions where you will want to create an index that allows duplicates. For example, if your application searches by lastname, it makes sense to build an index on the lastname key. Of course, you cannot guarantee that each lastname will be unique; and in any database of a reasonable size, duplicates are practically guaranteed.

MongoDB's indexing abilities don't end there, however. MongoDB can also create indexes on embedded documents. For example, if you store numerous addresses in the address key, you can create an index on the ZIP or postal code. This means that you can easily pull back a document based on any postal code—and do so very quickly.

MongoDB takes this a step further by allowing *composite indexes*. In a composite index, two or more keys are used to build a given index. For example, you might build an index that combines both the lastname and firstname tags. A search for a full name would be very quick because MongoDB can quickly isolate the lastname and then, just as quickly, isolate the firstname.

We will look at indexing in more depth in Chapter 10, but suffice it to say that MongoDB has you covered as far as indexing is concerned.

Leveraging Geospatial Indexes

One form of indexing worthy of special mention is *geospatial indexing*. This new, specialized indexing technique was introduced in MongoDB 1.4. You use this feature to index location-based data, enabling you to answer queries such as how many items are within a certain distance from a given set of coordinates.

As an increasing number of web applications start making use of location-based data, this feature will play an increasingly prominent role in everyday development. For now, though, geospatial indexing remains a somewhat niche feature; nevertheless, you will be very glad it's there if you ever find that you need it.

Profiling Queries

A built-in profiling tool lets you see how MongoDB works out which documents to return. This is useful because, in many cases, a query can be easily improved simply by adding an index. If you have a complicated query, and you're not really sure why it's running so slowly, then the query profiler can provide you with extremely valuable information. Again, you'll learn more about the MongoDB Profiler in Chapter 10.

Updating Information In-Place

When a database updates a row (or in the case of MongoDB, a document), it has a couple of choices about how to do it. Many databases choose the multi-version concurrency control (MVCC) approach, which allows multiple users to see different versions of the data. This approach is useful because it ensures that the data won't be changed partway through by another program during a given transaction.

The downside to this approach is that the database needs to track multiple copies of the data. For example, CouchDB provides very strong versioning, but this comes at the cost of writing the data out in its entirety. While this ensures that the data is stored in a robust fashion, it also increases complexity and reduces performance.

MongoDB, on the other hand, updates information *in-place*. This means that (in contrast to CouchDB) MongoDB can update the data wherever it happens to be. This typically means that no extra space needs to be allocated, and the indexes can be left untouched.

Another benefit of this method is that MongoDB performs *lazy writes*. Writing to and from memory is very fast, but writing to disk is thousands of times slower. This means that you want to limit reading and writing from the disk as much as possible. This isn't possible in CouchDB, because that program ensures that each document is quickly written to disk. While this approach guarantees that the data is written safely to disk, it also impacts performance significantly.

MongoDB only writes to disk when it has to, which is usually once every second or so. This means that if a value is being updated many times a second—a not uncommon scenario if you're using a value as a page counter or for live statistics—then the value will only be written once, rather than the thousands of times that CouchDB would require.

This approach makes MongoDB much faster, but, again, it comes with a tradeoff. CouchDB may be slower, but it does guarantee that data is stored safely on the disk. MongoDB makes no such guarantee, and this is why a traditional RDBMS is probably a better solution for managing critical data such as billing or accounts receivable.

Storing Binary Data

GridFS is MongoDB's solution to storing binary data in the database. BSON supports saving up to 4MB of binary data in a document, and this may well be enough for your needs. For example, if you want to store a profile picture or a sound clip, then 4MB might be more space than you need. On the other hand, if you want to store movie clips, high-quality audio clips, or even files that are several hundred megabytes in size, then MongoDB has you covered here, too.

GridFS works by storing the information about the file (called *metadata*) in the files collection. The data itself is broken down into pieces called *chunks* that are stored in the chunks collection. This approach makes storing data both easy and scalable; it also makes range operations (such as retrieving specific parts of a file) much easier to use.

Generally speaking, you would use GridFS through your programming language's MongoDB driver, so it's unlikely you'd ever have to get your hands dirty at such a low level. As with everything else in MongoDB, GridFS is designed for both speed and scalability. This means you can be confident that MongoDB will be up to the task if you want to work with large data files.

Replicating Data

When we talked about the guiding principles behind MongoDB, we mentioned that RDBMS databases offer certain guarantees for data storage that are not available in MongoDB. These guarantees weren't implemented for a handful of reasons. First, these features would slow the database down. Second, they would greatly increase the complexity of the program. Third, it was felt that the most common failure on a server would be hardware, which would render the data unusable anyway, even if the data were safely saved to disk.

Of course, none of this means that data safety isn't important. MongoDB wouldn't be of much use if you couldn't count on being able to access the data when you need it. Initially, MongoDB provided a safety net with a feature called master-slave replication, in which only one database is active for writing at any given time, an approach that is also fairly common in the RDBMS world. This feature has since been replaced with *replica sets*, and basic master-slave replication has been deprecated and should no longer be used.

Replica sets have one primary server (similar to a master), which handles all the write requests from clients. Because there is only one primary server in a given set, it can guarantee that all writes are handled properly. When a write occurs it is logged in the primary's 'oplog'.

The oplog is replicated by the secondary servers (of which there can be many) and used to bring themselves up to date with the master. Should the master fail at any given time, one of the secondaries will become the primary and take over responsibility for handling client write requests.

Implementing Sharding

For those involved with large-scale deployments, auto-sharding will probably prove one of MongoDB's most significant and oft-used features.

In an *auto-sharding* scenario, MongoDB takes care of all the data splitting and recombination for you. It makes sure the data goes to the right server and that queries are run and combined in the most efficient manner possible. In fact, from a developer's point of view, there is no difference between talking to a MongoDB database with a hundred shards and talking to a single MongoDB server. This feature is not yet production-ready; when it is, however, it will push MongoDB's scalability through the roof.

In the meantime, if you're just starting out or you're building your first MongoDB-based website, then you'll probably find that a single instance of MongoDB is sufficient for your needs. If you end up building the next Facebook or Amazon, however, you will be glad that you built your site on a technology that can scale so limitlessly. Sharding is the topic of Chapter 12 of this book.

Using Map and Reduce Functions

For many people, hearing the term *MapReduce* sends shivers down their spines. At the other extreme, many RDBMS advocates scoff at the complexity of map and reduce functions. It's scary for some because these functions require a completely different way of thinking about finding and sorting your data, and many professional programmers have trouble getting their heads around the concepts that underpin map and reduce functions. That said, these functions provide an extremely powerful way to query data. In fact, CouchDB supports only this approach, which is one reason it has such a high learning curve.

MongoDB doesn't require that you use map and reduce functions. In fact, MongoDB relies on a simple querying syntax that is more akin to what you see in MySQL. However, MongoDB does make these functions available for those who want them. The map and reduce functions are written in JavaScript and run on the server. The job of the map function is to find all the documents that meet a certain criteria. These results are then passed to the reduce function, which processes the data. The reduce function doesn't usually return a collection of documents; rather, it returns a new document that contains the information derived. As a general rule, if you would normally use GROUP BY in SQL, then the map and reduce functions are probably the right tools for the job in MongoDB.

■ **Note** You should not think of MongoDB's map and reduce functions as poor imitations of the approach adopted by CouchDB. If you so desired, you could use MongoDB's map and reduce functions for everything in lieu of MongoDB's innate query support.

The All-New Aggregation Framework

MapReduce is a very powerful tool, but it has one major drawback; it's not exactly easy to use. Many database systems are used for reporting, and SQL databases in particular make this very easy. If you want to group results or find the maximum and average, then it's very simple to express that idea and get the result you're looking for. Unfortunately, it's not quite so simple to do that in MapReduce, and you effectively have to do all the wiring up yourself. This can often mean that an otherwise simple task is unnecessary challenging.

In response to this, MongoDB Inc (previously 10gen) added the aggregation framework. It is pipeline-based, and allows you to take individual pieces of a query and string them together in order to get the result you're looking for. This maintains the benefits of MongoDB's document oriented design while still providing high performance.

So if you need all the power of MapReduce, you still have it at your beck and call. If you just want to do some basic statistics and number crunching, you're going to love the new aggregation framework. You'll learn more about the aggregation framework and its commands in Chapters 4 and 6.

Getting Help

MongoDB has a great community, and the core developers are very active and easily approachable, and they typically go to great lengths to help other members of the community. MongoDB is easy to use and comes with great documentation; however, it's still nice to know that you're not alone, and help is available, should you need it.

Visiting the Website

The first place to look for updated information or help is on the MongoDB website (`www://mongodb.org`). This site is updated regularly and contains all the latest MongoDB goodness. On this site, you can find drivers, tutorials, examples, frequently asked questions, and much more.

Chatting with the MongoDB Developers

The MongoDB developers hang out on Internet Relay Chat (IRC) at #MongoDB on the Freenode network (`www.freenode.net`). MongoDB's developers are based in New York, but they are often found chatting in this channel well into the night. Of course, the developers do need to sleep at some point (coffee only works for so long!); fortunately, there are also many knowledgeable MongoDB users from around the world who are ready to help out. Many people who visit the #MongoDB channel aren't experts; however, the general atmosphere is so friendly that they stick around anyway. Please feel free to join #MongoDB channel and chat with people there—you may find some great hints and tips. If you're really stuck, you'll probably be able to quickly get back on track.

Cutting and Pasting MongoDB Code

Pastie (`http://pastie.org`) is not strictly a MongoDB site; however, it is something you will come across if you float about in #MongoDB for any length of time. The Pastie site basically lets you cut and paste (hence the name) some output or program code, and then put it online for others to view. In IRC, pasting multiple lines of text can be messy or hard to read. If you need to post a fair bit of text (such as three lines or more), then you should visit `http://pastie.org`, paste in your content, and then paste the link to your new page into the channel.

Finding Solutions on Google Groups

MongoDB also has a Google group called `mongodb-user` (`http://groups.google.com/group/mongodb-user`). This group is a great place to ask questions or search for answers. You can also interact with the group via e-mail. Unlike IRC, which is very transient, the Google group is a great long-term resource. If you really want to get involved with the MongoDB community, joining the group is a great way to start.

Leveraging the JIRA Tracking System

MongoDB uses the JIRA issue-tracking system. You can view the tracking site at http://jira.mongodb.org/, and you are actively encouraged to report any bugs or problems that you come across to this site. Reporting such issues is viewed by the community as a genuinely good thing to do. Of course, you can also search through previous issues, and you can even view the roadmap and planned updates for the next release.

If you haven't posted to JIRA before, you might want to visit the IRC room first. You will quickly find out whether you've found something new, and if so, you will be shown how to go about reporting it.

Summary

This chapter has provided a whistle-stop tour of the benefits MongoDB brings to the table. We've looked at the philosophies and guiding principles behind MongoDB's creation and development, as well as the tradeoffs MongoDB's developers made when implementing these ideals. We've also looked at some of the key terms used in conjunction with MongoDB, how they fit together, and their rough SQL equivalents.

Next, we looked at some of the features MongoDB offers, including how and where you might want to use them. Finally, we wrapped up the chapter with a quick overview of the community and where you can go to get help, should you need it.

■ ■ ■

## CHAPTER 2

Installing MongoDB

In Chapter 1, you got a taste of what MongoDB can do for you. In this chapter, you will learn how to install and expand MongoDB to do even more, enabling you to use it in combination with your favorite programming language.

MongoDB is a cross-platform database, and you can find a significant list of available packages to download from the MongoDB website (www.mongodb.org). The wealth of available versions might make it difficult to decide which version is the right one for you. The right choice for you probably depends on the operating system your server uses, the kind of processor in your server, and whether you prefer a stable release or would like to take a dive into a version that is still in development but offers exciting new features. Perhaps you'd like to install both a stable and a forward-looking version of the database. It's also possible you're not entirely sure which version you should choose yet. In any case, read on!

Choosing Your Version

When you look at the Download section on the MongoDB website, you will see a rather straightforward overview of the packages available for download. The first thing you need to pay attention to is the operating system you are going to run the MongoDB software on. Currently, there are precompiled packages available for Windows, various flavors of the Linux operating system, Mac OS, and Solaris.

■ **Note** An important thing to remember here is the difference between the 32-bit release and the 64-bit release of the product. The 32-bit and 64-bit versions of the database currently have the same functionality, with one exception: the 32-bit release is limited to a total dataset size of approximately 2GB per server. The 64-bit version does not carry this restriction, however, so it's generally preferred over the 32-bit version for production environments. Also, the differences between these versions are subject to change.

You will also need to pay attention to the *version* of the MongoDB software itself: there are production releases, previous releases, and development releases. The *production* release indicates that it's the most recent stable version available. When a newer and generally improved or enhanced version is released, the prior most recent stable version will be made available as a *previous release*. This designation means the release is stable and reliable, but it usually has fewer features available in it. Finally, there's the *development release*. This release is generally referred to as the unstable version. This version is still in development, and it will include many changes, including significant new features. Although it has not been fully developed and tested yet, the developers of MongoDB have made it available to the public to test or otherwise try out.

Understanding the Version Numbers

MongoDB uses the "odd-numbered versions for development releases" approach. In other words, you can tell by looking at the second part of the version number (also called the release number) whether a version is a development version or a stable version. If the second number is even, then it's a *stable* release. If the second number is odd, then it's an *unstable*, or *development*, release.

Let's take a closer look at the three digits included in a version number's three parts, A, B, and C:

- A, the first (or leftmost) number: Represents the major version and only changes when there is a full version upgrade.

- B, the second (or middle) number: Represents the release number and indicates whether a version is a development version or a stable version. If the number is even, the version is stable; if the number is odd, the version is unstable and considered a development release.

- C, the third (or rightmost) number: Represents the revision number; this is used for bugs and security issues.

For example, at the time of writing, the following versions were available from the MongoDB website:

- 2.4.3 (Production release)

- 2.2.4 (Previous release)

- 2.5.0 (Development release)

Installing MongoDB on Your System

So far, you've learned which versions of MongoDB are available and—hopefully—were able to select one. Now you're ready to take a closer look at how to install MongoDB on your particular system. The two main operating systems for servers at the moment are based on Linux and Microsoft Windows, so this chapter will walk you through how to install MongoDB on both of these operating systems, beginning with Linux.

Installing MongoDB under Linux

The Unix-based operating systems are extremely popular choices at the moment for hosting services, including web services, mail services, and, of course, database services. In this chapter, we'll walk you through how to get MongoDB running on a popular Linux distribution: Ubuntu.

Depending on your needs, you have two ways of installing MongoDB under Ubuntu: you can install the packages automatically through so-called *repositories*, or you can install it manually. The next two sections will walk you through both options.

Installing MongoDB through the Repositories

Repositories are basically online directories filled with software. Every package contains information about the version number, prerequisites, and possible incompatibilities. This information is useful when you need to install a software package that requires another piece of software to be installed first because the prerequisites can be installed at the same time.

The default repositories available in Ubuntu (and other Debian-based distributions) contain MongoDB, but they may be out-of-date versions of the software. Therefore, let's tell apt-get (the software you use to install software from repositories) to look at a custom repository. To do this, you need to add the following line to your repository-list (/etc/apt/sources.list):

```
deb http://downloads-distro.mongodb.org/repo/ubuntu-upstart dist 10gen
```

Next, you need to import 10gen's public GPG key, used to sign the packages, ensuring their consistency; you can do so by using the apt-key command:

```
$ sudo apt-key adv --keyserver keyserver.ubuntu.com --recv 7F0CEB10
```

When that is done, you need to tell apt-get that it contains new repositories; you can do so using apt-get's update command:

```
$ sudo apt-get update
```

This line made aptitude aware of your manually added repository. This means you can now tell apt-get to install the software itself. You do this by typing the following command in the shell:

```
$ sudo apt-get install mongodb-10gen
```

This line installs the current stable (production) version from MongoDB. If you wish to install any other version from MongoDB instead, you need to specify the version number. For example, to install the current unstable (development) version from MongoDB, type in the following command instead:

```
$ sudo apt-get install mongodb-10gen=2.5.0
```

That's all there is to it. At this point, MongoDB has been installed and is (almost) ready to use!

■ **Note** Running apt-get update on a system running an older version of MongoDB will upgrade the software to the latest stable version available. You can prevent this from happening by running this command:

```
echo "mongodb-10gen hold" | sudo dpkg --set-selections
```

Installing MongoDB Manually

Next, we'll cover how to install MongoDB manually. Given how easy it is to install MongoDB with aptitude automatically, you might wonder why you would want to install the software manually. For starters, not all Linux distributions use apt-get. Sure, many of them do (including primarily the ones that are based on Debian Linux), but some don't. Also, the packaging remains a *work in progress*, so it might be the case that there are versions not yet available through the repositories. It's also possible that the version of MongoDB you want to use isn't included in the repository. Installing the software manually also gives you the ability to run multiple versions of MongoDB at the same time.

You've decided which version of MongoDB you would like to use, and you've downloaded it from their website, http://mongodb.org/downloads, to your Home directory. Next, you need to extract the package with the following command:

```
$ tar xzf mongodb-linux-x86_64-latest.tgz
```

This command extracts the entire contents of the package to a new directory called mongodb-linux-x86_64-xxxx-yy-zz; this directory is located under your current directory. This directory will contain a number of subdirectories and files. The directory that contains the executable files is called the bin directory. We will cover which applications perform which tasks shortly.

However, you don't need to do anything further to install the application. Indeed, it doesn't take much more time to install MongoDB manually—depending on what else you need to install, it might even be faster. Manually installing MongoDB does have some downsides, however. For example, the executables that you just extracted and found in the bin directory can't be executed from anywhere except the bin directory by default. Thus, if you want to run the mongod service, you will need to do so directly from the aforementioned bin directory. This downside highlights one of the benefits of installing MongoDB through repositories.

Installing MongoDB under Windows

Microsoft's Windows is also a popular choice for server software, including Internet-based services.

Windows doesn't come with a repository application like apt-get, so you'll need to download and extract the software from the MongoDB website to run it. Yes, the preceding information is correct. You do not need to walk through any setup process; installing the software is a simple matter of downloading the package, extracting it, and running the application itself.

For example, assume you've decided to download the latest stable version of MongoDB for your 64-bits Windows 2008 server. You begin by extracting the package (mongodb-win32-x86_64-x.y.x.zip) to the root of your C:\ drive. At this point, all you need to do is open a command prompt (Start ➤ Run ➤ cmd ➤ OK) and browse to the directory you extracted the contents to:

```
> cd C:\mongodb-win32-x86_64-x.y.z\
> cd bin\
```

Doing this brings you to the directory that contains the MongoDB executables. That's all there is to it: as I noted previously, no installation is necessary.

Running MongoDB

At long last, you're ready to get your hands dirty. You've learned where to get the MongoDB version that best suits your needs and hardware, and you've also seen how to install the software. Now it's finally time to look at running and using MongoDB.

Prerequisites

Before you can start the MongoDB service, you need to create a data directory for MongoDB to store its files in. By default, MongoDB stores the data in the /data/db directory on Unix-based systems (such as Linux and OS X) and in the C:\data\db directory on Windows.

■ **Note** MongoDB does not create these data directories for you, so you need to create them manually; otherwise, MongoDB will fail to run and throw an error message. Also, be sure that you set the permissions correctly: MongoDB must have read, write, and directory creation permissions to function properly.

If you wish to use a directory other than /data/db or C:\data\db, then you can tell MongoDB to look at the desired directory by using the --dbpath flag when executing the service.

Once you create the required directory and assign the appropriate permissions, you can start the MongoDB core database service by executing the *mongod* application. You can do this from the command prompt or the shell in Windows and Linux, respectively.

Surveying the Installation Layout

After you install or extract MongoDB successfully, you will have the applications shown in Table 2-1 available in the bin directory (in both Linux and Windows).

Table 2-1. *The Included MongoDB Applications*

Application	Function
-- bsondump	Reads contents of BSON-formatted rollback files.
-- mongo	The database shell.
-- mongod	The core database server.
-- mongodump	Database backup utility.
-- mongoexport	Export utility (JSON, CSV, TSV), not reliable for backup.
-- mongofiles	Manipulates files in GridFS objects.
-- mongoimport	Import utility (JSON, CSV, TSV), not reliable for recoveries.
-- mongooplog	Pulls oplog entries from another mongod instance.
-- mongoperf	Check disk I/O performance.
--mongorestore	Database backup restore utility.
--mongos	Mongodb shard process.
--mongosniff	Sniff/traces MongoDB database activity in real time, Unix-like systems only.
--mongostat	Returns counters of database operation.
--mongotop	Tracks/reports MongoDB read/write activities.
-- mongorestore	Restore/import utility.

Note: All applications are within the --bin directory.

The installed software includes 15 applications (or 14, under Microsoft Windows) that you will be using in conjunction with your MongoDB databases. The two "most important" applications are the mongo and mongod applications. The mongo application allows you to use the database shell; this shell enables you to accomplish practically anything you'd want to do with MongoDB.

The mongod application starts the service or *daemon*, as it's also called. There are also many flags you can set when launching the MongoDB applications. For example, the service lets you specify the path where the database is located (--dbpath), show version information (--version), and even print some diagnostic system information (with the --sysinfo flag)! You can view the entire list of options by including the --help flag when you launch the service. For now, you can just use the defaults and start the service by typing mongod in your shell or command prompt.

Using the MongoDB Shell

Once you create the database directory and start the mongod database application successfully, you're ready to fire up the shell and take a sneak peak at the powers of MongoDB.

Fire up your shell (Unix) or your command prompt (Windows); when you do so, make sure you are in the correct location, so that the mongo executable can be found. You can start the shell by typing mongo at the command prompt and hitting the Return key. You will be immediately presented with a blank window and a blinking cursor (see Figure 2-1). Ladies and gentlemen, welcome to MongoDB!

```
                              MongoDB
MongoDB shell version: 2.5.1-pre-
connecting to: test
> █
```

Figure 2-1. *The MongoDB shell*

If you start the MongoDB service with the default parameters, and start the shell with the default settings, you will be connected to the default test database running on your local host. This database is created automatically the moment you connect to it. This is one of MongoDB's most powerful features: if you attempt to connect to a database that does not exist, MongoDB will automatically create it for you. This can be either good or bad, depending on how well you handle your keyboard.

■ **Tip**   There's an on-line demo shell available on the MongoDB website where you can try out any of the commands listed.

Before taking any further steps, such as implementing any additional drivers that will enable you to work with your favorite programming language, you might find it helpful to take a quick peek at some of the more useful commands available in the MongoDB shell (see Table 2-2).

Table 2-2. *Basic Commands within the MongoDB Shell*

Command	Function
show dbs	Shows the names of the available databases.
show collections	Shows the collections in the current database.
show users	Shows the users in the current database.
use <db name>	Sets the current database to <db name>.

■ **Tip**   You can get a full list of commands by typing the help command in the MongoDB shell.

Installing Additional Drivers

You might think that you are ready to take on the world now that you have set up MongoDB and know how to use its shell. That's partially true; however, you probably want to use your preferred programming language rather than the shell when querying or otherwise manipulating the MongoDB database. 10gen offers multiple official drivers, and many more are offered in the community that let you do precisely that. For example, drivers for the following programming languages can be found on the MongoDB website:

- C
- C++
- C#

- Erlang

- Java

- JavaScript

- Node.js

- Perl

- PHP

- Python

- Ruby

- Scala

In this section, you will learn how to implement MongoDB support for two of the more popular programming languages in use today: PHP and Python.

■ **Tip** There are many community-driven MongoDB drivers available. A long list can be found on the MongoDB website, www.mongodb.org.

Installing the PHP Driver

PHP is one of the most popular programming languages in existence today. This language is specifically aimed at web development, and it can be incorporated into HTML easily. This fact makes the language the perfect candidate for designing a web application, such as a blog, a guestbook, or even a business-card database. The next few sections cover your options for installing and using the MongoDB PHP driver.

Getting MongoDB for PHP

Like MongoDB, PHP is a cross-platform development tool, and the steps required to set up MongoDB in PHP vary depending on the intended platform. Previously, this chapter showed you how to install MongoDB on both Ubuntu and Windows; we'll adopt the same approach here, demonstrating how to install the driver for PHP on both Ubuntu and Windows.

Begin by downloading the PHP driver for your operating system. Do this by firing up your browser and navigating to www.mongodb.org. At the time of writing, the website includes a separate menu option called Drivers. Click this option to bring up a list of currently available language drivers (see Figure 2-2).

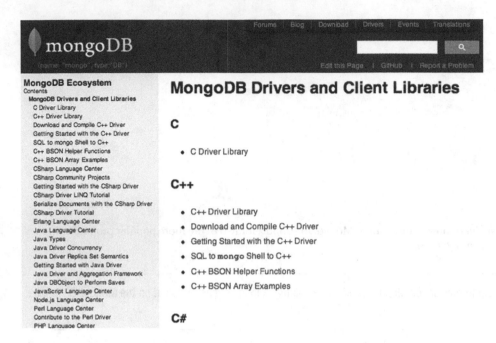

Figure 2-2. *A short list of currently available language drivers for MongoDB*

Next, select PHP from the list of languages and follow the links to download the latest (stable) version of the driver. Different operating systems will require different approaches for installing the MongoDB extension for PHP automatically. That's right; just as you were able to install MongoDB on Ubuntu automatically, you can do the same for the PHP driver. And just as when installing MongoDB under Ubuntu, you can also choose to install the PHP language driver manually. Let's look at the two options available to you.

Installing the PHP Driver on Unix-Based Platforms Automatically

The developers of PHP came up with a great solution that allows you to expand your PHP installation with other popular extensions: *PECL*. PECL is a repository solely designed for PHP; it provides a directory of all known extensions that you can use to download, install, and even develop PHP extensions. If you are already acquainted with the package-management system called aptitude (which you used previously to install MongoDB), then you will be pleased by how similar PECL's interface is to the one in aptitude.

Assuming that you have PECL installed on your system, open up a console and type the following command to install the MongoDB extension:

```
$ sudo pecl install mongo
```

Entering this command causes PECL to download and install the MongoDB extension for PHP automatically. In other words, PECL will download the extension for your PHP version and place it in the PHP extensions directory. There's just one catch: PECL does not automatically add the extension to the list of loaded extensions; you will need to do this step manually. To do so, open a text editor (vim, nano, or whichever text editor you prefer) and alter the file called php.ini, which is the main configuration file PHP uses to control its behavior, including the extensions it should load.

Next, open the php.ini file, scroll down to the extensions section, and add the following line to tell PHP to load the MongoDB driver:

```
extension=mongo.so
```

■ **Note**   The preceding step is mandatory; if you don't do this, then the MongoDB commands in PHP will not function. To find the php.ini file on your system, you can use the grep command in your shell: php -i | grep Configuration.

The "Confirming That Your PHP Installation Works" section later in this chapter will cover how to confirm that an extension has been loaded successfully.

That's all, folks! You've just installed the MongoDB extension for your PHP installation, and you are now ready to use it. Next, you will learn how to install the driver manually.

Installing the PHP Driver on Unix-Based Platforms Manually

If you would prefer to compile the driver yourself or for some reason are unable to use the PECL application as described previously (your hosting provider might not support this option, for instance), then you can also choose to download the source driver and compile it manually.

To download the driver, go to the github website (http://github.com). This site offers the latest source package for the PHP driver. Once you download it, you will need to extract the package, and *make* the driver by running the following set of commands:

```
$ tar zxvf mongodb-mongodb-php-driver-<commit_id>.tar.gz
$ cd mongodb-mongodb-php-driver-<commit_id>
$ phpize
$ ./configure
$ sudo make install
```

This process can take a while, depending on the speed of your system. Once the process completes, your MongoDB PHP driver is installed and ready to use! After you execute the commands, you will be shown where the driver has been placed; typically, the output looks something like this:

```
Installing '/ usr/lib/php/extensions/no-debug-zts-20060613/mongo.so'
```

You do need to confirm that this directory is the same directory where PHP stores its extensions by default. You can use the following command to confirm where PHP stores its extensions:

```
$ php -i | grep extension_dir
```

This line outputs the directory where all PHP extensions should be placed. If this directory doesn't match the one where the mongo.so driver was placed, then you must move the mongo.so driver to the proper directory, so PHP knows where to find it.

As before, you will need to tell PHP that the newly created extension has been placed in its extension directory, and that it should load this extension. You can specify this by modifying the php.ini file's extensions section; add the following line to that section:

```
extension=mongo.so
```

Finally, a restart of your web service is required. When using the Apache HTTPd service, you can accomplish this using the following service command:

```
sudo /etc/init.d/apache2 restart
```

That's it! This process is a little lengthier than using PECL's automated method; however, if you are unable to use PECL, or if you are a driver developer and interested in bug fixes, then you would want to use the manual method instead.

Installing the PHP Driver on Windows

You have seen previously how to install MongoDB on your Windows operating system. Now let's look at how to implement the MongoDB driver for PHP on Windows.

For Windows, there are precompiled binaries available for each release of the PHP driver for MongoDB. You can get these binaries from the previously mentioned github website (http://github.com). The biggest challenge in this case is choosing the correct package to install for your version of PHP (a wide variety of packages are available). If you aren't certain which package version you need, you can use the <? phpinfo(); ?> command in a PHP page to learn exactly which one suits your specific environment. We'll take a closer look at the phpinfo() command in the next section.

After downloading the correct package and extracting its contents, all you need to do is copy the driver file (called php_mongo.dll) to your PHP's extension directory; this enables PHP to pick it up.

Depending on your version of PHP, the extension directory may be called either Ext or Extensions. If you aren't certain which directory it should be, you can review the PHP documentation that came with the version of PHP installed on your system.

Once you place the driver DLL into the PHP extensions directory, you still need to tell PHP to load the driver. Do this by altering the php.ini file and adding the following line in the extensions section:

```
extension=php_mongo.dll
```

When done, restart the HTTP service on your system, and you are now ready to use the MongoDB driver in PHP. Before you start leveraging the magic of MongoDB with PHP, however, you need to confirm that the extension is loaded correctly.

Confirming That Your PHP Installation Works

So far you've successfully installed both MongoDB and the MongoDB driver in PHP. Now it's time to do a quick check to confirm whether the driver is being loaded correctly by PHP. PHP gives you a simple and straightforward method to accomplish this: the phpinfo() command. This command shows you an extended overview of all the modules loaded, including version numbers, compilation options, server information, OS information, and so on.

To use the phpinfo() command, open a text or HTML editor and type the following:

```
<? phpinfo(); ?>
```

Next, save the document in your webserver's www directory and call it whatever you like. For example, you might call it test.php or phpinfo.php. Now open your browser and go to your localhost or external server (that is, go to whatever server you are working on) and look at the page you just created. You will see a good overview of all PHP components and all sorts of other relevant information. The thing you need to focus on here is the section that displays your MongoDB information. This section will list the version number, port numbers, hostname, and so on (see Figure 2-3).

mongo

MongoDB Support		enabled	
Version		1.3.2	

Directive	Local Value	Master Value
mongo.allow_empty_keys	0	0
mongo.chunk_size	262144	262144
mongo.cmd	$	$
mongo.default_host	localhost	localhost
mongo.default_port	27017	27017
mongo.is_master_interval	*no value*	*no value*
mongo.long_as_object	0	0
mongo.native_long	0	0
mongo.ping_interval	*no value*	*no value*
mongo.utf8	1	1

Figure 2-3. *Displaying your MongoDB information in PHP*

Once you confirm that the installation was successful and that the driver loaded successfully, you're ready to write some PHP code and walk through a MongoDB example that leverages PHP.

Connecting to and Disconnecting from the PHP Driver

You've confirmed that the MongoDB PHP driver has been loaded correctly, so it's time to start writing some PHP code! Let's take a look at two simple yet fundamental options for working with MongoDB: initiating a connection between MongoDB and PHP, and then severing that connection.

You use the Mongo class to initiate a connection between MongoDB and PHP; this same class also lets you use the database server commands. A simple yet typical connection command looks like this:

```
$connection = new Mongo();
```

If you use this command without providing any parameters, it will connect to the MongoDB service on the default MongoDB port (27017) on your localhost. If your MongoDB service is running somewhere else, then you simply specify the hostname of the remote host you want to connect to:

```
$connection = new Mongo("example.com");
```

This line instantiates a fresh connection for your MongoDB service running on the server and listening to the example.com domain name (note that it will still connect to the default port: 27017). If you want to connect to a different port number, however (for example, if you don't want to use the default port, or you're already running another session of the MongoDB service on that port), you can do so by specifying the port number and hostname:

```
$connection = new Mongo("example.com:12345");
```

This example creates a connection to the database service. Next, you will learn how to disconnect from the service. Assuming you used the method just described to connect to your database, you can call $connection again to pass the close() command to terminate the connection, as in this example:

```
$connection->close();
```

The close doesn't need to be called, except in unusual circumstances. The reason for this is that the PHP driver closes the connection to the database once the Mongo object goes out of scope. Nevertheless, it is recommended that you call close() at the end of your PHP code; this helps you avoid keeping old connections from hanging around until they eventually time out. It also helps you ensure that any existing connection is closed, thereby enabling a new connection to happen, as in the following example:

```
$connection = new Mongo();
$connection->close();
$connection->connect();
```

The following snippet shows how this would look like in PHP:

```
<?php

// Establish the database connection
$connection = new Mongo()

// Close the database connection
$connection->close();

?>
```

Installing the Python Driver

Python is a general-purpose and easy-to-read programming language.

These qualities make Python a good language to start with when you are new to programming and scripting. It's also a great language to look into if you are familiar with programming, and you're looking for a multi-paradigm programming language that permits several styles of programming (object-oriented programming, structured programming, and so on). In the upcoming sections, you'll learn how to install Python and enable MongoDB support for the language.

Installing PyMongo under Linux

Python offers a specific package for MongoDB support called PyMongo. This package allows you to interact with the MongoDB database, but you will need to get this driver up and running before you can use this powerful combination. As when installing the PHP driver, there are two methods you can use to install PyMongo: an automated approach that relies on setuptools or a manual approach where you download the source code for the project. The following sections show you how to install PyMongo using both approaches.

Installing PyMongo Automatically

The pip application that comes bundled with the python-pip package lets you automatically download, build, install, and manage Python packages. This is incredibly convenient, enabling you to extend your Python modules installation even as it does all the work for you.

▪ **Note**   You must have setuptools installed before you can use the `pip` application. This will be done automatically when installing the python-pip package.

To install `pip`, all you need to do is tell `apt-get` to download and install it, like so:

```
$ sudo apt-get install python-pip
```

When this line executes, `pip` will detect the currently running version of Python and installs itself on the system. That's all there is to it. Now you are ready to use the `pip` command to download, make, and install the MongoDB module, as in this example:

```
$ sudo pip install pymongo
```

Again, that's all there is to it! PyMongo is now installed and ready to use.

▪ **Tip**   You can also install previous versions of the PyMongo module with pip using the `pip install pymongo=x.y.z` command. Here, $x.y.z$ denotes the version of the module.

Installing PyMongo Manually

You can also choose to install PyMongo manually. Begin by going to the download section of the site that hosts the PyMongo plugin (http://pypi.python.org/pypi/pymongo). Next, download the tarball and extract it. A typical download and extract procedure might look like this in your console:

```
$ wget http://pypi.python.org/packages/source/p/pymongo/pymongo-2.5.1.tar.gz
$ tar xzf pymongo-2.5.1.tar.gz
```

Once you successfully download and extract this file, make your way to the extracted contents directory and invoke the installation of PyMongo by running the `install.py` command with Python:

```
$ cd pymongo-2.5.1
$ sudo python setup.py install
```

The preceding snippet outputs the entire creation and installation process of the PyMongo module. Eventually, this process brings you back to your prompt, at which time you're ready to start using PyMongo.

Installing PyMongo under Windows

Installing PyMongo under Windows is a straightforward process. As when installing PyMongo under Linux, Easy Install can simplify installing PyMongo under Windows as well. If you don't have setuptools installed yet (this package includes the `easy_install` command), then go to the Python Package Index website (http://pypi.python.org) to locate the setuptools installer.

▪ **Caution**   The version of setuptools you download must match the version of Python installed on your system.

For example, assume you have Python version 2.7.5 installed on your system. You will need to download the setuptools package for v2.7.x. The good news is that you don't need to compile any of this; rather, you can simply download the appropriate package and double-click the executable to install setuptools on your system! It is that simple.

■ **Caution**   If you have previously installed an older version of setuptools, then you will need to uninstall that version using your system's Add/Remove Programs feature *before* installing the newer version.

Once the installation is complete, you will find the easy_install.exe file in Python's Scripts subdirectory. At this point, you're ready to install PyMongo on Windows.

Once you've successfully installed setuptools, you can open a command prompt and cd your way to Python's Scripts directory. By default, this is set to C:\Python*xy*\Scripts\, where *xy* represents your version number. Once you navigate to this location, you can use the same syntax shown previously for installing the Unix variant:

C:\Python27\Scripts> easy_install PyMongo

Unlike the output that you get when installing this program on a Linux machine, the output here is rather brief, indicating only that the extension has been downloaded and installed (see Figure 2-4). That said, this information is sufficient for your purposes in this case.

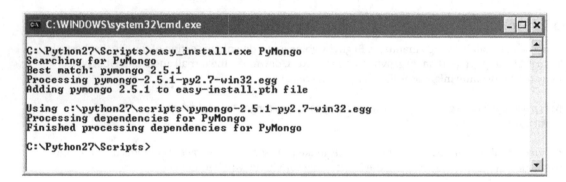

Figure 2-4. *Installing PyMongo under Windows*

Confirming That Your PyMongo Installation Works

To confirm whether the PyMongo installation has completed successfully, you can open up your Python shell. In Linux, you do this by opening a console and typing python. In Windows, you do this by clicking Start ➤ Programs ➤ Python *xy* ➤ Python (commandline). At this point, you will be welcomed to the world of Python (see Figure 2-5).

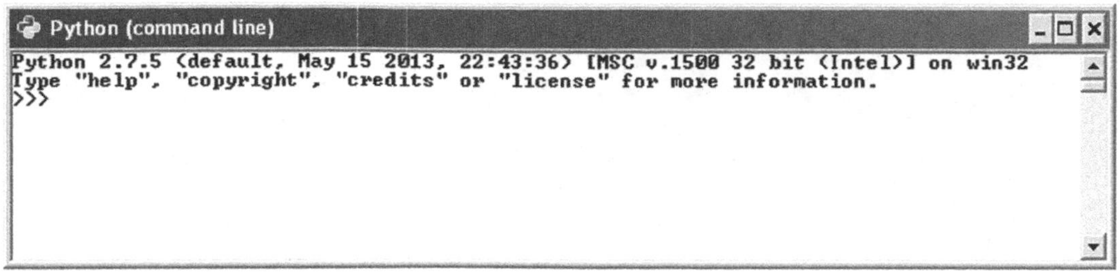

Figure 2-5. The Python shell

You can use the import command to tell Python to start using the freshly installed extension:

```
>>> import pymongo
>>>
```

■ **Note**   You must use the import pymongo command each time you want to use PyMongo.

If all went well, you will not see a thing, and you can start firing off some fancy MongoDB commands. If you received an error message, however, something went wrong, and you might need to review the steps just taken to discover where the error occurred.

Summary

In this chapter, we examined how to obtain the MongoDB software, including how to select the correct version you need for your environment. We also discussed the version numbers, how to install and run MongoDB, and how to install and run its prerequisites. Next, we covered how to establish a connection to a database through a combination of the shell, PHP, and Python.

We also explored how to expand MongoDB so it will work with your favorite programming languages, as well as how to confirm whether the language-specific drivers have installed correctly.

In the next chapter, we will explore how to design and structure MongoDB databases and data properly. Along the way, you'll learn how to index information to speed up queries, how to reference data, and how to leverage a fancy new feature called *geospatial indexing*.

CHAPTER 3

■ ■ ■

The Data Model

In the previous chapter, you learned how to install MongoDB on two commonly used platforms (Windows and Linux), as well as how to extend the database with some additional drivers. In this chapter, you will shift your attention from the operating system and instead examine the general design of a MongoDB database. Specifically, you'll learn what collections are, what documents look like, how indexes work and what they do, and finally, when and where to reference data instead of embedding it. We touched on some of these concepts briefly in Chapter 1, but in this chapter, we'll explore them in more detail. Throughout this chapter, you will see code examples designed to give you a good feeling for the concepts being discussed. Do not worry too much about the commands you'll be looking at, however, because they will be discussed extensively in Chapter 4.

Designing the Database

As you learned in the first two chapters, a MongoDB database is nonrelational and schemaless. This means that a MongoDB database isn't bound to any predefined columns or datatypes as relational databases are (such as MySQL). The biggest benefit of this implementation is that working with data is extremely flexible because there is no predefined structure required in your documents.

To put it more simply: you are perfectly capable of having one collection that contains hundreds or even thousands of documents that all carry a different structure—without breaking any of the MongoDB databases rules.

One of the benefits of this flexible schemaless design is that you won't be restricted when programming in a dynamically typed language such as Python or PHP. Indeed, it would be a severe limitation if your extremely flexible and dynamically capable programming language couldn't be used to its full potential because of the innate limitations of your database.

Let's take another glance at what the data design of a document in MongoDB looks like, paying particular attention to how flexible data in MongoDB is compared to data in a relational database. In MongoDB, a *document* is an item that contains the actual data, comparable to a row in SQL. In the following example, you will see how two completely different types of documents can coexist in a single collection named Media (note that a *collection* is roughly equivalent to a table in the world of SQL):

```
{
    "Type": "CD",
    "Artist": "Nirvana",
    "Title": "Nevermind",
    "Genre": "Grunge",
    "Releasedate": "1991.09.24",
```

```
    "Tracklist": [
        {
        "Track" : "1",
        "Title" : "Smells Like Teen Spirit",
        "Length" : "5:02"
        },
        {
        "Track" : "2",
        "Title" : "In Bloom",
        "Length" : "4:15"
        }
    ]
}
{
    "type": "Book",
    "Title": "Definitive Guide to MongoDB: A complete guide to dealing with Big Data using
MongoDB 2nd, The",
    "ISBN": "987-1-4302-5821-6",
    "Publisher": "Apress",
    "Author": [
        "Hows, David"
        "Plugge, Eelco",
        "Membrey, Peter",
        "Hawkins, Tim    ]
}
```

As you might have noticed when looking at this pair of documents, most of the fields aren't closely related to one another. Yes, they both have fields called Title and Type; but apart from that similarity, the documents are completely different. Nevertheless, these two documents are contained in a single collection called Media.

MongoDB is called a *schemaless* database, but that doesn't mean MongoDB's data structure is completely devoid of schema. For example, you do define collections and indexes in MongoDB (you will learn more about this later in the chapter). Nevertheless, you do not *need* to predefine a structure for any of the documents you will be adding, as is the case when working with MySQL, for example.

Simply stated, MongoDB is an extraordinarily dynamic database; the preceding example would never work in a relational database, unless you also added each possible field to your table. Doing so would be a waste of both space and performance, not to mention highly disorganized.

Drilling Down on Collections

As mentioned previously, *collection* is a commonly used term in MongoDB. You can think of a collection as a container that stores your documents (that is, your data), as shown in Figure 3-1.

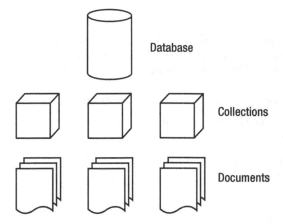

Figure 3-1. *The MongoDB database model*

Now compare the MongoDB database model to a typical model for a relational database (see Figure 3-2).

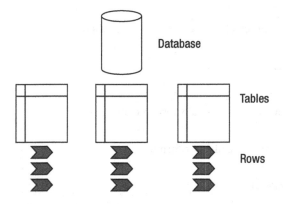

Figure 3-2. *A typical relational database model*

As you can see, the general structure is the same between the two types of databases; nevertheless, you do not use them in even remotely similar manners. There are several types of collections in MongoDB. The default collection type is expandable in size: the more data you add to it, the larger it becomes. It's also possible to define collections that are *capped*. These *capped collections* can only contain a certain amount of data before the oldest document is replaced by a newer document (you will learn more about these collections in Chapter 4).

Every collection in MongoDB has a unique name. This name should begin with a letter, or optionally, an underscore (_) when created using the createCollection function. The name can contain numbers and letters; however, the $ symbol is reserved by MongoDB. Similarly, using an empty string (" ") is not allowed; the null character cannot be used in the name and it cannot start with the "system." string. Generally, it's recommended that you keep the collection's name simple and short (to around nine characters or so); however, the maximum number of allowed characters in a collection name is 128. Obviously, there isn't much practical reason to create such a long name.

A single database has a default limit of 24,000 namespaces. Each collection accounts for at least two namespaces: one for the collection itself and one more for the first index created in the collection. If you were to add more indexes per collection, however, another namespace would be used. In theory, this means that each database can have up to 12,000 collections by default, assuming each collection only carries one index. However, this limit on the number of namespaces can be increased by providing the nssize parameter when executing the MongoDB service application (mongod).

Using Documents

Recall that a *document* consists of key-value pairs. For example, the pair "type" : "Book" consists of a key named type, and its value, Book. Keys are written as *strings*, but the values in them can vary tremendously. Values can be any of a rich set of datatypes, such as arrays or even binary data. Remember: MongoDB stores its data in BSON format (see Chapter 1 for more information on this topic).

Next, let's look at all of the possible types of data you can add to a document, and what you use them for:

- *String*: This commonly used datatype contains a string of text (or any other kind of characters). This datatype is used mostly for storing text values (for example, "Country" : "Japan"}.

- *Integer (32b and 64b)*: This type is used to store a numerical value (for example, { "Rank" : 1 }). Note that there are no quotes placed before or after the integer.

- *Boolean*: This datatype can be set to either TRUE or FALSE.

- *Double*: This datatype is used to store floating-point values.

- *Min/Max keys*: This datatype is used to compare a value against the lowest and highest BSON elements, respectively.

- *Arrays*: This datatype is used to store arrays (for example, ["Membrey, Peter","Plugge, Eelco","Hows, David"]).

- *Timestamp*: This datatype is used to store a timestamp. This can be handy for recording when a document has been modified or added.

- *Object*: This datatype is used for embedded documents.

- *Null*: This datatype is used for a Null value.

- *Symbol*: This datatype is used identically to a string; however, it's generally reserved for languages that use a specific symbol type.

- *Date* *: This datatype is used to store the current date or time in Unix time format (POSIX time).

- *Object ID* *: This datatype is used to store the document's ID.

- *Binary data* *: This datatype is used to store binary data.

- *Regular expression* *: This datatype is used for regular expressions. All options are represented by specific characters provided in alphabetical order. You will learn more about regular expressions in Chapter 4.

- *JavaScript Code* *: This datatype is used for JavaScript code.

The asterisks mean that the last five datatypes (date, object ID, binary data, regex, and JavaScript code) are non-JSON types; specifically, they are special datatypes that BSON allows you to use. In Chapter 4, you will learn how to identify your datatypes by using the $type operator.

In theory, this all probably sounds straightforward. However, you might wonder how you go about actually designing the document, including what information to put in it. Because a document can contain any type of data, you might think there is no need to reference information from inside another document. In the next section, we'll look at the pros and cons of embedding information in a document compared to referencing that information from another document.

Embedding vs. Referencing Information in Documents

You can choose either to embed information into a document or reference that information from another document. Embedding information simply means that you place a certain type of data (for example, an array containing more data) into the document itself. Referencing information means that you create a reference to another document that contains that specific data. Typically, you reference information when you use a relational database. For example, assume you wanted to use a relational database to keep track of your CDs, DVDs, and books. In this database, you might have one table for your CD collection and another table that stores the track lists of your CDs. Thus, you would probably need to query multiple tables to acquire a list of tracks from a specific CD.

With MongoDB (and other nonrelational databases), however, it would be much easier to embed such information instead. After all, the documents are natively capable of doing so. Adopting this approach keeps your database nice and tidy, ensures that all related information is kept in one single document, and even works much faster because the data is then co-located on the disk.

Now let's look at the differences between embedding and referencing information by looking at a real-world scenario: storing CD data in a database.

In the relational approach, your data structure might look something like this:

```
|_media
    |_cds
        |_id, artist, title, genre, releasedate
    |_ cd_tracklists
        |_cd_id, songtitle, length
```

In the nonrelational approach, your data structure might look something like this:

```
|_media
    |_items
        |_<document>
```

In the nonrelational approach, the document might look something like the following:

```
{
    "Type": "CD",
    "Artist": "Nirvana",
    "Title": "Nevermind",
    "Genre": "Grunge",
    "Releasedate": "1991.09.24",
    "Tracklist": [
        {
        "Track" : "1",
        "Title" : "Smells Like Teen Spirit",
        "Length" : "5:02"
        },
        {
        "Track" : "2",
        "Title" : "In Bloom",
        "Length" : "4:15"
        }
    ]
}
```

In this example, the track list information is embedded in the document itself. This approach is both incredibly efficient and well organized. All the information that you wish to store regarding this CD is added to a single document. In the relational version of the CD database, this requires at least two tables; in the nonrelational database, it requires only one collection and one document.

When information is retrieved for a given CD, that information only needs to be loaded from one document into RAM, not from multiple documents. Remember that every reference requires another query in the database.

■ **Tip** The rule of thumb when using MongoDB is to embed data whenever you can. This approach is far more efficient and almost always viable.

At this point, you might be wondering about the use case in which an application has multiple users. Generally speaking, a relational database version of the aforementioned CD app would require that you have one table that contains all your users and two tables for the items added. For a nonrelational database, it would be good practice to have separate collections for the users and the items added. For these kinds of problems, MongoDB allows you to create references in two ways: manually or automatically. In the latter case, you use the DBRef specification, which provides more flexibility in case a collection changes from one document to the next. You will learn more about these two approaches in Chapter 4.

Creating the _id Field

Every object within the MongoDB database contains a unique identifier to distinguish that object from every other object. This identifier is called the _id key, and it is added automatically to every document you create in a collection.

The _id key is the first attribute added in each new document you create. This remains true even if you do not tell MongoDB to create the key. For example, none of the code in the preceding examples used the _id key. Nevertheless, MongoDB created an _id key for you automatically in each document. It did so because _id key is a mandatory element for each document in the collection.

If you do not specify the _id value manually, the type will be set to a special BSON datatype that consists of a 12-byte binary value. Thanks to its design, this value has a reasonably high probability of being unique. The 12-byte value consists of a 4-byte timestamp (seconds since epoch, or January 1st, 1970), a 3-byte machine ID, a 2-byte process ID, and a 3-byte counter. It's good to know that the counter and timestamp fields are stored in *Big Endian* format. This is because MongoDB wants to ensure that there is an increasing order to these values, and a Big Endian approach suits this requirement best.

■ **Note** The terms *Big Endian* and *Little Endian* refer to how individual bytes/bits are stored in a longer data word in the memory. Big Endian simply means that the most significant value is saved first. Similarly, Little Endian means that the least significant value is saved first.

Figure 3-3 shows how the value of the _id key is built up and where the values come from.

0	1	2	3	4	5	6	7	8	9	10	11
Time				machine			Pid		inc		

Figure 3-3. Creating the _id key in MongoDB

Every additional supported driver that you load when working with MongoDB (such as the PHP driver or the Python driver) supports this special BSON datatype and uses it whenever new data is created. You can also invoke ObjectId() from the MongoDB shell to create a value for an _id key. Optionally, you can specify your own value by using ObjectId(*string*), where *string* represents the specified hex string.

Building Indexes

As mentioned in Chapter 1, an *index* is nothing more than a data structure that collects information about the values of specified fields in the documents of a collection. This data structure is used by MongoDB's query optimizer to quickly sort through and order the documents in a collection.

Remember that indexing ensures a quick lookup from data in your documents. Basically, you should view an index as a predefined query that was executed and had its results stored. As you can imagine, this enhances query-performance dramatically. The general rule of thumb in MongoDB is that you should create an index for the same sort of scenarios where you would want to have an index in MySQL.

The biggest benefit of creating your own indexes is that querying for often-used information will be incredibly fast because your query won't need to go through your entire database to collect this information.

Creating (or deleting) an index is relatively easy—once you get the hang of it, anyway. You will learn how to do so in Chapter 4, which covers working with data. You will also learn some more advanced techniques for taking advantage of indexing in Chapter 10, which covers how to maximize performance.

Impacting Performance with Indexes

You might wonder why you would ever need to delete an index, rebuild your indexes, or even delete all indexes within a collection. The simple answer is that doing so lets you clean up some irregularities. For instance, sometimes the size of a database can increase dramatically for no apparent reason. At other times, the space used by the indexes might strike you as excessive.

Another good thing to keep in mind: you can have a maximum of 40 indexes per collection. Generally speaking, this is far more than you should need, but you could potentially hit this limit someday.

■ **Note**   Adding an index increases query speed, but it reduces insertion or deletion speed. It's best to consider only adding indexes for collections where the number of reads is higher than the number of writes. When more writes occur than reads, indexes may even prove to be counterproductive.

Finally, all index information is stored in the system.indexes collection in your database. For example, you can run the db.indexes.find() command to take a quick peek at the indexes that have been stored so far. To see the indexes created for a specific collection, you can use the getIndexes command:

```
db.collection.getIndexes()
```

Implementing Geospatial Indexing

As Chapter 1 briefly mentioned, MongoDB has implemented *geospatial indexing* since version 1.4. This means that, in addition to normal indexes, MongoDB also supports geospatial indexes that are designed to work in an optimal way with location-based queries. For example, you can use this feature to find a number of closest known items to the user's current location. Or you might further refine your search to query for a specified number of restaurants near the current location. This type of query can be particularly helpful if you are designing an application where you want to find the closest available branch office to a given customer's ZIP code.

A document for which you want to add geospatial information must contain either a subobject or an array whose first element specifies the object type, followed by the item's longitude and latitude, as in the following example:

```
> db.restaurants.insert({name: "Kimono", loc: { type: "Point", coordinates: [ 52.37045
1, 5.217497]}})
```

Note that the type parameter can be used to specify the document's object type, which can be a Point, a LineString or a Polygon. As can be expected, the Point type is used to specify that the item (in this case, a restaurant) is located at exactly the spot given, thus requiring exactly two values, the longitute and latitude. The LineString type can be used to specify that the item extends along a specific line (say, a street), and thus requires a beginning and end point, as in the following example:

```
> db.streets.insert( {name: "Westblaak", loc: { type: "LineString", coordinates: [
[52.36881,4.890286],[52.368762,4.890021] ] } }  )
```

The Polygon type can be used to specify a (nondefault) shape (say, a shopping area). When using this type, you need to ensure that the first and last points are identical, to close the loop. Also, the point coordinates are to be provided as an array within an array, as in the following example:

```
> db.stores.insert( {name: "SuperMall", loc: { type: "Polygon", coordinates: [ [
[52.146917,5.374337], [52.146966,5.375471], [52.146722,5.375085], [52.146744,5.37437],
[52.146917,5.374337] ] ] } } )
```

In most cases, the Point type will be appropriate.

Once this geospatial information is added to a document, you can create the index (or even create the index beforehand, of course) and give the ensureIndex() function the 2dsphere parameter:

```
> db.restaurants.ensureIndex( { loc: "2dsphere" } )
```

■ **Note** The ensureIndex() function is used to add a custom index. Don't worry about the syntax of this function yet—you will learn how to use ensureIndex() in depth in the next chapter.

The 2dsphere parameter tells ensureIndex() that it's indexing a coordinate or some other form of two-dimensional information on an Earth-like sphere. By default, ensureindex() assumes that a latitude/longitude key is given, and it uses a range of -180 to 180. However, you can overwrite these values using the min and max parameters:

```
> db.restaurants.ensureIndex( { loc: "2dsphere" }, { min : -500 , max : 500 } )
```

You can also expand your geospatial indexes by using *secondary key* values (also known as *compound keys*). This structure can be useful when you intend to query on multiple values, such as a location (geospatial information) and a category (sort ascending):

```
> db.restaurants.ensureIndex( { loc: "2dsphere", category: 1 } )
```

■ **Note**   At this time, the geospatial implementation is based on the idea that the world is a perfect sphere. Thus, each degree of latitude and longitude is exactly 111km (69 miles) in length. However, this is only true exactly at the equator; the further you move away from the equator, the smaller each degree of longitude becomes, approaching zero at the poles.

Querying Geospatial Information

In this chapter, we are concerned primarily with two things: how to model the data and how a database works in the background of an application. That said, manipulating geospatial information is increasingly important in a wide variety of applications, so we'll take a few moments to explain how to leverage geospatial information in a MongoDB database.

Before getting started, a mild word of caution. If you are completely new to MongoDB and haven't had the opportunity to work with (geospatial) indexed data in the past, this section may seem a little overwhelming at first. Not to worry, however; you can safely skip it for now and come back to it later if you wish to. The examples given serve to show you a practical example of how (and why) to use geospatial indexing, making it easier to comprehend. With that out of the way, and if you are feeling brave, read on.

Once you've added data to your collection, and once the index has been created, you can do a geospatial query. For example, let's look at a few lines of simple yet powerful code that demonstrate how to use geospatial indexing.

Begin by starting up your MongoDB shell and selecting a database with the use function. In this case, the database is named restaurants:

```
> use restaurants
```

Once you've selected the database, you can define a few documents that contain geospatial information, and then insert them into the places collection (remember: you do not need to create the collection beforehand):

```
> db.restaurants.insert( { name: "Kimono", loc: { type: "Point", coordinates: [ 52.370451, 5.217497] } } )

> db.restaurants.insert( {name: "Shabu Shabu", loc: { type: "Point", coordinates: [51.915288,4.472786] } } )

> db.restaurants.insert( {name: "Tokyo Cafe", loc: { type: "Point", coordinates: [52.368736, 4.890530] } } )
```

After you add the data, you need to tell the MongoDB shell to create an index based on the location information that was specified in the loc key, as in this example:

```
> db.restaurants.ensureIndex ( { loc: "2dsphere" } )
```

Once the index has been created, you can start searching for your documents. Begin by searching on an exact value (so far this is a "normal" query; it has nothing to do with the geospatial information at this point):

```
> db.restaurants.find( { loc : [52,5] } )
>
```

The preceding search returns no results. This is because the query is *too* specific. A better approach in this case would be to search for documents that contain information *near* a given value. You can accomplish this using the $near operator. Note that this requires the type operator to be specified, as in the following example:

```
> db.restaurants.find( { loc : { $geoNear : { $geometry : { type : "Point", coordinates:
  [52.338433,5.513629] } } } } )
```

This produces the following output:

```
{
  "_id" : ObjectId("51ace0f380523d89efd199ac"),
  "name" : "Kimono",
  "loc" : {
    "type" : "Point",
    "coordinates" : [ 52.370451, 5.217497 ]
  }
}
{
  "_id" : ObjectId("51ace13380523d89efd199ae"),
  "name" : "Tokyo Cafe",
  "loc" : {
    "type" : "Point",
    "coordinates" : [ 52.368736, 4.89053 ]
  }
}
{
  "_id" : ObjectId("51ace11b80523d89efd199ad"),
  "name" : "Shabu Shabu",
  "loc" : {
    "type" : "Point",
    "coordinates" : [ 51.915288, 4.472786 ]
  }
}
```

Although this set of results certainly looks better, there's still one problem: all of the documents are returned! When used without any additional operators, $near returns the first 100 entries and sorts them based on their distance from the given coordinates. Now, while we can choose to limit our results to say, the first two items (or two hundred, if we want) using the limit function, even better would be to limit the results to those within a given range.

This can be achieved by appending the $maxDistance operator. Using this operator you can tell MongoDB to return only those results falling within a maximum distance (measured in meters) from the given point, as in the following example and its output:

```
> db.retaurants.find( { loc : { $geoNear : { $geometry : { type : "Point", coordinates:
[52.338433,5.513629] }, $maxDistance : 40000 } } } )
{
  "_id" : ObjectId("51ace0f380523d89efd199ac"),
  "name" : "Kimono",
  "loc" : {
    "type" : "Point",
    "coordinates" : [ 52.370451, 5.217497 ]
  }
}
```

As you can see, this returns only a single result: a restaurant located within 40 kilometers (or, roughly 25 miles) from the starting point.

■ **Note**   There is a direct correlation between the number of results returned and the time a given query takes to execute.

In addition to the $geoNear operator, MongoDB also includes a $geoWithin operator. You use this operator to find items in a particular shape. At this time, you can find items located in a $box, $polygon, $center and $centerSphere shape, where $box represents a rectangle, $polygon represents a specific shape of your choosing, $center represents a circle, and $centerSphere defines a circle on a sphere. Let's look at a couple of additional examples that illustrate how to use these shapes.

■ **Note**   With version 2.4 of MongoDB the $within operator was deprecated and replaced by $geoWithin. This operator does not strictly require a geospatial indexing. Also, unlike the $near operator, $geoWithin does not sort the returned results, improving their performance.

To use the $box shape, you first need to specify the lower-left, followed by the upper-right coordinates of the box, as in the following example:

```
> db.restaurants.find( { loc: { $geoWithin : { $box : [ [52.368549,4.890238],
[52.368849,4.89094] ] } } } )
```

Similarly, to find items within a specific polygon form, you need to specify the coordinates of your points as a set of nested arrays. Again note that the first and last coordinates must be identical to close the shape properly, as shown in the following example:

```
> db.restaurants.find( { loc :
  { $geoWithin :
    { $geometry :
      { type : "Polygon" ,
        coordinates : [ [
          [52.368739,4.890203],  [52.368872,4.890477],  [52.368726,4.890793],
          [52.368608,4.89049], [52.368739,4.890203]
        ] ]
      }
    }
  }
} )
```

The code to find items in a basic $circle shape is quite simple. In this case, you need to specify the center of the circle and its radius, measured in the units used by the coordinate system, before executing the find() function:

```
> db.restaurants.find( { loc: { $geoWithin : { $center : [ [52.370524, 5.217682], 10] } } } )
```

Note that ever since MongoDB version 2.2.3, the $center operator can be used without having a geospatial index in place. However, it is recommended to create one to improve performance.

Finally, to find items located within a circular shape on a sphere (say, our planet) you can use the $centerSphere operator. This operator is similar to $center, like so:

```
> db.restaurants.find( { loc: { $geoWithin : { $centerSphere : [ [52.370524, 5.217682], 10] } } } )
```

By default, the find() function is ideal for running queries. However, MongoDB also provides the geoNear() function, which works like the find() function, but also displays the distance from the specified point for each item in the results. The geoNear() function also includes some additional diagnostics. The following example uses the geoNear() function to find the two closest results to the specified position:

```
> db.runCommand( { geoNear : "restaurants", near : { type : "Point", coordinates:
[52.338433,5.513629] }, spherical : true})
```

It returns the following results:

```
{
  "ns" : "stores.restaurants",
  "results" : [
    {
      "dis" : 33155.517810497055,
      "obj" : {
        "_id" : ObjectId("51ace0f380523d89efd199ac"),
        "name" : "Kimono",
        "loc" : {
          "type" : "Point",
          "coordinates" : [
            52.370451,
            5.217497
          ]
        }
      }
    },
    {
      "dis" : 69443.96264213261,
      "obj" : {
        "_id" : ObjectId("51ace13380523d89efd199ae"),
        "name" : "Tokyo Cafe",
        "loc" : {
          "type" : "Point",
          "coordinates" : [
            52.368736,
            4.89053
          ]
        }
      }
    },
    {
      "dis" : 125006.87383713324,
      "obj" : {
        "_id" : ObjectId("51ace11b80523d89efd199ad"),
        "name" : "Shabu Shabu",
        "loc" : {
          "type" : "Point",
          "coordinates" : [
```

```
            51.915288,
            4.472786
          ]
        }
      }
    }
  ],
  "stats" : {
    "time" : 6,
    "nscanned" : 3,
    "avgDistance" : 75868.7847632543,
    "maxDistance" : 125006.87383713324
  },
  "ok" : 1
}
```

That completes our introduction to geospatial information for now; however, you'll see a few more examples that show you how to leverage geospatial functions in this book's upcoming chapters.

Using MongoDB in the Real World

Now that you have MongoDB and its associated plug-ins installed, and you have gained an understanding of the data model, it's time to get to work. In the next five chapters of the book, you will learn how to build, query, and otherwise manipulate a variety of sample MongoDB databases (see Table 3-1 for a quick view of the topics to come). Each chapter will stick primarily to using a single database that is unique to that chapter; we took this approach to make it easier to read this book in a modular fashion.

Table 3-1. *MongoDB Sample Databases Covered in This Book*

Chapter	Database Name	Topic
4	Library	Working with data and indexes
5	Test	GridFS
6	Contacts	PHP and MongoDB
7	Inventory	Python and MongoDB
8	Test	Advanced Queries

Summary

In this chapter, we looked at what's happening in the background of your database. We also explored the primary concepts of collections and documents in more depth; and we covered the datatypes supported in MongoDB, as well as how to embed and reference data.

Next, we examined what indexes do, including when and why they should be used (or not).

We also touched on the concepts of geospatial indexing. For example, we covered how geospatial data can be stored; we also explained how you can search for such data using either the regular find() function or the more geospatially based geoNear database command.

In the next chapter, we'll take a closer look at how the MongoDB shell works, including which functions can be used to insert, find, update, or delete your data. We will also explore how conditional operators can help you with all of these functions.

CHAPTER 4

■ ■ ■

Working with Data

In the previous chapter, you learned how the database works on the backend, what indexes are, how to use a database to quickly find the data you are looking for, and what the structure of a document looks like. You also saw a brief example that illustrated how to add data and find it again using the MongoDB shell. In this chapter, we will focus more on working with data from your shell.

We will use one database (named library) throughout this chapter, and we will perform actions such as adding data, searching data, modifying data, deleting data, and creating indexes. We'll also look at how to navigate the database using various commands, as well as what DBRef is and what it does. If you have followed the instructions in the previous chapters to set up the MongoDB software, you can follow the examples in this chapter to get used to the interface. Along the way, you will also attain a solid understanding of which commands can be used for what kind of operations.

Navigating Your Databases

The first thing you need to know is how to navigate your databases and collections. With traditional SQL databases, the first thing you would need to do is to create an actual database; however, as you probably remember from the previous chapters, this is not required with MongoDB because the program creates the database and underlying collection for you automatically the moment you store data in it.

To switch to an existing database or create a new one, you can use the use function in the shell, followed by the name of the database you would like to use, whether it exists or not. This snippet shows how to use the library database:

```
> use library
Switched to db library
```

The mere act of invoking the use function, followed by the database's name, sets your db (database) global variable to library. Doing this means that all the commands you pass down into the shell will automatically assume they need to be executed on the library database until you reset this variable to another database.

Viewing Available Databases and Collections

MongoDB automatically assumes a database needs to be created the moment you save data to it. It is also case-sensitive. For these reasons, it can be quite tricky to ensure that you're working in the correct database. Therefore, it's best to view a list of all current databases available to MongoDB prior to switching to one, in case you forgot the database's name or its exact spelling. You can do this using the show dbs function:

```
> show dbs
admin
local
```

Note that this function will only show a database that already exists. At this stage, the database does not contain any data yet, so nothing else will be listed. If you want to view all available collections for your current database, you can use the show collections function:

```
> show collections
system.indexes
```

Note that the system.indexes collection is created automatically the moment data is saved. This collection contains an index based on the _id key value from the document just inserted; it also includes any custom-created indexes that you've defined.

■ **Tip** To view the database you are currently working in, simply type **db** into the MongoDB shell.

Inserting Data into Collections

One of the most frequently used pieces of functionality you will want to learn about is how to insert data into your collection. All data is stored in BSON format (which is both compact and reasonably fast to scan), so you will need to insert the data in BSON format as well. You can do this in several ways. For example, you can define it first, and then save it in the collection using the insert function, or you can type the document while using the insert function on the fly:

```
> document = ( { "Type" : "Book", "Title" : "Definitive Guide to MongoDB 2nd ed.,
The", "ISBN" : "978-1-4302-5821-6", "Publisher" : "Apress", "Author": [
"Hows, David", "Plugge, Eelco", "Membrey, Peter", "Hawkins, Tim" ] } )
```

■ **Note** When you define a variable in the shell (for example, document = ({ ... })), the contents of the variable will be printed out immediately.

```
> db.media.insert(document)
```

Line breaks can also be used while typing in the shell. This can be convenient if you are writing a rather lengthy document, as in this example:

```
> document = ( { "Type" : "Book",
..."Title" : "Definitive Guide to MongoDB 2nd ed., The",
..."ISBN" : "978-1-4302-5821-6",
..."Publisher" : "Apress",
..."Author" : ["Hows, David", Plugge, Eelco", "Membrey, Peter"," "Hawkins, Tim"]
...} )
```

```
> db.media.insert(document)
```

As mentioned, the other option is to insert your data directly through the shell, without defining the document first. You can do this by invoking the insert function immediately, followed by the document's contents:

```
> db.media.insert( { "Type" : "CD", "Artist" : "Nirvana", "Title" : "Nevermind" })
```

Or you can insert the data while using line breaks, as before. For example, you can expand the preceding example by adding an array of tracks to it. Pay close attention to how the commas and brackets are used in the following example:

```
> db.media.insert( { "Type" : "CD",
..."Artist" : "Nirvana",
..."Title" : "Nevermind",
... "Tracklist" : [
... {
... "Track" : "1",
... "Title" : "Smells Like Teen Spirit",
... "Length" : "5:02"
... },
... {
... "Track" : "2",
... "Title" : "In Bloom",
... "Length" : "4:15"
... }
... ]
...}
... )
```

As you can see, inserting data through the Mongo shell is straightforward.

The process of inserting data is extremely flexible, but you must adhere to some rules when doing so. For example, the names of the keys while inserting documents have the following limitations:

- The $ character must not be the first character in the key name. Example: $tags
- The period [.] character must not appear anywhere in the key name. Example: ta.gs
- The name _id is reserved for use as a primary key ID; although it is not recommended, it can store anything unique as a value, such as a string or an integer.

Similarly, some restrictions apply when creating a collection. For example, the name of a collection must adhere to the following rules:

- The collection's name cannot exceed 128 characters.
- An empty string (" ") cannot be used as a collection name.
- The collection's name must start with either a letter or an underscore.
- The collection name system is reserved for MongoDB and cannot be used.
- The collection's name cannot contain the "\0" null character.

Querying for Data

You've seen how to switch to your database and how to insert data; next, you will learn how to query for data in your collection. Let's build on the preceding example and look at all the possible ways to get a good clear view of your data in a given collection.

■ **Note** When querying your data, you have an extraordinary range of options, operators, expressions, filters, and so on available to you. We will spend the next few sections reviewing these options.

The find() function provides the easiest way to retrieve data from multiple documents within one of your collections. This function is one that you will be using often.

Let's assume that you have inserted the preceding two examples into a collection called media in the library database. If you were to use a simple find() function on this collection, you would get all of the documents you've added so far printed out for you:

```
> db.media.find()
{ "_id" : "ObjectId("4c1a8a56c603000000007ecb"), "Type" : "Book", "Title" :
"Definitive Guide to MongoDB 2nd ed., The", "ISBN" : "978-1-4302-5821-6", "Publisher" :
"Apress", "Author" : ["Hows, David ", "Plugge, Eelco", "Membrey, Peter", "Hawkins, Tim"]}

{ "_id" : "ObjectId("4c1a86bb2955000000004076"), "Type" : "CD", "Artist" :
"Nirvana", "Title" : "Nevermind", "Tracklist" : [
    {
        "Track" : "1",
            "Title" : "Smells Like Teen Spirit",
            "Length" : "5:02"
    },
    {
        "Track" : "2",
        "Title" : "In Bloom",
        "Length" : "4:15"
    }
] }
```

This is simple stuff, but typically you would not want to retrieve all the information from all the documents in your collection. Instead, you probably want to retrieve a certain type of document. For example, you might want to return all the CDs from Nirvana. If so, you can specify that only the desired information is requested and returned:

```
> db.media.find ( { Artist : "Nirvana" } )
{ "_id" : "ObjectId("4c1a86bb2955000000004076"), "Type" : "CD", "Artist" :
 "Nirvana", "Title" : "Nevermind", "Tracklist" : [
    {
        "Track" : "1",
        "Title" : "Smells Like Teen Spirit",
        "Length" : "5:02"
    },
    {
        "Track" : "2",
        "Title" : "In Bloom",
        "Length" : "4:15"
    }
] }
```

Okay, so this looks much better! You don't have to see all the information from all the other items you've added to your collection, only the information that interests you. However, what if you're still not satisfied with the results returned? For example, assume you want to get a list back that shows only the titles of the CDs you have by Nirvana, ignoring any other information, such as track lists. You can do this by inserting an additional parameter into your query that specifies the name of the key that you want to return, followed by a 1:

```
> db.media.find ( {Artist : "Nirvana"}, {Title: 1} )
{ "_id" : ObjectId("4c1a86bb2955000000004076"), "Title" : "Nevermind" }
```

Inserting the { Title : 1 } information specifies that only the information from the title field should be returned. The results are sorted and presented to you in ascending order.

■ **Note** The ascending order is based upon the insertion order of the document.

You can also accomplish the opposite: inserting { Type : 0 } retrieves a list of all items you have stored from Nirvana, showing all information except for the Type field.

■ **Note** The _id field will by default remain visible, unless you explicitly ask it not to show itself.

Take a moment to run the revised query with the { Title : 1 } insertion; no unnecessary information is returned at all. This saves you time because you see only the information you want. It also spares your database the time required to return unnecessary information.

Using the Dot Notation

When you start working with more complex document structures such as documents containing arrays or embedded objects, you can begin using other methods for querying information from those objects as well. For example, assume you want to find all CDs that contain a specific song you like. The following code executes a more detailed query:

```
> db.media.find( { "Tracklist.Title" : "In Bloom" } )
{ "_id" : "ObjectId("4c1a86bb2955000000004076"), "Type" : "CD", "Artist" :
"Nirvana", "Title" : "Nevermind", "Tracklist" : [
    {
        "Track" : "1",
        "Title" : "Smells Like Teen Spirit",
        "Length" : "5:02"
    },
    {
        "Track" : "2",
        "Title" : "In Bloom",
        "Length" : "4:15"
    }
] }
```

Using a period [.] after the key's name tells your find function to look for information embedded in your documents. Things are a little simpler when working with arrays. For example, you can execute the following query if you want to find a list of books written by Peter Membrey:

```
> db.media.find( { "Author" : "Membrey, Peter" } )
{ "_id" : "ObjectId("4c1a8a56c603000000007ecb"), "Type" : "Book", "Title" :
"Definitive Guide to MongoDB 2nd ed., The", "ISBN" : "978-1-4302-5821-6", "Publisher" :
"Apress", "Author" : ["Hows, David ", "Plugge, Eelco", "Membrey, Peter", "Hawkins, Tim"] }
```

However, the following command will not match any documents, even though it might appear identical to the earlier track list query:

```
> db.media.find ( { "Tracklist" : {"Track" : "1" }} )
```

Subobjects must match exactly; therefore, the preceding query would only match a document that contains no other information, such as Track.Title:

```
{"Type" : "CD",
"Artist" : "Nirvana"
"Title" : "Nevermind",
"Tracklist" : [
    {
        "Track" : "1",
    },
    {
        "Track" : "2",
        "Title" : "In Bloom",
        "Length" : "4:15"
    }
]
}
```

Using the Sort, Limit, and Skip Functions

MongoDB includes several functions that you can use for more precise control over your queries. We'll cover how to use the sort, limit, and skip functions in this section.

You can use the sort function to sort the results returned from a query. You can sort the results in ascending or descending order using 1 or -1, respectively. The function itself is analogous to the ORDER BY statement in SQL, and it uses the key's name and sorting method as criteria, as in this example:

```
> db.media.find().sort( { Title: 1 })
```

This example sorts the results based on the Title key's value in ascending order. This is the default sorting order when no parameters are specified. You would add the -1 flag to sort in descending order.

■ **Note**   If you specify a key for sorting that does not exist, the values will be returned in their ascending insertion order.

You can use the limit() function to specify the maximum number of results returned. This function requires only one parameter: the number of the desired results returned. When you specify '0', all results will be returned. The following example returns only the first ten items in your media collection:

```
> db.media.find().limit( 10 )
```

Another thing you might want to do is skip the first *n* documents in a collection. The following example skips the first twenty documents in your media collection:

```
> db.media.find().skip( 20 )
```

As you probably surmised, this command returns all documents within your collection, except for the first twenty it finds. Remember: it finds documents in the order they were inserted.

MongoDB wouldn't be particularly powerful if it weren't able to combine these commands. However, practically any function can be combined and used in conjunction with any other function. The following example limits the results by skipping a few and then sorts the results in descending order:

```
> db.media.find().sort ( { Title : -1 } ).limit ( 10 ).skip ( 20 )
```

You might use this example if you want to implement paging in your application. As you might have guessed, this command wouldn't return any results in the media collection created so far, because the collection contains fewer documents than were skipped in this example.

■ **Note**   You can use the following shortcut in the `find()` function to skip and limit your results: `find ( {}, {}, 10, 20 )`. Here, you limit the results to 10 and skip the first 20 documents.

Working with Capped Collections, Natural Order, and $natural

There are some additional concepts and features you should be aware of when sorting queries with MongoDB, including capped collections, natural order, and $natural. We'll explain what all of these terms mean and how you can leverage them in your sorts in this section.

The *natural order* is the database's native ordering method for objects within a (normal) collection. So, when you query for items in a collection, the items are returned by default in the *forward natural order*. This is usually identical to the order in which items were inserted; however, that is not guaranteed to be the case, as data can move when it no longer fits on its old location after being modified.

A *capped collection* is a collection in your database where the natural order is guaranteed to be the order in which the documents were inserted. Guaranteeing that the natural order will always match the insertion order can be particularly useful when you're querying data and need to be absolutely certain that the results returned are already sorted based on their order of insertion.

Capped collections have another great benefit: they are a fixed size. Once a capped collection is full, the oldest data will be purged, and newer data will be added at the end, ensuring that the natural order follows the order in which the records were inserted. This type of collection can be used for logging and auto-archiving data.

Unlike a standard collection, a capped collection must be created explicitly, using the `createCollection` function. You must also supply parameters that specify the size (in bytes) of the collection you want to add. For example, imagine you want to create a capped collection named `audit` with a maximum size of 20480 bytes:

```
> db.createCollection("audit", {capped:true, size:20480})
{ "ok" : 1 }
```

Given that a capped collection guarantees that the natural order matches the insertion order, you don't need to include any special parameters or any other special commands or functions when querying the data either, except of course when you want to reverse the default results. This is where the $natural parameter comes in. For example, assume you want to find the ten *most recent* entries from your capped collection that lists failed login attempts. You could use the $natural parameter to find this information:

```
> db.audit.find().sort( { $natural: -1 } ).limit ( 10 )
```

■ **Note**   Documents already added to a capped collection can be updated, but they must not grow in size. The update will fail if they do. Deleting documents from a capped collection is also not possible; instead, the entire collection must be dropped and re-created if you want to do this. You will learn more about dropping a collection later in this chapter.

You can also limit the number of items added into a capped collection using the max: parameter when you create the collection. However, you must take care to ensure that there is enough space in the collection for the number of items you want to add. If the collection becomes full before the number of items has been reached, the oldest item in the collection will be removed. The MongoDB shell includes a utility that lets you see the amount of space used by an existing collection, whether it's capped or uncapped. You invoke this utility using the validate() function. This can be particularly useful if you want to estimate how large a collection might become.

As stated previously, you can use the max: parameter to cap the number of items that can be inserted into a collection, as in this example:

```
> db.createCollection("audit100", { capped:true, size:20480, max: 100})
{ "ok" : 1 }
```

Next, use the validate() function to check the size of the collection:

```
> db.audit100.validate()
{
    "ns" : "media.audit100",
    "result" : "
        validate
        capped:1 max:100
        firstExtent:0:54000 ns:media.audit100
        lastExtent:0:54000 ns:media.audit100
        # extents:1
        datasize?:0 nrecords?:0 lastExtentSize:20736
        padding:1
        first extent:
        loc:0:54000 xnext:null xprev:null
        nsdiag:media.audit100
        size:20736 firstRecord:null lastRecord:null
        capped outOfOrder:0 (OK)
        0 objects found, nobj:0
        0 bytes data w/headers
        0 bytes data wout/headers
        deletedList: 1100000000000000000
        deleted: n: 2 size: 20560
        nIndexes:0
    ",
    "ok" : 1,
    "valid" : true,
    "lastExtentSize" : 20736
}
```

The resulting output shows that the table (named audit100) is a capped collection with a maximum of 100 items to be added, and it currently contains zero items.

Retrieving a Single Document

So far we've only looked at examples that show how to retrieve multiple documents. If you want to receive only one result, however, querying for all documents—which is what you generally do when executing a find() function—would be a waste of CPU time and memory. For this case, you can use the findOne() function to retrieve a single item from your collection. Overall, the result is identical to what occurs when you append the limit(1) function, but why make it harder on yourself than you should?

The syntax of the findOne() function is identical to the syntax of the find() function:

```
> db.media.findOne()
```

It's generally advised to use the findOne() function if you expect only one result.

Using the Aggregation Commands

MongoDB comes with a nice set of aggregation commands. You might not see their significance at first, but once you get the hang of them, you will see that the aggregation commands form an extremely powerful set of tools. For instance, you might use them to get an overview of some basic statistics about your database. In this section, we will take a closer look at how to use three of the functions from the available aggregate commands: count, distinct, and group.

In addition to these three basic aggregation commands, MongoDB also includes an aggregation framework. This powerful feature will allow you to calculate aggregated values without needing to use the—often overly complex—map/reduce framework. The aggregation framework will be discussed in Chapter 5.

Returning the Number of Documents with count()

The count() function returns the number of documents in the specified collection. So far we've added a number of documents in the *media* collection. The count() function can tell you exactly how many:

```
> db.media.count()
2
```

You can also perform additional filtering by combining count() with conditional operators, as shown here:

```
> db.media.find( { Publisher : "Apress", Type: "Book" } ).count()
1
```

This example returns only the number of documents added in the collection that are published by Apress and of the type Book. Note that the count() function ignores a skip() or limit() parameter by default. To ensure that your query doesn't skip these parameters and that your count results will match the limit and/or skip parameters, use count(true):

```
> db.media.find( { Publisher: "Apress", Type: "Book" }).skip ( 2 ) .count (true)
0
```

Retrieving Unique Values with distinct()

The preceding example shows a great way to retrieve the total number of documents from a specific publisher. However, this approach is definitely not precise. After all, if you own more than one book with the same title (for instance, the hardcopy and the e-book), then you would technically have just one book. This is where distinct() can help you: it will only return unique values.

For the sake of completeness, you can add an additional item to the collection. This item carries the same title, but has a different ISBN number:

```
> document = ( { "Type" : "Book","Title" : "Definitive Guide to MongoDB 2nd ed., The", ISBN:
"978-1-4302-5821-6", "Publisher" : "Apress", "Author" :
["Hows, David","Membrey, Peter","Plugge, Eelco","Hawkins, Tim"] } )
> db.media.insert (document)
```

At this point, you should have two books in the database with identical titles. When using the distinct() function on the titles in this collection, you will get a total of two unique items. However, the titles of the two books are unique, so they will be grouped into one item. The other result will be the title of the album "Nevermind:"

```
> db.media.distinct( "Title")
[ "Definitive Guide to MongoDB, The", "Nevermind" ]
```

Similarly, you will get two results if you query for a list of unique ISBN numbers:

```
> db.media.distinct ("ISBN")
[ "1-4302-3051-7", "987-4302-3051-9" ]
```

The distinct() function also takes nested keys when querying; for instance, this command will give you a list of unique titles of your CDs:

```
> db.media.distinct ("Tracklist.Title")
[ "In Bloom", "Smells Like Teen Spirit" ]
```

Grouping Your Results

Last but not least, you can group your results. MongoDB's group() function is similar to SQL's GROUP BY function, although the syntax is a little different. The purpose of the command is to return an array of grouped items. The group() function takes three parameters: key, initial, and reduce.

The key parameter specifies which results you want to group. For example, assume you want to group results by Title. The initial parameter lets you provide a base for each grouped result (that is, the base number of items to start off with). By default, you want to leave this parameter at zero if you want an exact number returned. The reduce parameter groups all similar items together. Reduce takes two arguments: the current document being iterated over and the aggregation counter object. These arguments are called items and prev in the example that follows. Essentially, the reduce parameter adds a 1 to the sum of every item it encounters that matches a title it has already found.

The group() function is ideal when you're looking for a *tagcloud* kind of function. For example, assume you want to obtain a list of all unique titles of *any* type of item in your collection. Additionally, assume you want to group them together if any doubles are found, based on the title:

```
> db.media.group (
{
    key: {Title : true},
    initial: {Total : 0},
```

```
    reduce : function (items,prev)
    {
        prev.Total += 13
    }
}
)

[
    {
        "Title" : "Nevermind",
        "Total" : 1
    },
    {
        "Title" : "Definitive Guide to MongoDB, The",
        "Total" : 2
    }
]
```

In addition to the key, initial, and reduce parameters, you can specify three more optional parameters:

- keyf: You can use this parameter to replace the key parameter if you do not wish to group the results on an existing key in your documents. Instead, you would group them using another function you design that specifies how to do grouping.

- cond: You can use this parameter to specify an additional statement that must be true before a document will be grouped. You can use this much as you use the find() query to search for documents in your collection. If this parameter isn't set (the default), then all documents in the collection will be checked.

- finalize: You can use this parameter to specify a function you want to execute before the final results are returned. For instance, you might calculate an average or perform a count and include this information in the results.

■ **Note** The group() function does not currently work in sharded environments. For these, you should use the mapreduce() function instead. Also, the resulting output cannot contain more than 10,000 keys in all with the group() function, or an exception will be raised. This too, can be bypassed by using mapreduce().

Working with Conditional Operators

MongoDB supports a large set of conditional operators to better filter your results. The following sections provide an overview of these operators, including some basic examples that show you how to use them. Before walking through these examples, however, you should add a few more items to the database; doing so will let you see the effects of these operators more plainly:

```
dvd = ( { "Type" : "DVD", "Title" : "Matrix, The", "Released" : 1999,
    "Cast" : ["Keanu Reeves","Carrie-Anne Moss","Laurence Fishburne","Hugo
    Weaving","Gloria Foster","Joe Pantoliano"] } )
{
        "Type" : "DVD",
        "Title" : "Matrix, The",
```

```
            "Released" : 1999,
            "Cast" : [
                    "Keanu Reeves",
                    "Carrie-Anne Moss",
                    "Laurence Fishburne",
                    "Hugo Weaving",
                    "Gloria Foster",
                    "Joe Pantoliano"
            ]
}
> db.media.insert(dvd)

> dvd = ( { "Type" : "DVD", Title : "Blade Runner", Released : 1982 } )
{ "Type" : "DVD", "Title" : "Blade Runner", "Released" : 1982 }
> db.media.insert(dvd)

> dvd = ( { "Type" : "DVD", Title : "Toy Story 3", Released : 2010 } )
{ "Type" : "DVD", "Title" : "Toy Story 3", "Released" : 2010 }
> db.media.insert(dvd)
```

Performing Greater-Than and Less-Than Comparisons

You can use the following special parameters to perform greater-than and less-than comparisons in queries: $gt, $lt, $gte, and $lte. In this section, we'll look at how to use each of these parameters.

The first one we'll cover is the $gt (greater than) parameter. You can use this to specify that a certain integer should be greater than a specified value in order to be returned:

```
> db.media.find ( { Released : {$gt : 2000} }, { "Cast" : 0 } )
{ "_id" : ObjectId("4c4369a3c603000000007ed3"), "Type" : "DVD", "Title" :
"Toy Story 3", "Released" : 2010 }
```

Note that the year 2000 itself will not be included in the preceding query. For that, you use the $gte (greater than or equal to) parameter:

```
> db.media.find ( { Released : {$gte : 1999 } }, { "Cast" : 0 } )
{ "_id" : ObjectId("4c43694bc603000000007ed1"), "Type" : "DVD", "Title" :
"Matrix, The", "Released" : 1999 }
{ "_id" : ObjectId("4c4369a3c603000000007ed3"), "Type" : "DVD", "Title" :
"Toy Story 3", "Released" : 2010 }
```

Likewise, you can use the $lt (less than) parameter to find items in your collection that predate the year 1999:

```
> db.media.find ( { Released : {$lt : 1999 } }, { "Cast" : 0 } )
{ "_id" : ObjectId("4c436969c603000000007ed2"), "Type" : "DVD", "Title" : "Blade Runner",
"Released" : 1982 }
```

You can also get a list of items older than or equal to the year 1999 by using the $lte (less than or equal to) parameter:

```
> db.media.find( {Released : {$lte: 1999}}, { "Cast" : 0 })
{ "_id" : ObjectId("4c43694bc603000000007ed1"), "Type" : "DVD", "Title" :
"Matrix, The", "Released" : 1999 }
{ "_id" : ObjectId("4c436969c603000000007ed2"), "Type" : "DVD", "Title" :
"Blade Runner", "Released" : 1982 }
```

You can also combine these parameters to specify a range:

```
> db.media.find( {Released : {$gte: 1990, $lt : 2010}}, { "Cast" : 0 })
{ "_id" : ObjectId("4c43694bc603000000007ed1"), "Type" : "DVD", "Title" :
"Matrix, The", "Released" : 1999 }
```

These parameters might strike you as relatively simple to use; however, you will be using them a lot when querying for a specific range of data.

Retrieving All Documents but Those Specified

You can use the $ne (not equals) parameter to retrieve every document in your collection, except for the ones that match certain criteria. For example, you can use this snippet to obtain a list of all books where the author is not Eelco Plugge:

```
> db.media.find( { Type : "Book", Author: {$ne : "Plugge, Eelco"}})
```

Specifying an Array of Matches

You can use the $in operator to specify an array of possible matches. The SQL equivalent is the IN operator.
    You can use the following snippet to retrieve data from the media collection using the $in operator:

```
> db.media.find( {Released : {$in : [1999,2008,2009] } }, { "Cast" : 0 } )
{ "_id" : ObjectId("4c43694bc603000000007ed1"), "Type" : "DVD", "Title" : "Matrix, The",
"Released" : 1999 }
```

This example returns only one item, because only one item matches the release year of 1999, and there are no matches for the years 2008 and 2009.

Finding a Value Not in an Array

The $nin operator functions similarly to the $in operator, except that it searches for the objects where the specified field does *not* have a value in the specified array:

```
> db.media.find( {Released : {$nin : [1999,2008,2009] },Type : "DVD" },
{ "Cast" : 0 } )
{ "_id" : ObjectId("4c436969c603000000007ed2"), "Type" : "DVD", "Title" :
"Blade Runner", "Released" : 1982 }
{ "_id" : ObjectId("4c4369a3c603000000007ed3"), "Type" : "DVD", "Title" :
"Toy Story 3", "Released" : 2010 }
```

Matching All Attributes in a Document

The $all operator also works similarly to the $in operator. However, $all requires that all attributes match in the documents, whereas only one attribute must match for the $in operator. Let's look at an example that illustrates these differences. First, here's an example that uses $in:

```
> db.media.find ( { Released : {$in : ["2010","2009"] } }, { "Cast" : 0 } )
{ "_id" : ObjectId("4c4369a3c603000000007ed3"), "Type" : "DVD", "Title" :
"Toy Story 3", "Released" : 2010 }
```

One document is returned for the $in operator because there's a match for 2010, but not for 2009. However, the $all parameter doesn't return any results, because there are no matching documents with 2009 in the value:

```
> db.media.find ( { Released : {$all : ["2010","2009"] } }, { "Cast" : 0 } )
```

Searching for Multiple Expressions in a Document

You can use the $or operator to search for multiple expressions in a single query, where only one criterion needs to match to return a given document. Unlike the $in operator, $or allows you to specify both the key and the value, rather than only the value:

```
> db.media.find({ $or : [ { "Title" : "Toy Story 3" }, { "ISBN" :
"987-1-4302-3051-9" } ] } )
{ "_id" : ObjectId("4c5fc7d8db290000000067c5"), "Type" : "Book", "Title" :
"Definitive Guide to MongoDB, The", "ISBN" : "987-1-4302-3051-9",
"Publisher" : "Apress", "Author" : ["Hows, David", "Membrey, Peter", "Plugge, Eelco",
"Hawkins, Tim" ] }
{ "_id" : ObjectId("4c5fc943db290000000067ca"), "Type" : "DVD", "Title" :
"Toy Story 3", "Released" : 2010 }
```

It's also possible to combine the $or operator with another query parameter. This will restrict the returned documents to only those that match the first query (mandatory), and then either of the two key/value pairs specified at the $or operator, as in this example:

```
> db.media.find({ "Type" : "DVD", $or : [ { "Title" : "Toy Story 3" }, {
"ISBN" : "987-1-4302-3051-9" } ] })
{ "_id" : ObjectId("4c5fc943db290000000067ca"), "Type" : "DVD", "Title" :
"Toy Story 3", "Released" : 2010 }
```

You could say that the $or operator allows you to perform two queries at the same time, combining the results of two otherwise unrelated queries.

Retrieving a Document with $slice

You can use the $slice operator to retrieve a document that includes a specific area from an array in that document. This can be particularly useful if you want to limit a certain set of items added to save bandwidth. The operator also lets you retrieve the results *n* items per page, a feature generally known as *paging*.

In theory, the $slice operator combines the capabilities of the limit() and skip() functions; however, limit() and skip()do not work on an array, whereas $slice does. The operator takes two parameters; the first indicates the total number of items to be returned. The second parameter is optional; if used, it ensures that the *first* parameter defines the offset, while the *second* defines the limit. The limit parameter can also indicate a negative condition.

The following example limits the items from the Cast list to the first three items:

```
> db.media.find({"Title" : "Matrix, The"}, {"Cast" : {$slice: 3}})
{ "_id" : ObjectId("4c5fcd3edb290000000067cb"), "Type" : "DVD", "Title" :
"Matrix, The", "Released" : 1999, "Cast" : [ "Keanu Reeves", "Carrie-Anne
Moss", "Laurence Fishburne" ] }
```

You can also get only the last three items by making the integer negative:

```
> db.media.find({"Title" : "Matrix, The"}, {"Cast" : {$slice: -3}})
{ "_id" : ObjectId("4c5fcd3edb290000000067cb"), "Type" : "DVD", "Title" :
"Matrix, The", "Released" : 1999, "Cast" : [ "Hugo Weaving", "Gloria Foster",
"Joe Pantoliano" ] }
```

Or you can skip the first two items and limit the results to three from that particular point (pay careful attention to the brackets):

```
> db.media.find({"Title" : "Matrix, The"}, {"Cast" : {$slice: [2,3] }})
{ "_id" : ObjectId("4c5fcd3edb290000000067cb"), "Type" : "DVD", "Title" :
"Matrix, The", "Released" : 1999, "Cast" : [ "Laurence Fishburne", "Hugo
Weaving", "Gloria Foster" ] }
```

Finally, when specifying a negative integer, you can skip to the last five items and limit the results to four, as in this example:

```
> db.media.find({"Title" : "Matrix, The"}, {"Cast" : {$slice: [-5,4] }})
{ "_id" : ObjectId("4c5fcd3edb290000000067cb"), "Type" : "DVD", "Title" :
"Matrix, The", "Released" : 1999, "Cast" : [ "Carrie-Anne Moss","Laurence
Fishburne","Hugo Weaving","Gloria Foster"] }
```

■ **Note**   With version 2.4 MongoDB also introduced the $slice operator for $push operations, allowing you to limit the number of array elements when appending values to an array. This operator is discussed later in this chapter. Do not confuse the two, however.

Searching for Odd/Even Integers

The $mod operator lets you search for specific data that consists of an even or uneven number. This works because the operator takes the modulus of 2 and checks for a remainder of 0, thereby providing even-numbered results only.

For example, the following code returns any item in the collection that has an even-numbered integer set to its Released field:

```
> db.media.find ( { Released : { $mod: [2,0] } }, {"Cast" : 0 } )
{ "_id" : ObjectId("4c45b5c18e0f0000000062aa"), "Type" : "DVD", "Title" :
"Blade Runner", "Released" : 1982 }
{ "_id" : ObjectId("4c45b5df8e0f0000000062ab"), "Type" : "DVD", "Title" :
"Toy Story 3", "Released" : 2010 }
```

Likewise, you can find any documents containing an uneven value in the Released field by changing the parameters in $mod, as follows:

```
> db.media.find ( { Released : { $mod: [2,1] } }, { "Cast" : 0 } )
{ "_id" : ObjectId("4c45b5b38e0f0000000062a9"), "Type" : "DVD", "Title" :
"Matrix, The", "Released" : 1999 }
```

■ **Note**   The $mod operator only works on integer values, not on strings that contain a numbered value. For example, you can't use the operator on { Released : "2010" }, because it's in quotes and therefore a string.

Filtering Results with $size

The $size operator lets you filter your results to match an array with the specified number of elements in it. For example, you might use this operator to do a search for those CDs that have exactly two songs on them:

```
> db.media.find ( { Tracklist : {$size : 2} } )
{ "_id" : ObjectId("4c1a86bb2955000000004076"), "Type" : "CD", "Artist" :
"Nirvana", "Title" : "Nevermind", "Tracklist" : [
        {
                "Track" : "1",
                "Title" : "Smells Like Teen Spirit",
                "Lenght" : "5:02"
        },
        {
                "Track" : "2",
                "Title" : "In Bloom",
                "Length" : "4:15"
        }
] }
```

■ **Note**   You cannot use the $size operator to find a range of sizes. For example, you cannot use it to find arrays with more than one element in them.

Returning a Specific Field Object

The $exists operator allows you to return a specific object if a specified field is either missing or found. The following example returns all items in the collection with a key named Author:

```
> db.media.find ( { Author : {$exists : true } } )
```

Similarly, if you invoke this operator with a value of false, then all documents that don't have a key named Author will be returned:

```
> db.media.find ( { Author : {$exists : false } } )
```

■ **Warning**   Currently, the $exists operator is unable to use an index; therefore, using it requires a full table scan.

Matching Results Based on the BSON Type

The $type operator lets you match results based on their BSON type. For instance, the following snippet lets you find all items that have a track list of the type Embedded Object (that is, it contains a list of information):

```
> db.media.find ( { Tracklist: { $type : 3 } } )
{ "_id" : ObjectId("4c1a86bb2955000000004076"), "Type" : "CD", "Artist" :
"Nirvana", "Title" : "Nevermind", "Tracklist" : [
        {
                "Track" : "1",
                "Title" : "Smells Like Teen Spirit",
                "Lenght" : "5:02"
        },
        {

                "Track" : "2",
                "Title" : "In Bloom",
                "Length" : "4:15"
        }
] }
```

The known data types are defined in Table 4-1.

Table 4-1. *Known BSON Types and Codes*

Code	Data Type
–1	MiniKey
1	Double
2	Character string (UTF8)
3	Embedded object
4	Embedded array
5	Binary Data
7	Object ID
8	Boolean type
9	Date type
10	Null type
11	Regular Expression
13	JavaScript Code
14	Symbol
15	JavaScript Code with scope
16	32-bit integer
17	Timestamp
18	64-bit integer
127	MaxKey
255	MinKey

Matching an Entire Array

If you want to match an entire array within a document, you can use the $elemMatch operator. This is particularly useful if you have multiple documents within your collection, some of which have some of the same information. This can make a default query incapable of finding the exact document you are looking for. This is because the standard query syntax doesn't restrict itself to a single document within an array.

Let's look at an example that illustrates this principle. For this to work, we need to add another document to the collection, one that has an identical item in it, but is otherwise different. Specifically, we'll add another CD from Nirvana that happens to have the same track on it as the aforementioned CD ("Smells Like Teen Spirit"). However, on this version of the CD, the song is track 5, not track 1:

```
{
        "Type" : "CD",
        "Artist" : "Nirvana",
        "Title" : "Nirvana",
        "Tracklist" : [
                {
                        "Track" : "1",
                        "Title" : "You know you're right",
                        "Length" : "3:38"
                },
                {
                        "Track" : "5",
                        "Title" : "Smells like teen spirit",
                        "Length" : "5:02"
                }
        ]
}
```

```
> nirvana = ( { "Type" : "CD", "Artist" : "Nirvana", "Title" : "Nirvana",
"Tracklist" : [ { "Track" : "1", "Title" : "You Know You're Right", "Length"
: "3:38"}, {"Track" : "5", "Title" : "Smells Like Teen Spirit", "Length" :
"5:02" } ] } )
```

```
> db.media.insert(nirvana)
```

If you want to search for an album from Nirvana that has the song "Smells Like Teen Spirit" as Track 1 on the CD, you might think that the following query would do the job:

```
> db.media.find ( { "Tracklist.Title" : "Smells Like Teen Spirit",
"Tracklist.Track" : "1" } )
```

Unfortunately, the preceding query will return both documents. The reason for this is that both documents have a track with the title called "Smells Like Teen Spirit" and both have a track number 1. If you want to match an entire document within the array, you can use $elemMatch, as in this example:

```
> db.media.find ( { Tracklist: { "$elemMatch" : { Title:
"Smells like teen spirit", Track : "1" } } } )
```

```
{ "_id" : ObjectId("4c1a86bb2955000000004076"), "Type" : "CD", "Artist" :
"Nirvana", "Title" : "Nevermind", "Tracklist" : [
```

```
{
            "Track" : "1",
            "Title" : "Smells Like Teen Spirit",
            "Lenght" : "5:02"
    },
    {
            "Track" : "2",
            "Title" : "In Bloom",
            "Length" : "4:15"
    }
] }
```

This query gave the desired result and only returned the first document.

$not (meta-operator)

You can use the $not meta-operator to negate any check performed by a standard operator. The following example returns all documents in your collection, except for the one seen in the $elemMatch example:

```
> db.media.find ( { Tracklist : { $not : { "$elemMatch" : { Title:
"Smells Like Teen Spirit", "Track" : "1" } } } } )
```

Specifying Additional Query Expressions

Apart from the structured query syntax you've seen so far, you can also specify additional query expressions in JavaScript. The big advantage of this is that JavaScript is extremely flexible and allows you to do tons of additional things. The downside of using JavaScript is that it's a tad slower than the native operators baked into MongoDB.

For example, assume you want to search for a DVD within your collection that is older than 1995. All of the following code examples would return this information:

```
db.media.find ( { "Type" : "DVD", "Released" : { $lt : 1995 } } )

db.media.find ( { "Type" : "DVD", $where: "this.Released < 1995" } )

db.media.find ("this.Released < 1995")

f = function() { return this.Released < 1995 }
db.media.find(f)
```

And *that's* how flexible MongoDB is! Using these operators should enable you to find just about anything throughout your collections.

Leveraging Regular Expressions

Regular expressions are another powerful tool you can use to query information. *Regular expressions—regex*, for short—are special text strings that you can use to describe your search pattern. These work much like wildcards, but they are far more powerful and flexible.

MongoDB allows you to use these regular expressions when searching for data in your collections; however, it will attempt to use an index whenever possible for simple prefix queries.

The following example uses regex in a query to find all items in the media collection that start with the word "Matrix:"

```
> db.media.find ( { Title : /Matrix*/i } )
```

Using regular expressions from MongoDB can make your life much simpler, so we'd recommend exploring this feature in greater detail as time permits or your circumstances can benefit from it.

Updating Data

So far you've learned how to insert and query for data in your database. Next, you'll learn how to update that data. MongoDB supports quite a few update operators that you'll learn how to use in the following sections.

Updating with update()

MongoDB comes with the update() function for performing updates to your data. The update() function takes three primary arguments: criteria, objNew and options.

The criteria argument lets you specify the query that selects the record you want to update. You use the objNew argument to specify the updated information; or you can use an operator to do this for you. The options argument lets you specify your options when updating the document, and has two possible values: upsert and multi. The upsert option lets you specify whether the update should be an *upsert*—that is, it tells MongoDB to update the record if it exists, and create it if it doesn't. Finally, the multi option lets you specify whether all matching documents should be updated or just the first one (the default action).

The following simple example uses the update() function without any fancy operators:

```
> db.media.update( { "Title" : "Matrix, The"}, {"Type" : "DVD", "Title" :
"Matrix, The", "Released" : 1999, "Genre" : "Action"}, { upsert: true} )
```

This example overwrites the document in the collection and saves it with the new values specified. Note that any fields that you leave out are removed (the document is basically being rewritten). Because the upsert argument is specified as true, any fields that do not exist yet will be added (the Genre key/value pair, in this case).

In case there happen to be multiple documents matching the criteria and you wish to upsert them all, the upsert and multi options can be added while using the $set modifier operator as shown here:

```
> db.media.update( { "Title" : "Matrix, The"}, {$set: {"Type" : "DVD", "Title" :
"Matrix, The", "Released" : 1999, "Genre" : "Action"} }, {upsert: true, multi: true} )
```

■ **Note** An upsert tells the database to "update a record if a document is present or to insert the record if it isn't."

Implementing an Upsert with the save() Command

You can also perform an upsert with the save() command. To do this, you need to specify the _id value; you can have this value added automatically or specify it manually yourself. If you do not specify the _id value, the save() command will assume it's an insert and simply add the document into your collection.

The main benefit of using the save() command is that you do not need to specify that the upsert method should be used in conjunction with the update() command. Thus, the save() command gives you a quicker way to upsert data. In practice, the save() and update() commands look similar:

```
> db.media.update( { "Title" : "Matrix, The"}, {"Type" : "DVD", "Title" :
"Matrix, The", "Released" : "1999", "Genre" : "Action"}, { upsert: true} )

> db.media.save( { "Title" : "Matrix, The"}, {"Type" : "DVD", "Title" :
"Matrix, The", "Released" : "1999", "Genre" : "Action"})
```

Obviously, this example assumes that the Title value acts as the id field.

Updating Information Automatically

You can use the modifier operations to update information quickly and simply in your documents, but without needing to type everything in manually. For example, you might use these operations to increase a number or to remove an element from an array.

We'll be exploring these operators next, providing practical examples that show you how to use them.

Incrementing a Value with $inc

The $inc operator enables you to perform an (atomic) update on a key to increase the value by the given increment, assuming that the field exists. If the field doesn't exist, it will be created. To see this in action, begin by adding another document to the collection:

```
> manga = ( { "Type" : "Manga", "Title" : "One Piece", "Volumes" : 612,
"Read" : 520 } )
{
        "Type" : "Manga",
        "Title" : "One Piece",
        "Volumes" : "612",
        "Read" : "520"
}
> db.media.insert(manga)
```

Now you're ready to update the document. For example, assume you've read another four volumes of the One Piece manga, and you want to increment the number of Read volumes in the document. The following example shows you how to do this:

```
> db.media.update ( { "Title" : "One Piece"}, {$inc: {"Read" : 4} } )
> db.media.find ( { "Title" : "One Piece" } )
{
        "Type" : "Manga",
        "Title" : "One Piece ",
        "Volumes" : "612",
        "Read" : "524"
}
```

Setting a Field's Value

You can use the $set operator to set a field's value to one you specify. This goes for any datatype, as in the following example:

```
> db.media.update ( { "Title" : "Matrix, The" }, {$set : { Genre :
"Sci-Fi" } } )
```

This snippet would update the genre in the document created earlier, setting it to Sci-Fi instead.

Deleting a Specified Field

The $unset operator lets you delete a given field, as in this example:

```
> db.media.update ( {"Title": "Matrix, The"}, {$unset : { "Genre" : 1 } } )
```

This snippet would delete the Genre key and its value from the document.

Appending a Value to a Specified Field

The $push operator allows you to append a value to a specified field. If the field is an existing array, then the value will be added. If the field doesn't exist yet, then the field will be set to the array value. If the field exists, but it isn't an array, then an error condition will be raised.

Begin by adding another author to your entry in the collection:

```
> db.media.update ( {"ISBN" : "978-1-4302-5821-6"}, {$push: { Author : "Griffin,
Stewie"} } )
```

The next snippet raises an error message because the Title field is not an array:

```
> db.media.update ( {"ISBN" : "978-1-4302-5821-6"}, {$push: { Title :
"This isn't an array"} } )
Cannot apply $push/$pushAll modifier to non-array
```

The following example shows how the document looks in the meantime:

```
> db.media.find ( { "ISBN" : "978-1-4302-5821-6" } )
{
    "Author" :
    [
        "Hows, David",
        "Membrey, Peter",
        "Plugge, Eelco",
        "Griffin, Stewie",
    ],
    "ISBN" : "978-1-4302-5821-6",
    "Publisher" : "Apress",
    "Title" : "Definitive Guide to MongoDB 2nd ed., The",
    "Type" : "Book",
    "_id" : ObjectId("4c436231c603000000007ed0")
}
```

Specifying Multiple Values in an Array

When working with arrays, the $push operator will append the value specified to the given array, expanding the data stored within the given element. If you wish to add several separate values to the given array, you can use the optional $each modifier as in this example:

```
> db.media.update( { "ISBN" : "978-1-4302-5821-6" }, { $push: { Author : { $each:
["Griffin, Peter", "Griffin, Brian"] } } } )
{
    "Author" :
    [
        "Hows, David",
        "Membrey, Peter",
        "Plugge, Eelco",
        "Hawkins, Tim",
        "Griffin, Stewie",
        "Griffin, Peter",
        "Griffin, Brian"
    ],
    "ISBN" : "978-1-4302-5821-6",
    "Publisher" : "Apress",
    "Title" : "Definitive Guide to MongoDB 2nd ed., The",
    "Type" : "Book",
    "_id" : ObjectId("4c436231c603000000007ed0")
}
```

Optionally, you can use the $slice operator when using $each. This allows you to limit the number of elements within an array during a $push operation. $slice takes either a negative number or zero. Using a negative number ensures that only the last *n* elements will be kept within the array, whereas using zero would empty the array. Note that the $slice operator has to be the first modifier to the $push operator in order to function as such:

```
> db.media.update( { "ISBN" : "978-1-4302-5821-6" }, { $push: { Author : { $each:
["Griffin, Meg", "Griffin, Louis"], $slice: -2 } } } )
{
    "Author" :
    [
        "Griffin, Meg",
        "Griffin, Louis"
    ],
    "ISBN" : "978-1-4302-5821-6",
    "Publisher" : "Apress",
    "Title" : "Definitive Guide to MongoDB 2nd ed., The",
    "Type" : "Book",
    "_id" : ObjectId("4c436231c603000000007ed0")
}
```

As you can see, the $slice operator ensured that not only were the two new values pushed, the data kept within the array was also limited to the value specified (two). The $slice operator can be a valuable tool when working with fixed-sized arrays.

Adding Data to an Array with $addToSet

The $addToSet operator is another command that lets you add data to an array. However, this operator only adds the data to the array if the data is not already there. In this way, $addToSet is unlike $push. By default, the $addToSet operator takes one argument. However, you can use the $each operator to specify additional arguments when using t$addToSet. The following snippet adds the author Griffin, Brian into the authors array because it isn't there yet:

```
> db.media.update( { "ISBN" : "1-4302-3051-7" }, {$addToSet : { Author :
"Griffin, Brian" } } )
```

Executing the snippet again won't change anything because the author is already in the array.

To add more than one value, however, you should take a different approach and use the $each operator, as well:

```
> db.media.update( { "ISBN" : "1-4302-3051-7" }, {$addToSet : { Author :
{ $each : ["Griffin, Brian","Griffin, Meg"] } } } )
```

At this point, our document, which once looked tidy and trustworthy, has been transformed into something like this:

```
{
    "Author" :
    [
        "Hows, David",
        "Membrey, Peter",
        "Plugge, Eelco",
        "Hawkins, Tim",
        "Griffin, Stewie",
        "Griffin, Peter",
        "Griffin, Brian",
        "Griffin, Louis",
        "Griffin, Meg"
    ],
    "ISBN" : "1-4302-3051-7",
    "Publisher" : "Apress",
    "Title" : "Definitive Guide to MongoDB, The",
    "Type" : "Book",
    "_id" : ObjectId("4c436231c603000000007ed0")
}
```

Removing Elements from an Array

MongoDB also includes several methods that let you remove elements from an array, including $pop, $pull, $pullAll. In the sections that follow, you'll learn how to use each of these methods for removing elements from an array.

The $pop operator lets you remove a single element from an array. This operator lets you remove the first or last value in the array, depending on the parameter you pass down with it. For example, the following snippet removes the last element from the array:

```
> db.media.update( { "ISBN" : "1-4302-3051-7" }, {$pop : {Author : 1 } } )
```

In this case, the $pop operator will *pop* Meg's name off the list of authors. Passing down a negative number would remove the first element from the array. The following example removes Peter Membrey's name from the list of authors:

```
> db.media.update( { "ISBN" : "1-4302-3051-7" }, {$pop : {Author : -1 } } )
```

■ **Note**   Specifying a value of -2 or 1000 wouldn't change which element gets removed. Any negative number would remove the first element, while any positive number would remove the last element. Using the number 0 removes the last element from the array.

Removing Each Occurrence of a Specified Value

The $pull operator lets you remove each occurrence of a specified value from an array. This can be particularly useful if you have multiple elements with the same value in your array. Let's begin this example by using the $push parameter to add Stewie back to the list of authors:

```
> db.media.update ( {"ISBN" : "1-4302-3051-7"}, {$push: { Author :
"Griffin, Stewie"} } )
```

Stewie will be in and out of the database a couple more times as we walk through this book's examples. You can remove all occurrences of this author in the document with the following code:

```
> db.media.update ( {"ISBN" : "1-4302-3051-7"}, {$pull : { Author : "Griffin,
Stewie" } } )
```

Removing Multiple Elements from an Array

You can also remove multiple elements with different values from an array. The $pullAll operator enables you to accomplish this. The $pullAll operator takes an array with all the elements you want to remove, as in the following example:

```
> db.media.update( { "ISBN" : "1-4302-3051-7"}, {$pullAll : { Author :
["Griffin, Louis","Griffin, Peter","Griffin, Brian"] } } )
```

The field from which you remove the elements (Author in the preceding example) needs to be an array. If it isn't, you'll receive an error message.

Specifying the Position of a Matched Array

You can use the $ operator in your queries to specify the position of the matched array item in your query. You can use this operator for data manipulation after finding an array member. For instance, assume you've added another track to your track list, but you accidentally made a typo when entering the track number:

```
> db.media.update( { "Title" : "Nirvana" }, {$addToSet : { Tracklist :
{"Track" : 2,"Title": "Been a Son", "Length":"2:23"} } } )
{
    "Artist" : "Nirvana",
    "Title" : "Nirvana",
```

```
    "Tracklist" : [
        {
                "Track" : "1",
                "Title" : "You Know You're Right",
                "Length" : "3:38"
        },
        {
                "Track" : "5",
                "Title" : "Smells Like Teen Spirit",
                "Length" : "5:02"
        },
        {
                "Track" : 2,
                "Title" : "Been a Son",
                "Length" : "2:23"
        }
    ],
    "Type" : "CD",
    "_id" : ObjectId("4c443ad6c603000000007ed5")
}
```

It so happens you know that the track number of the most recent item should be 3 rather than 2. You can use the $inc method in conjunction with the $ operator to increase the value from 2 to 3, as in this example:

```
> db.media.update( { "Tracklist.Title" : "Been a son"},
{$inc:{"Tracklist.$.Track" : 1} } )
```

Note that only the first item it matches will be updated. Thus, if there are two identical elements in the comments array, only the first element will be increased.

Atomic Operations

MongoDB supports atomic operations executed against single documents. An *atomic operation* is a set of operations that can be combined in such a way that the set of operations appears to be merely one single operation to the rest of the system. This set of operations will have either a positive or a negative outcome as the final result.

You can call a set of operations an atomic operation if it meets the following pair of conditions:

1. No other process knows about the changes being made until the entire set of operations has completed.

2. If one of the operations fails, the entire set of operations (the entire atomic operation) will fail, resulting in a full rollback, where the data is restored to its state prior to running the atomic operation.

A standard behavior when executing atomic operations is that the data will be *locked* and therefore unable to be reached by other queries. However, MongoDB does not support locking or complex transactions for a number of reasons:

- In sharded environments (see Chapter 12 for more information on such environments), distributed locks can be expensive and slow. MongoDB's goal is to be lightweight and fast, so expensive and slow goes against the principle.

- MongoDB developers don't like the idea of deadlocks. In their view, it's preferable for a system to be simple and predictable instead.

- MongoDB is designed to work well for real-time problems. When an operation is executed that locks large amounts of data, it would also stop some smaller light queries for an extended period of time. Again, this goes against the MongoDB goal of speed.

MongoDB includes several update operators (as noted previously), all of which can atomically update an element:

- $set: Sets a particular value.

- $unset: Removes a particular value.

- $inc: Increments a particular value by a certain amount.

- $push: Appends a value to an array.

- $pull: Removes one or more values from an existing array.

- $pullAll: Removes several values from an existing array.

Using the Update if Current Method

Another strategy that atomic update uses is the *update-if-current* method. This method takes the following three steps:

1. It fetches the object from the document.

2. It modifies the object locally (with any of the previously mentioned operations, or a combination of them).

3. It sends an update request to update the object to the new value, in case the current value still matches the old value fetched.

You can use the getlasterror method to check whether all went well. Note that all of this happens automatically. Let's take a new look at an example shown previously:

```
> db.media.update( { "Tracklist.Title" : "Been a son"},
{$inc:{"Tracklist.$.Track" : 1} } )
```

Now you can use the getlasterror command to check whether the update went smoothly:

```
> db.$cmd.findOne({getlasterror:1})
```

If the atomic update executes successfully, you get the following result back:

```
{ "err" : null, "updatedExisting" : true, "n" : 1, "ok" : 1 }
```

In this example, you incremented `Tracklist.Track` using the track list title as an identifier. But now consider what happens if the track list data is changed by another user using the same method while MongoDB was modifying your data. Because `Tracklist.Title` remains the same, you might assume (incorrectly) that you are updating the original data, when in fact you are overwriting the changes.

This is known as *the ABA problem*. This scenario might seem unlikely, but in a multi-user environment, where many applications are working on data at the same time, this can be a significant problem.

To avoid this problem, you can do one of the following:

- Use the entire object in the update's query expression, instead of just the _id and `comments.by` field.

- Use `$set` to set the field you care about. If other fields have changed, they won't be affected by this.

- Put a version variable in the object and increment it on each update.

- When possible, use a $ operator instead of an update-if-current sequence of operations.

■ **Note** MongoDB does not support updating multiple documents atomically in a single operation. Instead, you can use nested objects, which effectively make them one document for atomic purposes.

Modifying and Returning a Document Atomically

The `findAndModify` command also allows you to perform an atomic update on a document. This command modifies the document and returns it. The command takes three main operators: `<query>`, which you use to specify the document you're executing it against; `<sort>`, used to sort the matching documents when multiple match, and `<operations>`, which you use to specify what needs to be done.

Now let's look at a handful of examples that illustrate how to use this command. The first example finds the document you're searching for and removes it once it is found:

```
> db.media.findAndModify( { "Title" : "One Piece",sort:{"Title": -1}, remove:
true} )
{
        "_id" : ObjectId("4c445218c603000000007ede"),
        "Type" : "Manga",
        "Title" : "One Piece",
        "Volumes" : 612,
        "Read" : 524
}
```

This code returned the document it found matching the criteria. In this case, it found and removed the first item it found with the title "One Piece." If you execute a `find()` function now, you will see that the document is no longer within the collection.

The next example modifies the document rather than removing it:

```
> db.media.findAndModify( { query: { "ISBN" : "987-1-4302-3051-9" }, sort:
{"Title":-1}, update: {$set: {"Title" : " Different Title"} } } )
```

The preceding example updates the title from "Definitive Guide to MongoDB," The to "Different Title"—and returns the old document (as it was before the update) to your shell. If you would rather see the results of the update on the document instead, you can add the new operator after your query:

```
> db.media.findAndModify( { query: { "ISBN" : "987-1-4302-3051-9" }, sort:
{"Title":-1}, update: {$set: {"Title" : " Different Title"} }, new:true } )
```

Note that you can use any modifier operation with this command, not just $set.

Renaming a Collection

It might happen that you discover you have named a collection incorrectly, but you've already inserted some data into it. This might make it troublesome to remove and read the data again from scratch.

Instead, you can use the renameCollection() function to rename your existing collection. The following example shows you how to use this simple and straightforward command:

```
> db.media.renameCollection("newname")
{ "ok" : 1 }
```

If the command executes successfully, an OK will be returned. If it fails, however (if the collection doesn't exist, for example), then the following message is returned:

```
{ "errmsg" : "assertion: source namespace does not exist", "ok" : 0 }
```

The renameCollection command doesn't take many parameters (unlike some commands you've seen so far); however, it can be quite useful in the right circumstances.

Removing Data

So far we've explored how to add, search for, and modify data. Next, we'll examine how to *remove* documents, entire collections, and the databases themselves.

Previously, you learned how to remove data from a specific document (using the $pop command, for instance). In this section, you will learn how to remove full documents and collections. Just as the insert() function is used for inserting and update() is used for modifying a document, remove() is used to remove a document.

To remove a single document from your collection, you need to specify the criteria you'll use to find the document. A good approach is to perform a find() first; this ensures that the criteria used are specific to your document. Once you are sure of the criterion, you can invoke the remove() function using that criterion as a parameter:

```
> db.newname.remove( { "Title" : "Different Title" } )
```

This statement removes the book added previously or any other item in your collection that has the same title. The fact this statement removes all books by that title is one reason why it's best to specify the item's _id value—it's always unique.

Or you can use the following snippet to remove all documents from the newname library (remember, we renamed the media collection this previously):

```
> db.newname.remove({})
```

■ **Warning** When removing a document, you need to remember that any reference to that document will remain within the database. For this reason, be sure you manually delete or update those references as well; otherwise, these references will return null when evaluated. Referencing will be discussed in the next section.

If you want to remove an entire collection, you can use the drop() function. The following snippet removes the entire newname collection, including all of its documents:

```
> db.newname.drop()
true
```

The drop() function returns either true or false, depending on whether the operation has completed successfully. Likewise, if you want to remove an entire database from MongoDB, you can use the dropDatabase() function, as in this example:

```
> db.dropDatabase()
{ "dropped" : "library", "ok" : 1 }
```

Note that this snippet will remove the database you are currently working in (again, be sure to check db to see which database is your current database).

Referencing a Database

At this point, you have an empty database again. You're also familiar with inserting various kinds of data into a collection. Now you're ready to take things a step further and learn about *database referencing*. As you've already seen, there are plenty of scenarios where embedding data into your document will suffice for your application (such as the track list or the list of authors in the book entry). However, sometimes you do need to reference information in another document. The following sections will explain how to go about doing so.

Just as with SQL, references between documents in MongoDB are resolved by performing additional queries on the server. MongoDB gives you two ways to accomplish this: referencing them manually or using the DBRef standard, which many drivers also support.

Referencing Data Manually

The simplest and most straightforward way to reference data is to do so manually. When referencing data manually, you store the value from the _id of the other document in your document, either through the full ID or through a simpler common term. Before proceeding with an example, let's add a new document and specify the publisher's information in it (pay close attention to the _id field:

```
> apress = ( { "_id" : "Apress", "Type" : "Technical Publisher", "Category" :
["IT", "Software","Programming"] } )
{
        "_id" : "Apress",
        "Type" : "Technical Publisher",
```

```
        "Category" : [
                "IT",
                "Software",
                "Programming"
        ]
}
> db.publisherscollection.insert(apress)
```

Once you add the publisher's information, you're ready to add an actual document (for example, a book's information) into the media collection. The following example adds a document, specifying Apress as the name of the publisher:

```
> book = ( { "Type" : "Book", "Title" : "Definitive Guide to MongoDB 2nd ed., The",
"ISBN" : "987-1-4302-5821-6", "Publisher" : "Apress","Author" : ["Hows, David",""Plugge,
Eelco","Membrey,Peter",Hawkins, Tim"] } )
{
        "Type" : "Book",
        "Title" : "Definitive Guide to MongoDB 2nd ed., The",
        "ISBN" : "987-1-4302-5821-6",
        "Publisher": "Apress",
        "Author" : [
                "Hows, David"
                "Membrey, Peter",
                "Plugge, Eelco",
                "Hawkins, Tim"
        ]
}
> db.media.insert(book)
```

All the information you need has been inserted into the publisherscollection and media collections, respectively. You can now start using the database reference. First, specify the document that contains the publisher's information to a variable:

```
> book = db.media.findOne()
{
        "_id" : ObjectId("4c458e848e0f00000000628e"),
        "Type" : "Book",
        "Title" : "Definitive Guide to MongoDB, The",
        "ISBN" : "987-1-4302-3051-9",
        "Publisher" : "Apress",
        "Author" : [
                "Hows, David"
                "Membrey, Peter",
                "Plugge, Eelco",
                "Hawkins, Tim"
        ]
}
```

To obtain the information itself, you combine the findOne function with some dot notation:

```
> db.publisherscollection.findOne( { _id : book.Publisher } )
{
        "_id" : "Apress",
        "Type" : "Technical Publisher",
        "Category" : [
                "IT",
                "Software",
                "Programming"
        ]
}
```

As this example illustrates, referencing data manually is straightforward and doesn't require much brainwork. Here, the _id in the documents placed in the users collection has been manually set and has not been generated by MongoDB (otherwise, the _id would be an object ID).

Referencing Data with DBRef

The DBRef standard provides a more formal specification for referencing data between documents. The main reason for using DBRef over a manual reference is that the collection can change from one document to the next. So, if your referenced collection will always be the same, the referencing data manually (as just described) is fine.

With DBRef, the database reference is stored as a standard embedded (JSON/BSON) object. Having a standard way to represent references means that drivers and data frameworks can add helper methods that manipulate the references in standard ways.

The syntax for adding a DBRef reference value looks like this:

```
{ $ref : <collectionname>, $id : <id value>[, $db : <database name>] }
```

Here, <collectionname> represents the name of the collection referenced (for example, publisherscollection); <id value> represents the value of the _id field for the object you are referencing; and the optional $db allows you to reference documents that are placed in other databases.

Let's look at another example using DBRef from scratch. Begin by emptying your two collections and adding a new document:

```
> db.publisherscollection.drop()
true
> db.media.drop()
true
> apress = ( { "Type" : "Technical Publisher", "Category" :
["IT","Software","Programming"] } )
{
        "Type" : "Technical Publisher",
        "Category" : [
                "IT",
                "Software",
                "Programming"
        ]
}
> db.publisherscollection.save(apress)
```

So far you've defined the variable apress and saved it using the save() function. Next, display the updated contents of the variable by typing in its name:

```
> apress
{
"Type" : "Technical Publisher",
"Category" : [
        "IT",
        "Software",
        "Programming"
],
"_id" : ObjectId("4c4597e98e0f000000006290")
}
```

So far you've defined the publisher and saved it to the publisherscollection collection. Now you're ready to add an item to the *media* collection that references the data:

```
> book = { "Type" : "Book", "Title" : "Definitive Guide to MongoDB 2nd ed., The",
"ISBN" : "978-1-4302-5821-6", "Author": ["Hows, David","Membrey, Peter","Plugge,
Eelco","Hawkins, Tim"], Publisher : [ new DBRef ('publisherscollection',
apress._id) ] }
{
        "Type" : "Book",
        "Title" : "Definitive Guide to MongoDB 2nd ed., The",
        "ISBN" : "987-1-4302-5821-6",
        "Author" : [
                "Hows, David"
                "Membrey, Peter",
                "Plugge, Eelco",
                "Hawkins, Tim"

        ],
        "Publisher" : [
                DBRef("publishercollection", "Apress")
        ]
}
> db.media.save(book)
```

And that's it! Granted, the example looks a little less simple than the manual method of referencing data; however, it's a good alternative for cases where collections can change from one document to the next.

Implementing Index-Related Functions

In the previous chapter, you took a brief look at what indexes can do for your database. Now it's time to briefly learn how to create and use indexes. Indexing will be discussed in greater detail in Chapter 10, but for now let's look at the basics. MongoDB includes a fair number of functions available for maintaining your indexes; we'll begin by creating an index with the ensureIndex() function.

The ensureIndex() function takes at least one parameter, which is the name of a key in one of your documents that you will use to build the index. In the previous example, you added a document to the media collection that used the Title key. This collection would be well served by an index on this key.

■ **Tip** The rule of thumb in MongoDB is to create an index for the same sort of scenarios where you'd want to create one in MySQL.

You can create an index for this collection by invoking the following command:

```
> db.media.ensureIndex( { Title : 1 } )
```

This command ensures that an index will be created for all the Title values from all documents in the media collection. The :1 at the end of the line specifies the direction of the index: 1 stores the items in ascending order, whereas -1 stores them in descending order.

```
// Ensure ascending index
db.media.ensureIndex( { Title :1 } )

// Ensure descending index
db.media.ensureIndex( { Title :-1 } )
```

■ **Tip** Searching through indexed information is fast. Searching for non-indexed information is slow, as each document needs to be checked to see if it's a match.

BSON allows you to store full arrays in a document; however, it would also be beneficial to be able to create an index on an embedded key. Luckily, the developers of MongoDB thought of this, too, and added support for this feature. Let's build on one of the earlier examples in this chapter, adding another document into the database that has embedded information:

```
> db.media.insert( { "Type" : "CD", "Artist" : "Nirvana","Title" :
"Nevermind", "Tracklist" : [ { "Track" : "1", "Title" : "Smells Like Teen
Spirit", "Length" : "5:02" }, {"Track" : "2","Title" : "In Bloom", "Length" :
"4:15" } ] } )

{ "_id" : ObjectId("4c45aa2f8e0f000000006293"), "Type" : "CD", "Artist" :
"Nirvana", "Title" : "Nevermind", "Tracklist" : [
        {
                "Track" : "1",
                "Title" : "Smells Like Teen Spirit",
                "Length" : "5:02"
        },
        {
                "Track" : "2",
                "Title" : "In Bloom",
                "Length" : "4:15"
        }
] }
```

Next, you can create an index on the Title key for all entries in the track list:

```
> db.media.ensureIndex( { "Tracklist.Title" : 1 } )
```

The next time you perform a search for any of the titles in the collection—assuming they are nested under Tracklist—the titles will show up instantly. Next, you can take this concept one step further and use an entire (sub) document as a key, as in this example:

```
> db.media.ensureIndex( { "Tracklist" : 1 } )
```

This statement indexes each element of the array, which means you can now search for any object in the array. These types of keys are also known as *multi keys*. You can also create an index based on multiple keys in a set of documents. This process is known as *compound indexing*. The method you use to create a compound index is mostly the same; the difference is that you specify several keys instead of one, as in this example:

```
> db.media.ensureIndex({"Tracklist.Title": 1, "Tracklist.Length": -1})
```

The benefit of this approach is that you can make an index on multiple keys (as in the previous example, where you indexed an entire subdocument). Unlike the subdocument method, however, compound indexing lets you specify whether you want one of the two fields to be indexed in descending order. If you perform your index with the subdocument method, you are limited to ascending or descending order only. There is more on compound indexes in Chapter 10.

Surveying Index-Related Commands

So far you've taken a quick glance at one of the index-related commands, ensureIndex(). Without a doubt, this is the command you will primarily use to create your indexes. However, you might also find a pair of additional functions useful: hint() and min()/max(). You use these functions to query for data. We haven't covered them to this point because they won't function without a custom index. But now let's take a look at what they can do for you.

Forcing a Specified Index to Query Data

You can use the hint() function to force the use of a specified index when querying for data. The intended benefit of using this command is to improve the query performance. To see this principle in action, try performing a find with the hint() function without defining an index:

```
> db.media.find( { ISBN: " 978-1-4302-5821-6"} ) . hint ( { ISBN: -1 } )
error: { "$err" : "bad hint", "code" : 10113 }
```

If you create an index on ISBN numbers, this technique will be more successful. Note that the first command's background parameter ensures that the indexing is done on the background:

```
> db.media.ensureIndex({ISBN: 1}, {background: true});
> db.media.find( { ISBN: " 978-1-4302-5821-6"} ) . hint ( { ISBN: 1 } )

{ "_id" : ObjectId("4c45a5418e0f000000006291"), "Type" : "Book", "Title" : "Definitive Guide to
MongoDB, The", "ISBN" : " 978-1-4302-5821-6", "Author" : ["Hows, David","Membrey, Peter",
"Plugge, Eelco","Hawkins,Tim"], "Publisher" : [
        {
                "$ref" : "publisherscollection",
                "$id" : ObjectId("4c4597e98e0f000000006290")
        }
] }
```

To confirm that the given index is being used, you can optionally add the explain() function, returning information about the query plan chosen. Here, the indexBounds value tells you about the index used:

```
> db.media.find( { ISBN: " 978-1-4302-5821-6"} ) . hint ( { ISBN: 1 } ).explain()
{
    "cursor" : "BtreeCursor ISBN_1",
    "isMultiKey" : false,
    "n" : 1,
    "nscannedObjects" : 1,
    "nscanned" : 1,
    "nscannedObjectsAllPlans" : 1,
    "nscannedAllPlans" : 1,
    "scanAndOrder" : false,
    "indexOnly" : false,
    "nYields" : 0,
    "nChunkSkips" : 0,
    "millis" : 0,
    "indexBounds" : {
        "ISBN" : [
            [
                {
                    "$minElement" : 1
                },
                {
                    "$maxElement" : 1
                }
            ]
        ]
    },
    "server" : "localhost:27017"
}
```

Constraining Query Matches

The min() and max() functions enable you to constrain query matches to only those that have index keys between the min and max keys specified. Therefore, you will need to have an index for the keys you are specifying. Also, you can either combine the two functions or use them separately. Let's begin by adding a few documents that enable you to take advantage of these functions. First, create an index on the Released field:

```
> db.media.insert( { "Type" : "DVD", "Title" : "Matrix, The", "Released" :
1999} )
> db.media.insert( { "Type" : "DVD", "Title" : "Blade Runner", "Released" :
1982 } )
> db.media.insert( { "Type" : "DVD", "Title" : "Toy Story 3", "Released" :
2010} )
> db.media.ensureIndex( { "Released": 1 } )
```

You can now use the max() and min() commands, as in this example:

```
> db.media.find() . min ( { Released: 1995 } ) . max ( { Released : 2005 } )
{ "_id" : ObjectId("4c45b5b38e0f0000000062a9"), "Type" : "DVD", "Title" :
"Matrix, The", "Released" : 1999 }
```

If no index is created, then an error message will be returned, saying that no index has been found for the specified key pattern. Obviously, you will need to define which index must be used with the hint() function:

```
> db.media.find() . min ( { Released: 1995 } ) .
max ( { Released : 2005 } ). hint ( { Released : 1 } )
{ "_id" : ObjectId("4c45b5b38e0f0000000062a9"), "Type" : "DVD", "Title" :
"Matrix, The", "Released" : 1999 }
```

■ **Note**   The min() value will be *included* in the results, whereas the max() value will be *excluded* from the results.

Generally speaking, it is recommended that you use $gt and $lt (greater than and less than, respectively) rather than min() and max() because $gt and $lt don't require an index. The min() and max() functions are used primarily for compound keys.

Summary

In this chapter, we've taken a look at the most commonly used commands and options that can be performed with the MongoDB shell to manipulate data. We also examined how to search for, add, modify, and delete data, and how to modify your collections and databases. Next, we took a quick look at atomic operations, how to use aggregation, and when to use operators such as $elemMatch. Finally, we explored how to create indexes and when to use them. We examined what indexes are used for, how you can drop them, how to search for your data using the indexes created, and how to check for running indexing operations.

In the next chapter, we'll look into the fundamentals of GridFS, including what it is, what it does, and how it can be used to your benefit.

## CHAPTER 5

GridFS

We live in a world of high-definition video, 12MP cameras, and storage media that can hold 50GB of data on a disc the size of a CD-ROM. In that context, the 16MB limit for the maximum size of a MongoDB document might seem laughably inadequate. Indeed, you might wonder why MongoDB, which has been designed as a database for today's high-tech age, has such a seemingly strange limitation. The short answer is performance.

If data were stored in the document itself, it would obviously get very large, which in turn would make the data harder to work with. For example, pulling back the whole document would require loading the files in the document, as well. You could work around this issue, but you would still need to pull back the entire file whenever you accessed it, even if you only wanted a small section of it. You can't ask for a chunk of data in the middle of a document—it's an all-or-nothing proposition. Fortunately, MongoDB features a unique and somewhat elegant solution to this problem. MongoDB enables you to store large files quite easily, yet it also allows you to access parts of the file without retrieving the entire thing—all while maintaining high performance. It achieves this by leveraging a specification known as GridFS.

■ **Note**   One interesting thing about GridFS is that it isn't actually a software feature. For example, there isn't any special server-side code in MongoDB that manages GridFS. Instead, GridFS is a simple specification used by all of the supported drivers on MongoDB. The key benefit of such a specification is that files stored by one driver can be accessed by any other driver that follows the same convention.

This approach adheres closely to the MongoDB principle of keeping things simple. Because GridFS uses standard MongoDB features, it's easy to implement and work with the specification from the driver's point of view. It also means you can poke around by hand if you really want to, as to MongoDB files in the GridFS specification are just normal collections containing documents.

Filling in Some Background

Chapter 1 touched on the fact that we have been taught to use databases for even simple storage for many years. For example, the book one of us bought to help improve his PHP more than 15 years ago introduced MySQL in Chapter 3. Considering the complexity of SQL and databases in the real world (not to mention in theory), you might wonder why a book intended for beginners would practically start off with SQL. After all, it was a PHP book and not a MySQL book.

One thing most people don't appreciate until they try it is that reading and writing data directly to disk is hard. Some people don't agree with us on this point—after all, opening and reading files in Python might seem trivial. And it is: in simpler scenarios, working with files is rather painless when using PHP. If all you want to do is read in lines and process them, you're unlikely to have any trouble.

On the other hand, things become a lot harder if you want to search a file or store complicated or structured data. Even if you can work out how to do this and create a solution, your solution is unlikely to be faster or more efficient than relying on a database instead. Today's applications depend on finding and storing data quickly—and databases make this possible for those of us who can't or don't want to write such a system ourselves.

One area that is glossed over by many books is the storing of files. Most books that teach you to use a database to store your data also teach you to read and write to the filesystem instead when you need to store files. In some ways, this isn't usually a problem, because it's much easier to read and write simple files than to process what's in them. There are some issues, however. First, the developer must have permission to write those files in the first place, and that requires giving the web server permission to write to the local filesystem. This might not seem likely to pose a problem, but it gives system administrators nightmares—getting files onto a server is the first stage in being able to compromise it.

Databases can store binary files; typically, it's just not elegant for them to do so. MySQL has a special column type called BLOB. PostgreSQL requires special procedures to be followed to store such files—and the data isn't stored in the table itself. In other words, it's messy. These solutions are obviously bolt-ons. Thus, it's not surprising that people choose to write data to the disk instead. But that approach also has issues. Apart from the problems with security, it adds another directory that needs to be backed up, and you must also ensure that this information is replicated to all the appropriate servers. There are filesystems that provide the ability to write to disk and have that content fully replicated (including GFS); but these solutions are complex and add overhead; moreover, these features typically make your solution harder to maintain.

MongoDB, on the other hand, enforces a maximum document size of 16MB. This is more than enough for storing rich documents, and it might have sufficed a few years ago for storing many other types of files as well. However, this limit is wholly inadequate for today's environment.

Working with GridFS

Next, we'll take a brief look at how GridFS is implemented. As the MongoDB website points out, you do not need to understand or be aware of the underlying implementation of GridFS to use it. In fact, you can simply let the driver handle the heavy lifting for you. For the most part, the drivers that support GridFS implement file handling in a language-specific way. For example, the MongoDB driver for Python works in a manner that is wholly consistent with Python, as you'll see shortly. If the ins-and-outs of GridFS don't interest you, then just skip ahead to the next section. We promise you won't miss anything that enables you to use MongoDB effectively!

GridFS consists of two parts. More specifically, it consists of two collections. One collection holds the filename and related information such as size (called metadata), while the other collection holds the file data itself, usually in 256K chunks. The specification calls for these to be named files and chunks, respectively. By default, the files and chunks collections are created in the fs namespace, but this can be changed. The ability to change the default namespace is useful if you want to store different types of files. For example, you might want to keep image and movie files separate.

Getting Started with the Command-Line Tools

Now that we have some of the background out of the way, let's look at how to get started with GridFS by exploring the command-line tools available to leverage it. First, we will need a file to play with. To keep things simple, let's use the dictionary file. On Ubuntu, you can find this at /usr/share/dict/words. However, there are various levels of symbolic links, so you might want to run this command first:

```
root@core2:/usr/share/dict# cat words > /tmp/dictionary
```

▪ **Note** In Ubuntu, you might need to use apt-get install wbritish to get the dictionary file installed.

This command copies all the contents of the file to a nice and simple path that you can use easily. Of course, you can use any file that you wish for this example; it doesn't need to be any particular size or type.

Rather than describe all the options you can use with mongofiles, let's jump right in and start playing with some of the tool's features. This book assumes that you're running mongofiles on the same machine as MongoDB. If you're not, then you'll need to use the -h option to specify the host that MongoDB is running on. You'll learn about the other options available in the mongofiles command after putting it through its paces.

First, let's list all the files in the database. We're not expecting any files to be in there yet, but let's make sure. The list command lists the files in the database so far:

```
$ mongofiles list
connected to: 127.0.0.1
$
```

OK, so that probably wasn't very exciting. Keep in mind that mongofiles is a proof-of-concept tool; it's probably not a tool you will use much with your own applications. However, mongofiles is great for learning and testing. Once you create a file, you can use the tool to explore the files and chunks that are created.

Let's kick things up a notch and the put command to add the dictionary file created previously (remember: you can use any file that you like for this example):

```
$ mongofiles put /tmp/dictionary
connected to: 127.0.0.1
added file: { _id: ObjectId('51cb61b26487b3d8ce7af440'), filename: "/tmp/dictionary", chunkSize:
262144, uploadDate: new Date(1372283314621), md5: "40c0825855792bd20e8a2d515fe9c3e3", length:
4953699 }}}
done!
$
```

This example returns some useful information; however, let's double-check the information it shows by confirming that the file is there. Do so by rerunning the list command:

```
$ mongofiles list
connected to: 127.0.0.1
/tmp/dictionary          4953699
$
```

This example shows the dictionary file, along with its size. The information clearly comes from the files collection, but we're getting ahead of ourselves. Let's take a moment to step back and examine the output returned from the put command in this example.

Using the _id Key

As you know, each document in MongoDB includes a unique identifier stored in the _id key. Like MySQL's auto_increment field, the _id key is not of much direct interest, apart from the fact that it allows you to pick out a specific file.

Working with Filenames

The output from the put command also shows a Filename key, which itself needs a little explanation. Generally, you will want to keep this field unique to help prevent major confusion; however, that's not entirely necessary. In fact, if you run the put command again, you'll end up with two documents that look identical. In this case, the files and metadata are identical, apart from the _id key. You might be surprised by this and wonder why MongoDB doesn't update the file that exists rather than create a new one. The reason is that there could be many cases where you would have filenames that are identical. For example, if you built a system to store student assignments, then chances are pretty good that at least some of the filenames would be the same. MongoDB cannot assume that identical filenames (even those with identical sizes) are in fact the same file. Thus, there are many cases where it would be a mistake for MongoDB to update the file. Of course, you can use the _id key to update a specific file; and you'll learn more about this topic in the upcoming Python-based experiments.

Determining a File's Length

The put command also returns a file's length, which is both useful information and critical to how GridFS works. While it is nice to know how big a file is for reference, the file's size also plays a big part when you write your own applications. For example, when sending a file over the Web (through HTTP, for example), you need to specify how big the file is. Not all servers do this; for example, when downloading files from certain sites, you may have noticed that your browser can tell you the speed you're downloading the file at, but not how long it will take to finish downloading the file. This is because the server did not provide size information.

Knowing the size of your file is important in one other respect. Earlier, we mentioned that a file is broken up into *chunks*—that is, the file is split into smaller pieces. By default, the chunk size is 256K, but that can be changed to another value if you wish. To work out how many chunks a file takes up, you need to know two things. First you must know how big each chunk is; and second, you must know the file size, so that you can tell how many chunks there are.

You might think that this shouldn't be important. After all, if you have a 1MB file and the chunk size is 256K, then you know that you must start with chunk number four if you want to access data starting at the 800K mark. Yet you still need to know how big the overall file is for the following reason: if you don't know the size, you cannot work out how many valid chunks there are. In the previous example, there's nothing to stop you asking for data that starts at 1.26MB (that is, the sixth chunk). In this case, that chunk doesn't exist, but there is no way to know that without a reference to the file size. Of course, the driver handles all of this for you, so there's no need to worry too much about it; however, knowing how GridFS works "behind the scenes" will certainly help when it comes to debugging your applications.

Working with Chunk Sizes

The put command also returns the chunk size because, although there is a default chunk size, this default can be changed on a file-by-file basis. This allows flexible sizing. If your website streams video, you might want to have many chunks so that you can easily skip to any part of a given video with ease. If you had one big file, you would have to return the whole file, and then find the starting point for the specified section in it. With GridFS, you can pull back data at the chunk level. If you're using the default size, then you can start retrieving data from any 256K chunk. Of course, you can also specify the bit of data you actually want (for example, you might want only five minutes in the middle of a sixty-minute movie). This is a very efficient system, and 256K is a pretty good chunk size for most purposes. If you decide to change it, you should have a good reason for doing so. As always, don't forget to benchmark and test the performance of your custom chunk size; it's not uncommon for theoretically better systems to fail to live up to expectations.

■ **Note** MongoDB has a 16MB restriction on document size. Because GridFS is simply a different way of storing files in the standard MongoDB framework, this restriction also exists in GridFS. That is, you can't create chunks larger than 16MB. This shouldn't pose a problem, because the whole point of GridFS is to alleviate the need for huge document sizes. If you're worried that you're storing huge files, and this will give you too many chunk documents, you needn't worry— there are MongoDB systems in production with significantly more than a billion documents!

Tracking the Upload Date

The `uploadDate` key does exactly what its name suggests: it stores the date the file was created in MongoDB. This is a good time to mention that the `files` collection is just a normal MongoDB collection, containing normal documents. This means that you can add any additional key and value pairs that you need, in the same way you would for any other collection.

For example, consider the case of a real-world application that needs to store text content that you extract from various files. You might need to do this so you could perform some additional indexing and searching. To accomplish this, you might add a `file_text` key and store the text in there. The elegance of the GridFS system means that you can do anything with this system you can do with any other MongoDB documents. Elegance and power are two of the defining characteristics of working in MongoDB.

Hashing Your Files

MongoDB ships with the MD5 hashing algorithm. You may have come across the algorithm previously when downloading software over the Internet. The theory behind MD5 is that each file has a unique signature. Changing a single bit anywhere in that file will drastically (and noticeably) change the signature. This signature is used for two reasons: security and integrity. For security, if you know what the MD5 hash is supposed to be and you trust the source (perhaps a friend gave it to you), then you can be assured that the file has not been altered if the hash (often called the *checksum*) is correct. This also ensures that the file integrity has been maintained and that no data has been lost or damaged. The MD5 hash of a particular file acts like a fingerprint for a file. The hash can be also used to identify files that have different filenames but have the same contents.

■ **Warning**   The MD5 algorithm is no longer considered secure, and it has been demonstrated that it is possible to create two different files that have the same MD5 checksum, even though their contents are different. In cryptographic terms, this is called a *collision*. Such collisions are bad because they mean it is possible for an attacker to alter a file in such a way that it cannot be detected. This caveat remains somewhat theoretical because a great deal of effort and time would be required to create such collisions intentionally; and even then, the files could be so different as to be obviously not the same file. For this reason, MD5 is still the preferred method of determining file integrity because it is so widely supported. However, if you want to use hashing for its security benefits, you are much better off using one of the SHA family specifications—ideally SHA-256 or SHA-512. Even these hashing families have some theoretical vulnerabilities; however, no one has yet demonstrated a practical case of creating intentional collisions for the SHA family of hashes. MongoDB uses MD5 to ensure file integrity, which is fine for most purposes. However, if you want to hash important data (such as user passwords), you should probably consider using the SHA family of hashes instead.

Looking Under MongoDB's Hood

At this point, you have some data in a MongoDB database. Now let's take a closer look at that data under the covers. To do this, you'll again use some command-line tools to connect to the database and query it. For example, try running the `find()` command against the file created earlier:

```
$ mongo test
MongoDB shell version: 2.5.1-pre
connecting to: test
```

```
> db.fs.files.find()
{ "_id" : ObjectId("51cb61b26487b3d8ce7af440"), "filename" : "/tmp/dictionary",
"chunkSize" : 262144, "uploadDate" : ISODate("2013-06-26T21:48:34.621Z"), "md5" :
"40c0825855792bd20e8a2d515fe9c3e3", "length" : 4953699 }
>
```

The output should look familiar—after all, it's the same data that you saw earlier in this chapter. Now you can see that the information printed by `mongofiles` was taken from the file's entry in the `fs.files` collection.

Next, let's take a look at the `chunks` collection (we have to add a filter; otherwise, it will show us all of the raw binary data as well):

```
$ mongo test
MongoDB shell version: 2.5.1-pre
connecting to: test
> db.fs.chunks.find({},{"data":0});
{ "_id" : ObjectId("51cb61b29b2daad9857ca205"), "files_id" : ObjectId("51cb61b26487b3d8ce7af440"), "n" : 4 }
{ "_id" : ObjectId("51cb61b29b2daad9857ca206"), "files_id" : ObjectId("51cb61b26487b3d8ce7af440"), "n" : 5 }
{ "_id" : ObjectId("51cb61b29b2daad9857ca207"), "files_id" : ObjectId("51cb61b26487b3d8ce7af440"), "n" : 6 }
{ "_id" : ObjectId("51cb61b29b2daad9857ca208"), "files_id" : ObjectId("51cb61b26487b3d8ce7af440"), "n" : 7 }
{ "_id" : ObjectId("51cb61b29b2daad9857ca209"), "files_id" : ObjectId("51cb61b26487b3d8ce7af440"), "n" : 8 }
{ "_id" : ObjectId("51cb61b29b2daad9857ca20a"), "files_id" : ObjectId("51cb61b26487b3d8ce7af440"), "n" : 9 }
{ "_id" : ObjectId("51cb61b29b2daad9857ca20b"), "files_id" : ObjectId("51cb61b26487b3d8ce7af440"), "n" : 10 }
{ "_id" : ObjectId("51cb61b29b2daad9857ca20c"), "files_id" : ObjectId("51cb61b26487b3d8ce7af440"), "n" : 11 }
{ "_id" : ObjectId("51cb61b29b2daad9857ca20d"), "files_id" : ObjectId("51cb61b26487b3d8ce7af440"), "n" : 12 }
{ "_id" : ObjectId("51cb61b29b2daad9857ca20e"), "files_id" : ObjectId("51cb61b26487b3d8ce7af440"), "n" : 13 }
{ "_id" : ObjectId("51cb61b29b2daad9857ca20f"), "files_id" : ObjectId("51cb61b26487b3d8ce7af440"), "n" : 14 }
{ "_id" : ObjectId("51cb61b29b2daad9857ca210"), "files_id" : ObjectId("51cb61b26487b3d8ce7af440"), "n" : 15 }
{ "_id" : ObjectId("51cb61b29b2daad9857ca211"), "files_id" : ObjectId("51cb61b26487b3d8ce7af440"), "n" : 16 }
{ "_id" : ObjectId("51cb61b29b2daad9857ca212"), "files_id" : ObjectId("51cb61b26487b3d8ce7af440"), "n" : 17 }
{ "_id" : ObjectId("51cb61b29b2daad9857ca201"), "files_id" : ObjectId("51cb61b26487b3d8ce7af440"), "n" : 0 }
{ "_id" : ObjectId("51cb61b29b2daad9857ca202"), "files_id" : ObjectId("51cb61b26487b3d8ce7af440"), "n" : 1 }
{ "_id" : ObjectId("51cb61b29b2daad9857ca203"), "files_id" : ObjectId("51cb61b26487b3d8ce7af440"), "n" : 2 }
{ "_id" : ObjectId("51cb61b29b2daad9857ca204"), "files_id" : ObjectId("51cb61b26487b3d8ce7af440"), "n" : 3 }
{ "_id" : ObjectId("51cb61b29b2daad9857ca213"), "files_id" : ObjectId("51cb61b26487b3d8ce7af440"), "n" : 18 }>
```

You might wonder why the output here has so many entries. As noted previously, GridFS is just a specification. That is, it uses what MongoDB already provides. While we were testing the commands for the book, the dictionary file was added a couple of times. Later, this file was deleted when we emptied the `fs.files` collection. You can see for yourself what happened next! The fact that some documents were removed from a collection has no bearing on what happens in another collection. Remember: MongoDB doesn't treat these documents or collections in any special way. If the file had been deleted properly through a driver or the `mongofiles` tool, that tool would also have cleaned up the chunks collection.

■ **Warning** Accessing documents and collections directly is a powerful feature, but you need to be careful. This feature also makes it much easier to shoot yourself in both feet at the same time. Make sure you know what you're doing and that you perform a great deal of testing if you decide to edit these documents and collections manually. Also, keep in mind that the GridFS support in MongoDB's drivers won't know anything about any customizations that you've made.

Using the search Command

Next, let's take a closer look at MongoDB's search command. Thus far, there is only a single file in the database, which greatly limits the types of searches you might conduct! So let's add something else. The following snippet copies the dictionary to another file, and then imports that file:

```
$ cp /tmp/dictionary /tmp/hello_world
$ mongofiles put /tmp/hello_world
connected to: 127.0.0.1
added file: { _id: ObjectId('51cb63d167961ebc919edbd5'), filename: "/tmp/hello_world", chunkSize:
262144, uploadDate: new Date(1372283858021), md5: "40c0825855792bd20e8a2d515fe9c3e3", length:
4953699 }done!
root@core2:~# mongofiles list
connected to: 127.0.0.1
/tmp/dictionary     4953699
/tmp/hello_world    4953699
$
```

The first line copies the file, and the second line imports it into MongoDB. As in the earlier example, the put command prints out the new document that MongoDB has created. Next, you might run the mongofiles command list to check that the files were correctly stored. If you do so, you can see that there are now two files in the collection; unsurprisingly, both files have the same size.

The search command works exactly as you would expect. All you need to do is tell mongofiles what you are looking for, and it will try to find it for you, as in this example:

```
$  mongofiles search hello
connected to: 127.0.0.1
/tmp/hello_world    4953699
$  mongofiles search dict
connected to: 127.0.0.1
/tmp/dictionary     4953699
$
```

Again, nothing too exciting happens here. However, there is an important takeaway that's worth noting. MongoDB can be as simple or as complex as you need it to be. The mongofiles tool is only for reference use, and it includes very basic debugging. The good news: MongoDB makes it easy to perform simple searches against your files. The even better news: MongoDB also has your back if you want to write some insanely complicated searches.

Deleting

The mongofiles command delete doesn't require much explanation, but it does deserve a big warning. This command deletes files based on the filename. Thus, if you have more than one file with the same name, this command will delete *all* of them. The following snippet shows how to use the delete command:

```
$ mongofiles delete /tmp/hello_world
connected to: 127.0.0.1
$ mongofiles list
connected to: 127.0.0.1
/tmp/dictionary         4953699
$
```

■ **Note** Many people have commented in connection with this issue that deleting multiple files with the same name is not a problem because no application would have duplicate names. This is simply not true; and in many cases, it doesn't even make sense to enforce unique names. For example, if your app lets users upload photos to their profiles, there's a good chance that half the files you receive will be called photo.jpg or me.png.

Of course, if you are unlikely to use mongofiles to manage your live data—and in truth no one ever expected it to be used that way—then you just need to be careful when deleting data in general.

Retrieving Files from MongoDB

So far, you haven't actually pulled any files out from MongoDB. The most important feature of any database is that it lets you find and retrieve data once it's been put in. The following snippet retrieves a file from MongoDB using the mongofiles command get:

```
$ mongofiles get /tmp/dictionary
connected to: 127.0.0.1
done write to: /tmp/dictionary
$
```

This example includes an intentional mistake. Because it specifies the full name and path of the file you want to retrieve (as required), mongofiles writes the data to a file with the same name and path. Effectively, this overwrites the original dictionary file! This isn't exactly a great loss, because it is being overwritten by the same file—and the dictionary file was only a temporary copy in the first place. Nevertheless, this behavior could give you a rather nasty shock if you accidentally erase two weeks of work. Trust us, you won't figure out where all your work went until sometime after the event! As when using the delete command, you need to be careful when using the get command.

Summing Up mongofiles

The mongofiles utility is a useful tool for quickly looking at what's in your database. If you've written some software, and you suspect something might be amiss with it, then you can use mongofiles to double-check what's going on.

It's an extremely simple implementation, so it doesn't require any fancy logic that could complicate accomplishing the task at hand. Whether you would use mongofiles in a production environment is a matter of personal taste. It's not exactly a Swiss army knife; however, it does provide a useful set of commands that you'll be grateful to have if your application begins misbehaving. In short, you should be familiar with this tool because someday it might be exactly the tool you require to solve an otherwise nettlesome problem.

Exploiting the Power of Python

At this point, you have a solid idea of how GridFS works. Next, you will learn how to access GridFS from Python. Chapter 2 covered how to install PyMongo; if you have any trouble with the examples, please refer back to Chapter 2 and make sure everything is installed correctly.

If you've been following along with the previous examples in this chapter, you should now have one file in GridFS. You'll also recall that the file is a dictionary file, so it contains a list of words. In this section, you will learn how to write a simple Python script that prints out all the words in the dictionary file. Sure, it would be simpler and more efficient to simply cat the original file—but where would the fun be in that?

Begin by firing up Python:

```
Python 2.6.6 (r266:84292, Oct 12 2012, 14:23:48)
[GCC 4.4.6 20120305 (Red Hat 4.4.6-4)] on linux2
Type "help", "copyright", "credits" or "license" for more information.>>>
```

The standard driver for Python is called PyMongo, and it was written by Mike Dirolf. Because the PyMongo driver is supported directly by MongoDB, Inc., the company that publishes MongoDB, you can rest assured that it will be regularly updated and maintained. So, let's go ahead and import the library. You should see something like the following:

```
>>> from pymongo import Connection
>>> import gridfs
>>>
```

If PyMongo isn't installed correctly, you will get an error similar to this:

```
>>> import gridfs
Traceback (most recent call last):
  File "<stdin>", line 1, in <module>
ImportError: No module named gridfs
>>>
```

If you see the latter message, chances are something was missed during installation. In that case, pop back to Chapter 2 and follow the instructions to install PyMongo again.

Connecting to the Database

Before you can retrieve information from a database, you must first establish a connection to it. When you were using the mongofiles utility earlier in this chapter, you probably noticed the reference to 127.0.0.1. This value is also known as the *localhost*, and it represents your computer's loopback address. This value is simply a shortcut for telling a computer to talk to itself. The reason mongofiles mentioned this IP address is that it was actually connecting to MongoDB through the network. The default is to connect to the local machine on the default MongoDB port. Because you haven't changed the default settings, mongofiles can find and connect to your database without any trouble.

When using MongoDB with Python, however, you need to connect to the database and then set up GridFS. Fortunately, this is easy to do:

```
>>> db = Connection().test
>>> fs = gridfs.GridFS(db)
>>>
```

The first line opens the connection and selects the database. By default, mongofiles uses the test database; hence, you'll find your dictionary file in test. The second line sets up GridFS and prepares it for use.

Accessing the Words

In its original implementation, the PyMongo driver used a file-like interface to leverage GridFS. This is somewhat different from what you saw in this chapter's earlier examples with mongofiles, which were more FTP-like in nature. In the original implementation of PyMongo, you could read and write data just as you do for a normal file.

This made PyMongo very much like Python to use, and it allowed for easy integration with existing scripts. However, this behavior was changed in version 1.6 of the driver, and this functionality is no longer supported. While very Python-like, the behavior had some problems that made the tool less effective overall.

Generally speaking, the PyMongo driver attempts to make GridFS files look and feel like ordinary files on the filesystem. On the one hand, this is nice because it means there's no learning curve, and the driver is usable with any method that requires a file. On the other hand, this approach is somewhat limiting and doesn't give a good feel for how powerful GridFS is. Important changes were made to how PyMongo works in version 1.6, particularly in how get and put work.

■ **Note** This revised version of PyMongo isn't too dissimilar from previous versions of the tool, and many people who used the previous API have found it easy to adapt to the revised version. That said, Mike's changes haven't gone down well with everybody. For example, some people found the file-based keying in the old API to be extremely useful and easy to use. The revised version of PyMongo supports the ability to create filenames, so the missing behavior can be replicated in the revised version; however, doing so does require a bit more code.

Putting Files into MongoDB

Getting files into GridFS through PyMongo is straightforward and intentionally similar to the way you do so using command-line tools. MongoDB is all about throughput, and the changes to the API in the revised version of PyMongo reflect this. Not only do you get better performance, but the changes also bring the Python driver in line with the other GridFS implementations.

Let's put the dictionary into GridFS (again):

```
>>> with open("/tmp/dictionary") as dictionary:
...    uid = fs.put(dictionary)
...
>>> uid
ObjectId('51cb65be2f50332093f67b98') >>>
```

In this example, you use the put method to insert the file. It's important that you capture the result from this method because it contains the document _id for your file. PyMongo takes a different approach than mongofiles, which assumes the filename is effectively the key (even though you can have duplicates). Instead, PyMongo references files based on their _id. If you don't capture this information, then you won't be able to reliably find the file again. Actually, that's not strictly true—you could *search* for a file quite easily—but if you want to link this file to a particular user account, then you need this _id.

Two useful arguments that can be used in conjunction with the put command are filename and content_type. As you might expect, these arguments let you set the filename and the content type of the file, respectively. This is useful for loading files directly from disk. However, it is even handier when you're handling files that have been received over the Internet or generated in memory because, in those cases, you can use file-like semantics, but without actually having to create a real file on the disk.

Retrieving Files from GridFS

At long last, you're now ready to return your data! At this point, you have your unique _id, so finding the file is easy. The get method retrieves a file from GridFS:

```
>>> new_dictionary = fs.get(uid)
```

That's it! The preceding snippet returns a file-like object; thus, you can print all the words in the dictionary using the following snippet:

```
>>> for word in new_dictionary:
...    print word
```

Now watch in awe as a list of words quickly scrolls up the screen! Okay, so this isn't exactly rocket science. However, the fact that it isn't rocket science or in any way difficult is part of the beauty of GridFS—it does work as advertised, and it does so in an intuitive and easily understood way!

Deleting Files

Deleting a file is also easy. All you have to do is call fs.delete() and pass the _id of the file, as in the following example:

```
>>> fs.delete(uid)
>>> new_dictionary = fs.get(uid)
Traceback (most recent call last):
  File "<stdin>", line 1, in <module>
  File "/usr/lib/python2.6/site-packages/pymongo-2.5.2-py2.6-linux-x86_64.egg/gridfs/__init__.py",
line 140, in get
    return GridOut(self.__collection, file_id)
  File "/usr/lib/python2.6/site-packages/pymongo-2.5.2-py2.6-linux-x86_64.egg/gridfs/grid_file.py",
line 392, in __init__
    (files, file_id))
gridfs.errors.NoFile: no file in gridfs collection Collection(Database(Connection('localhost',
27017), u'test'), u'fs.files') with _id ObjectId('51cb65be2f50332093f67b98') >>>
```

These results could look a bit scary, but they are just PyMongo's way of saying that it couldn't find the file. This isn't surprising, because you just deleted it!

Summary

In this chapter, you undertook a fast-paced tour of GridFS. You learned what GridFS is, how it fits together with MongoDB, and how to use its basic syntax. This chapter didn't explore GridFS in great depth, but in the next chapter, you'll learn how to integrate GridFS with a real application using PHP. For now, it's enough to understand how GridFS can save you time and hassle when storing files and other large pieces of data.

In the next chapter, you'll start putting what you've learned to real use—specifically, you'll learn how to build a fully functional address book!

PART 2

■ ■ ■

Developing with MongoDB

CHAPTER 6

■ ■ ■

PHP and MongoDB

Through the first five chapters, you've learned how to perform all sorts of actions in the MongoDB shell. For example, you've learned how to add, modify, and delete a document. You've also learned about the workings of DBRef and GridFS, including how to use them.

So far, however, most of the things you've learned about have taken place in the MongoDB shell. It is a very capable application, but the MongoDB software also comes with a vast number of additional drivers (see Chapter 2 for more information on these) that let you step outside the shell to accomplish many other sorts of tasks programmatically.

One such tool is the PHP driver, which allows you to extend your PHP installation to connect, modify, and manage your MongoDB databases when you want to use PHP rather than the shell. This can be helpful when you need to design a web application, or don't have access to the MongoDB shell. As this chapter will demonstrate, most of the actions you can perform with the PHP driver closely resemble functions you can execute in the MongoDB shell; however, the PHP driver requires that the options be specified in an array, rather than between two curly brackets. Similarities notwithstanding, you will need to be aware of quite a few *however*s when working with the PHP driver. This chapter will walk you through the benefits of using PHP with MongoDB, as well as how to overcome the aforementioned "howevers."

This chapter brings you back to the beginning in many ways. You will start by learning to navigate the database and use collections in PHP. Next you will learn how to insert, modify, and delete posts in PHP. You will also learn how to use GridFS and DBRef again; this time, however, the focus will be on how to use them in PHP, rather than the theory behind these technologies.

Comparing Documents in MongoDB and PHP

As you've learned previously, a document in a MongoDB collection is stored using a JSON-like format that consists of keys and values. This is similar to the way PHP defines an associative array, so it shouldn't be too difficult to get used to this format.

For example, assume a document looks like the following in the MongoDB shell:

```
contact = ( {
    "First Name" : "Philip",
    "Last Name" : "Moran",
    "Address" : [
        {
        "Street" : "681 Hinkle Lake Road",
        "Place" : "Newton",
        "Postal Code" : "MA 02160",
        "Country" : "USA"
        }
    ],
```

```
    "E-Mail" : [
        "pm@example.com",
        "pm@office.com",
        "philip@example.com",
        "philip@office.com",
        "moran@example.com",
        "moran@office.com",
        "pmoran@example.com",
        "pmoran@office.com"
    ],
    "Phone" : "617-546-8428",
    "Age" : 60
})
```

The same document would look like this when contained in an array in PHP:

```
$contact = array(
    "First Name" => "Philip",
    "Last Name" => "Moran",
    "Address" => array(
        "Street" => "681 Hinkle Lake Road",
        "Place" => "Newton",
        "Postal Code" => "MA 02160",
        "Country" => "USA"
    )
    ,
    "E-Mail" => array(
        "pm@example.com",
        "pm@office.com",
        "philip@example.com",
        "philip@office.com",
        "moran@example.com",
        "moran@office.com",
        "pmoran@example.com",
        "pmoran@office.com"
    ),
    "Phone" => "617-546-8428",
    "Age" => 60
);
```

The two versions of the document look a lot alike. The obvious difference is that the colon (:) is replaced as the key/value separator by an arrow-like symbol (=>) in PHP. You will get used to these syntactical differences relatively quickly.

MongoDB Classes

The PHP driver for MongoDB contains four core classes, a few others for dealing with GridFS, and several more to represent MongoDB datatypes. The core classes make up the most important part of the driver. Together, these classes allow you to execute a rich set of commands. The four core classes available are as follows:

- MongoClient: Initiates a to the database and provides database server commands such as connect(), close(), listDBs(), selectDBs(), and selectCollection().

- MongoDB: Interacts with the database and provides commands such as createCollection(), selectCollection(), createDBRef(), getDBRef(), drop(), and getGridFS().

- MongoCollection: Interacts with the collection. It includes commands such as count(), find(), findOne(), insert(), remove(), save(), and update().

- MongoCursor: Interacts with the results returned by a find() command and includes commands such as getNext(), count(), hint(), limit(), skip(), and sort().

In this chapter, we'll look at all of the preceding commands; without a doubt, you'll use these commands the most.

■ **Note**   This chapter will not discuss the preceding commands grouped by class; instead, the commands will be sorted in as logical an order as possible.

Connecting and Disconnecting

Let's begin by examining how to use the MongoDB driver to connect to and select a database and a collection. You establish connections using the Mongo class, which is also used for database server commands. The following example shows how to quickly connect to your database in PHP:

```
// Connect to the database
$c = new MongoClient();
// Select the database you want to connect to, e.g contacts
$c->contacts;
```

The Mongo class also includes the selectDB() function, which you can use to select a database:

```
// Connect to the database
$c = new MongoClient();
// Select the database you want to connect to, e.g. contacts
$c->selectDB("contacts");
```

The next example shows how to select the collection you want to work with. The same rules apply as when working in the shell: if you select a collection that does not exist yet, it will be created when you save data to it. The process for selecting the collection you want to connect to is similar to that for connecting to the database; in other words, you use the (->) syntax to literally point to the collection in question, as in the following example:

```
// Connect to the database
$c = new Mongo();
// Selecting the database ('contacts') and collection ('people') you want
// to connect to
$c->contacts->people;
```

The selectCollection() function also lets you select—or switch—collections, as in the following example:

```
// Connect to the database
$c = new Mongo();
// Selecting the database ('contacts') and collection ('people') you want
// to connect to
$c-> selectDB("contacts")->selectCollection("people");
```

Before you can select a database or a collection, you sometimes need to find the desired database or collection. The Mongo class includes two additional commands for listing the available databases, as well as the available collections. You can acquire a list of available databases by invoking the listDBs() function and printing the output (which will be placed in an array):

```
// Connecting to the database
$c = new Mongo();
// Listing the available databases
print_r($c->listDBs());
```

Likewise, you can use listCollections() to get a list of available collections in a database:

```
// Connecting to the database
$c = new Mongo();
// Listing the available collections within the 'contacts' database
print_r($c->contacts->listCollections());
```

■ **Note** The print_r command used in this example is a PHP command that prints the contents of an array. The listDBs() function returns an array directly, so the command can be used as a parameter of the print_r function.

The MongoClient class also contains a close() function that you can use to disconnect the PHP session from the database server. However, using it is generally not required, except in unusual circumstances, because the driver will automatically close the connection to the database cleanly whenever the Mongo object goes out of scope.

Sometimes you may not want to forcibly close a connection. For example, you may not be sure of the actual state of the connection, or you may wish to ensure that a new connection can be established. In this case, you can use the close() function, as shown in the following example:

```
// Connecting to the database
$c = new Mongo();
// Closing the connection
$c->close();
```

Inserting Data

So far you've seen how to establish a connection to the database. Now it's time to learn how to insert data into your collection. The process for doing this is no different in PHP than when using the MongoDB shell. The process has two steps. First, you define the document in a variable. Second, you insert it using the insert() function.

Defining a document is not specifically related to MongoDB—instead, you create an array with keys and values stored in it, as in the following example:

```
$contact = array(
    "First Name" => "Philip",
    "Last Name" => "Moran",
    "Address" => array(
        "Street" => "681 Hinkle Lake Road",
        "Place" => "Newton",
        "Postal Code" => "MA 02160",
        "Country" => "USA"
    )
    ,
    "E-Mail" => array(
        "pm@example.com",
        "pm@office.com",
        "philip@example.com",
        "philip@office.com",
        "moran@example.com",
        "moran@office.com",
        "pmoran@example.com",
        "pmoran@office.com"
    ),
    "Phone" => "617-546-8428",
    "Age" => 60
);
```

■ **Warning**   Strings sent to the database need to be UTF-8 formatted to prevent an exception from occurring.

Once you've assigned your data properly to a variable—called $contact in this case—you can use the insert() function to insert it in the MongoCollection class:

```
// Connect to the database
$c = new MongoClient();
// Select the collection 'people'
$collection = $c->contacts->people;
// Insert the document '$contact' into the people collection '$collection'
$collection->insert($contact);
```

The insert() function takes five options, specified in an array: fsync, j, w, wtimeout and timeout. The fsync option can be set to TRUE or FALSE; FALSE is the default value for this option. If set to TRUE, fsync forces the data to be written to the hard disk before it indicates the insertion was a success. This option will override any setting for the option w, setting it to 0. The j option can be set to TRUE or FALSE, where FALSE is the default. If set, the j option will force the data to be written to the journal before indicating the insertion was a success. If you are unfamiliar with journaling, think of it as a log file that keeps track of the changes made to your data, before it is finally written to disk. This ensures that, were mongod to stop unexpectedly, it will be able to recover the changes written to the journal, thereby preventing your data from entering an inconsistent state.

The w option can be used to acknowledge or unacknowledge a write operation (making this option also applicable for remove() and update() operations). If w is set to 0, the write operation will not be acknowledged; set it to 1 and the write will be acknowledged by the (primary) server. When working with replica sets, w can also be set to n, ensuring that the primary server acknowledges the write operation when successfully replicated to n nodes. w can also be set to 'majority'—a reserved string—ensuring that the majority of the replica set will acknowledge the write, or to a specific tag, ensuring that those tagged nodes will acknowledge the write. For this option also, the default setting is 1. The wtimeout option can be used to specify how long the server is to wait for receiving acknowledgement (in milliseconds). By default, this option is set to 10000. Lastly, the timeout option allows you to specify how long (in milliseconds) the client needs to wait for a response from the database.

The following example illustrates how to use the w and wtimeout options to insert data:

```php
// Define another contact
$contact = array(
        "Fir't Name" => "Victoria",
        "Last Name" => "Wood",
        "Address" => array(
                        "Street" => "50 Ash lane",
                        "Place" => "Ystradgynlais",
                        "Postal Code" => "SA9 6XS",
                        "Country" => "UK"
        )
        ,
        "E-Mail" => array(
                "vw@example.com",
                "vw@office.com"
        ),
        "Phone" => "078-8727-8049",
        "Age" => 28
);
// Connect to the database
$c = new MongoClient();
// Select the collection 'people'
$collection = $c->contacts->people;
// Specify the w and wtimeout options
$options = array("w" => 1, "wtimeout" => 5000);
// Insert the document '$contact' into the people collection '$collection'
$collection->insert($contact,$options);
```

And that's all there is to inserting data into your database with the PHP driver. For the most part, you will probably be working on defining the array that contains the data, rather than injecting the data into the array.

Listing Your Data

Typically, you will use the find() function to query for data. It takes a parameter that you use to specify your search criteria; once you specify your criteria, you execute find() to get the results. By default, the find() function simply returns all documents in the collection. This is similar to the shell examples discussed in Chapter 4. Most of the time, however, you will not want to do this. Instead, you will want to define specific information to return results for. The next sections will cover commonly used options and parameters that you can used with the find() function to filter your results.

Returning a Single Document

Listing a single document is easy: simply executing the findOne() function without any parameters specified will grab the first document it finds in the collection. The findOne function stores the returned information in an array and leaves it for you to print it out again, as in this example:

```
// Connect to the database
$c = new MongoClient();
// Select the collection 'people' from the database 'contacts'
$collection = $c->contacts->people;
// Find the very first document within the collection, and print it out
// using print_r
print_r($collection->findOne());
```

As noted previously, it's easy to list a single document in a collection: all you will need to do is define the findOne() function itself. Naturally, you can use the findOne() function with additional filters. For instance, if you know the last name of a person you're looking for, you can specify it as an option in the findOne() function:

```
// Connect to the database
$c = new MongoClient();
// Select the collection 'people' from the database 'contacts'
$collection = $c->contacts->people;
// Define the last name of the person in the $lastname variable
$lastname = array("Last Name" => "Moran");
// Find the very first person in the collection with the last name "Moran"
print_r($collection->findOne($lastname));
```

Of course, many more options exist for filtering the data; you'll learn more about these additional options later in this chapter. Let's begin by looking at some sample output returned by using the print_r() command (the example adds a few line breaks for the sake of making the code easier to read):

```
Array (
    [_id] => MongoId Object ( )
    [First Name] => Philip
    [Last Name] => Moran
    [Address] => Array (
        [Street] => 681 Hinkle Lake Road
        [Place] => Newton
        [Postal Code] => MA 02160
        [Country] => USA
    )
    [E-Mail] => Array (
        [0] => pm@example.com
        [1] => pm@office.com
        [2] => philip@example.com
        [3] => philip@office.com
        [4] => moran@example.com
        [5] => moran@office.com
```

```
        [6] => pmoran@example.com
        [7] => pmoran@office.com
    )
    [Phone] => 617-546-8428
    [Age] => 60
)
```

Listing All Documents

While you can use the findOne() function to list a single document, you will use the find() function for pretty much everything else. Don't misunderstand, please: you *can* find a single document with the find() function by limiting your results; but if you are unsure about the number of documents to be returned, or if you are expecting more than one document, then the find() function is your friend.

As detailed in the previous chapters, the find() function has many, many options that you can use to filter your results to suit just about any circumstance you can imagine. We'll start off with a few simple examples and build from there.

First, let's see how you can display all the documents in a certain collection using PHP and the find() function. The only thing that you should be wary of when printing out multiple documents is that each document is returned in an array, and that each array needs to be printed individually. You can do this using PHP's while() function. As just indicated, you will need to instruct the function to print each document before proceeding with the next one. The getNext() command gets the next document in the cursor from MongoDB; this command effectively returns the next object in the cursor and advances the cursor. The following snippet lists all the documents found in a collection:

```php
// Connect to the database
$c = new MongoClient();
// Select the collection 'people' from the database 'contacts'
$collection = $c->contacts->people;
// Execute the query and store it under the $cursor variable
$cursor = $collection->find();
// For each document it finds within the collection, print the contents
while ($document = $cursor->getNext())
{
        print_r($document);
}
```

■ **Note** You can implement the syntax for the preceding example several different ways. For example, a faster way to execute the preceding command would look like this: $cursor = $c->contacts->people->find(). For the sake of clarity, however, code examples like this one will be split up into two lines in this chapter, leaving more room for comments.

At this stage, the resulting output would still show only two arrays, assuming you have added the documents described previously in this chapter (and nothing else). If you were to add more documents, then each document would be printed in its own array. Granted, this doesn't look pretty; however, that's nothing you can't fix with a little additional code.

Using Query Operators

Whatever you can do in the MongoDB shell, you can also accomplish using the PHP driver. As you've seen in the previous chapters, the shell includes dozens of options for filtering your results. For example, you can use dot notation; sort or limit the results; skip, count, or group a number of items; or even use regular expressions, among many other things. The following sections will walk you through how to use most of these options with the PHP driver.

Querying for Specific Information

As you might remember from Chapter 4, you can use dot notation to query for specific information in an embedded object in a document. For instance, if you want to find one of your contacts for which you know a portion of the address details, you can use dot notation to find this, as in the following example:

```
// Connect to the database
$c = new MongoClient();
// Select the collection 'people' from the database 'contacts'
$collection = $c->contacts->people;
// Use dot notation to search for a document in which the place
// is set to "Newton"
$address = array("Address.Place" => "Newton");
// Execute the query and store it under the $cursor variable
$cursor = $collection->find($address);
// For each document it finds within the collection, print the ID
// and its contents
while ($document = $cursor->getNext())
{
    print_r($document);
}
```

In a similar fashion, you can search for information in a document's array by specifying one of the items in that array, such as an e-mail address. Because an e-mail address is (usually) unique, the findOne() function will suffice in this example:

```
// Connect to the database
$c = new MongoClient();
// Select the collection 'people' from the database 'contacts'
$collection = $c->contacts->people;
// Define the e-mail address you want to search for under $email
$email = array("E-Mail" => "vw@example.com");
// Find the very first person in the collection matching the e-mail address
print_r($collection->findOne($email));
```

As expected, this example returns the first document that matches the e-mail address vw@example.com—the address of Victoria Wood in this case. The document is returned in the form of an array:

```
Array (
    [_id] => MongoId Object ( )
    [First Name] => Victoria
    [Last Name] => Wood
    [Address] => Array (
        [Street] => 50 Ash lane
        [Place] => Ystradgynlais
```

```
            [Postal Code] => SA9 6XS
            [Country] => UK
        )
    [E-Mail] => Array (
            [0] => vw@example.com
            [1] => vw@office.com
        )
    [Phone] => 078-8727-8049
    [Age] => 28
)
```

Sorting, Limiting, and Skipping Items

The MongoCursor class provides sort(), limit(), and skip() functions, which allow you to sort your results, limit the total number of returned results, and skip a specific number of results, respectively. Let's use the PHP driver to examine each function and how it is used.

PHP's sort() function takes one array as a parameter. In that array, you can specify the field by which it should sort the documents. As when using the shell, you use the value 1 to sort the results in ascending order and -1 to sort the results in descending order. Note that you execute these functions on an existing cursor—that is, against the results of a previously executed find() command.

The following example sorts your contacts based on their age in ascending order:

```php
// Connect to the database
$c = new MongoClient();
// Select the collection 'people' from the database 'contacts'
$collection = $c->contacts->people;
// Execute the query and store it under the $cursor variable
$cursor = $collection->find();
// Use the sort command to sort all results in $cursor, based on their age
$cursor->sort(array('Age' => 1));
// Print the results
while($document = $cursor->getNext())
{
    print_r($document);
}
```

You execute the limit() function on the actual cursor; this takes a stunning total of *one* parameter, which specifies the number of results you would like to have returned. The limit() command returns the first number of *n* items it finds in the collection that match your search criteria. The following example returns only one document (granted, you could use the findOne() function for this instead, but limit() does the job):

```php
// Connect to the database
$c = new MongoClient();
// Select the collection 'people' from the database 'contacts'
$collection = $c->contacts->people;
// Execute the query and store it under the $cursor variable
$cursor = $collection->find();
// Use the limit function to limit the number of results to 1
$cursor->limit(1);
```

```
//Print the result
while($document = $cursor->getNext())
{
    print_r($document);
}
```

Finally, you can use the skip() function to skip the first *n* results that match your criteria. This function also works on a cursor:

```
// Connect to the database
$c = new MongoClient();
// Select the collection 'people' from the database 'contacts'
$collection = $c->contacts->people;
// Execute the query and store it under the $cursor variable
$cursor = $collection->find();
// Use the skip function to skip the first result found
$cursor->skip(1);
// Print the result
while($document = $cursor->getNext())
{
    print_r($document);
}
```

Counting the Number of Matching Results

You can use PHP's count() function to count the number of documents matching your criteria and return the number of items in an array. This function is part of the MongoCursor class and thus operates on the cursor. The following example shows how to get a count of contacts in the collection for people who live in the United States:

```
// Connect to the database
$c = new MongoClient();
// Select the collection 'people' from the database 'contacts'$collection = $c->contacts->people;
// Specify the search parameters
$country = array("Address.Country" => "USA");
// Execute the query and store under the $cursor variable for further processing
$cursor = $collection->find($country);
// Count the results and return the value
print_r($cursor->count());
```

This query returns one result. Such counts can be useful for all sorts of operations, whether it's counting comments, the total number of registered users, or anything else.

Grouping Data with the Aggregation Framework

The aggregation framework is easily one of the more powerful features built into MongoDB, as it allows you to calculate aggregated values without needing to use the—often overly complex—Map/Reduce functionality. One of the most useful pipeline operators the framework includes is the $group operator, which can loosely be compared to SQL's GROUP BY functionality. This operator allows you to calculate aggregate values based upon a collection of documents. For example, the aggregation function $max can be used to find and return a group's highest value; the $min function to find and return the lowest value, and $sum to calculate the total number of occurrences of a given value.

Let's say that you want to get a list of all contacts in your collection, grouped by the country where they live. The aggregation framework lets you do this easily. Let's take a look at an example:

```
// Connect to the database
$c = new MongoClient();
// Select the collection 'people' from the database 'contacts'
$collection = $c->contacts->people;
// Execute the query and store it under the $result variable
$result = $collection->aggregate(array(
        '$group' => array(
                '_id' => '$Address.Country',
                'total' => array('$sum' => 1)
        )
));
// Count the results and return the value
print_r($result);
```

As you can see, the aggregate function accepts one (or more) arrays with pipeline operators (in this case, the $group operator). Here, you can specify how the resulting output is returned, and any optional aggregation functions to execute: in this case the $sum function. In this example a unique document is returned for every unique country found, represented by the document's _id field. Next, the total count of each country is summarized using the $sum function, and returned using the total field. Note that the $sum function is represented by an array, and given the value of 1 as we want every match to increase the total by 1.

You might wonder what the resulting output will look like. Here's an example of the output, given that there are two contacts living in the United Kingdom and one in the United States:

```
Array (
    [result] => Array (
        [0] => Array (
            [_id] => UK [total] => 2
        )
        [1] => Array (
            [_id] => USA [total] => 1
        )
    )
    [ok] => 1
)
```

This example is but a simple one, but the aggregation framework is quite powerful indeed, as you will see when we look into it more closely in Chapter 8.

Specifying the Index with Hint

You use PHP's hint() function to specify which index should be used when querying for data; doing so can help you increase query performance. For instance, assume you have thousands of contacts in your collection, and you generally search for a person based upon last name. In this case, it's recommended that you create an index on the Last Name key in the collection.

■ **Note** The hint() example shown next will not return anything if no index is created first.

To use the hint() function, you must apply it to the cursor, as in the following example:

```
// Connect to the database
$c = new MongoClient();
// Select the collection 'people' from the database 'contacts'
$collection = $c->contacts->people;
// Execute the query and store it under the $cursor variable
$cursor = $collection->find(array("Last Name" => "Moran"));
// Use the hint function to specify which index to use
$cursor->hint(array("Last Name" => -1));
//Print the result
while($document = $cursor->getNext())
{
    print_r($document);
}
```

■ **Note**   See Chapter 4 for more details on how to create an index. It is also possible to use the PHP driver's
ensureIndex() function to create an index, as discussed there.

Refining Queries with Conditional Operators

You can use conditional operators to refine your queries. PHP comes with a nice set of default conditional operators, such as < (less than), > (greater than), <= (less than or equal to), and >= (greater than or equal to). Now for the bad news: you cannot use these operators with the PHP driver. Instead, you will need to use MongoDB's version of these operators. Fortunately, MongoDB itself comes with a vast set of conditional operators (you can find more information about these operators in Chapter 4). You can use all of these operators when querying for data through PHP, passing them on through the find() function.

While you can use all these operators with the PHP driver, you must use specific syntax to do so; that is, you must place them in an array, and pass this array to the find() function. The following sections will walk you through how to use several commonly used operators.

Using the $lt, $gt, $lte, and $gte Operators

MongoDB's $lt, $gt, $lte, and $gte operators allow you to perform the same actions as the <, >, <=, and >= operators, respectively. These operators are useful in situations where you want to search for documents that store integer values.

You can use the $lt (less than) operator to find any kind of data for which the integer value is less than n, as shown in the following example:

```
// Connect to the database
$c = new MongoClient();
// Select the collection 'people' from the database 'contacts'
$collection = $c->contacts->people;
// Specify the conditional operator
$cond = array('Age' => array('$lt' => 30));
// Execute the query and store it under the $cursor variable
$cursor = $collection->find($cond);
```

```
//Print the results
while($document = $cursor->getNext())
{
    print_r($document);
}
```

The resulting output shows only one result in the current documents: the contact information for Victoria Wood, who happens to be younger than 30:

```
Array (
    [_id] => MongoId Object ( )
    [First Name] => Victoria
    [Last Name] => Wood
        Address] => Array (
        [Street] => 50 Ash lane
        [Place] => Ystradgynlais
        [Postal Code] => SA9 6XS
        [Country] => UK
    )
    [E-Mail] => Array (
        [0] => vw@example.com
        [1] => vw@office.com
    )
    [Phone] => 078-8727-8049
    [Age] => 28
)
```

Similarly, you can use the $gt operator to find any contacts who are older than 30. This following example does that by changing the $lt variable to $gt (greater than), instead:

```
// Connect to the database
$c = new MongoClient();
// Select the collection 'people' from the database 'contacts'
$collection = $c->contacts->people;
// Specify the conditional operator
$cond = array('Age' => array('$gt' => 30));
// Execute the query and store it under the $cursor variable
$cursor = $collection->find($cond);
//Print the results
while($document = $cursor->getNext())
{
    print_r($document);
}
```

This will return the document for Philip Moran because he's older than 30:

```
Array (
    [_id] => MongoId Object ( )
    [First Name] => Philip
    [Last Name] => Moran
```

```
        [Address] => Array (
            [Street] => 681 Hinkle Lake Road
            [Place] => Newton
            [Postal Code] => MA 02160
            [Country] => USA
        )
        [E-Mail] => Array (
            [0] => pm@example.com
            [1] => pm@office.com
            [2] => philip@example.com
            [3] => philip@office.com
            [4] => moran@example.com
            [5] => moran@office.com
            [6] => pmoran@example.com
            [7] => pmoran@office.com
        )
        [Phone] => 617-546-8428
        [Age] => 60
)
```

You can use the $lte operator to specify that the value must either match exactly or be lower than the value specified. Remember: $lt will find anyone who is younger than 30, but not anyone who is exactly 30. The same goes for the $gte operator, which finds any value that is greater than or equal to the integer specified. Now let's look at a pair of examples.

The first example will return both items from your collection to your screen:

```
// Connect to the database
$c = new MongoClient();
// Select the collection 'people' from the database 'contacts'
$collection = $c->contacts->people;
// Specify the conditional operator
$cond = array('Age' => array('$lte' => 60));
// Execute the query and store it under the $cursor variable
$cursor = $collection->find($cond);
//Print the results
while($document = $cursor->getNext())
{
    print_r($document);
}
```

The second example will display only one document because the collection only holds one contact who is either 60 or older:

```
// Connect to the database
$c = new MongoClient();
// Select the collection 'people' from the database 'contacts'
$collection = $c->contacts->people;
// Specify the conditional operator
$cond = array('Age' => array('$gte' => 60));
```

```
// Execute the query and store it under the $cursor variable
$cursor = $collection->find($cond);
//Print the results
while($document = $cursor->getNext())
{
    print_r($document);
}
```

Finding Documents that *Don't* Match a Value

You can use the $ne (not equals) operator to find any documents that don't match the value specified in the $ne operator. The syntax for this operator is straightforward. The next example will display any contact whose age is not equal to 28:

```
// Connect to the database
$c = new MongoClient();
// Select the collection 'people' from the database 'contacts'
$collection = $c->contacts->people;
// Specify the conditional operator
$cond = array('Age' => array('$ne' => 28));
// Execute the query and store it under the $cursor variable
$cursor = $collection->find($cond);
//Print the results
while($document = $cursor->getNext())
{
    print_r($document);
}
```

Matching Any of Multiple Values with $in

The $in operator lets you search for documents that match any of several possible values added to an array, as in the following example:

```
// Connect to the database
$c = new MongoClient();
// Select the collection 'people' from the database 'contacts'
$collection = $c->contacts->people;
// Specify the conditional operator
$cond = array('Address.Country' => array('$in' => array("USA","UK")));
// Execute the query and store it under the $cursor variable
$cursor = $collection->find($cond);
//Print the results
while($document = $cursor->getNext())
{
    print_r($document);
}
```

The resulting output would show any contact information from any person you add, whether that person lives in the US or the UK. Note that the list of possibilities is actually added in an array; it cannot be typed in "just like that."

Matching All Criteria in a Query with $all

Like the $in operator, the $all operator lets you compare against multiple values in an additional array. The difference is that the $all operator requires that all items in the array match a document before it returns any results. The following example shows how to conduct such a query:

```
// Connect to the database
$c = new MongoClient();
// Select the collection 'people' from the database 'contacts'
$collection = $c->contacts->people;
// Specify the conditional operator
$cond = array('E-Mail' => array('$all' => array("vw@example.com","vw@office.com")));
// Execute the query and store it under the $cursor variable
$cursor = $collection->find($cond);
//Print the results
while($document = $cursor->getNext())
{
    print_r($document);
}
```

Searching for Multiple Expressions with $or

You can use the $or operator to specify multiple expressions a document can contain to return a match. The difference between the two operators is that the $in operator doesn't allow you to specify both a key and value, whereas the $or operator does. You can combine the $or operator with any other key/value combination. Let's look at two examples.

The first example searches for and returns any document that contains either an Age key with the integer value of 28 or an Address.Country key with the value of USA:

```
// Connect to the database
$c = new MongoClient();
// Select the collection 'people' from the database 'contacts'
$collection = $c->contacts->people;
// Specify the conditional operator
$cond = array('$or' => array(
    array("Age" => 28),
    array("Address.Country" => "USA")
) );
// Execute the query and store it under the $cursor variable
$cursor = $collection->find($cond);
//Print the results
while($document = $cursor->getNext())
{
    print_r($document);
}
```

The second example searches for and returns any document that has the Address.Country key set to USA (mandatory), as well as a key/value set either to "Last Name" : "Moran" or to "E-Mail" : "vw@example.com":

```
// Connect to the database
$c = new MongoClient();
// Select the collection 'people' from the database 'contacts'
$collection = $c->contacts->people;
// Specify the conditional operator
$cond = array(
    "Address.Country" => "USA",
    '$or' => array(
        array("Last Name" => "Moran"),
        array("E-Mail" => "vw@example.com")
    )
);
// Execute the query and store it under the $cursor variable
$cursor = $collection->find($cond);
//Print the results
while($document = $cursor->getNext())
{
    print_r($document);
}
```

The $or operator allows you to conduct two searches at once and then combine the resulting output, even if the searches have nothing in common.

Retrieving a Specified Number of Items with $slice

You can use the $slice projection operator to retrieve a specified number of items from an array in your document. This function is similar to the skip() and limit() functions detailed previously in this chapter. The difference is that the skip() and limit() functions work on full documents, whereas the $slice operator allows you to work on an array rather than a single document.

The $slice projection operator is a great method for limiting the number of items per page (this is generally known as *paging*). The next example shows how to limit the number of e-mail addresses returned from one of the contacts specified earlier (Philip Moran); in this case, you only return the first three e-mail addresses:

```
// Connect to the database
$c = new MongoClient();
// Select the collection 'people' from the database 'contacts'
$collection = $c->contacts->people;
// Specify our search operator
$query = array("Last Name" => "Moran");
// Create a new object from an array using the $slice operator
$cond = (object)array('E-Mail' => array('$slice' => 3));
// Execute the query and store it under the $cursor variable
$cursor = $collection->find($query, $cond);
// For each document it finds within the collection, print the contents
while ($document = $cursor->getNext())
{
        print_r($document);
}
```

Similarly, you can get only the *last* three e-mail addresses in the list by making the integer negative, as shown in the following example:

```
// Connect to the database
$c = new MongoClient();
// Select the collection 'people' from the database 'contacts'
$collection = $c->contacts->people;
// Specify our search operator
$query = array("Last Name" => "Moran");
// Specify the conditional operator
$cond = (object)array('E-Mail' => array('$slice' => -3));
// Execute the query and store it under the $cursor variable
$cursor = $collection->find($query, $cond);
// For each document it finds within the collection, print the contents
while ($document = $cursor->getNext())
{
        print_r($document);
}
```

Or, you can skip the first two entries and limit the results to three:

```
// Connect to the database
$c = new MongoClient();
// Select the collection 'people' from the database 'contacts'
$collection = $c->contacts->people;
// Specify our search operator
$query = array("Last Name" => "Moran");
// Specify the conditional operator
$cond = (object)array('E-Mail' => array('$slice' => array(2, 3)));
// Execute the query and store it under the $cursor variable
$cursor = $collection->find($query, $cond);
// For each document it finds within the collection, print the contents
while ($document = $cursor->getNext())
{
        print_r($document);
}
```

The $slice operator is a great method for limiting the number of items in an array; you'll definitely want to keep this operator in mind when programming with the MongoDB driver and PHP.

Determining Whether a Field Has a Value

You can use the $exists operator to return a result based on whether a field holds a value (regardless of the value of this field). As illogical as this may sound, it's actually very handy. For example, you can search for contacts where the Age field has not been set yet; or you can search for contacts for whom you have a street name.

The following example returns any contacts that do not have an Age field set:

```
// Connect to the database
$c = new MongoClient();
// Select the collection 'people' from the database 'contacts'
$collection = $c->contacts->people;
```

```
// Specify the conditional operator
$cond = array('Age' => array('$exists' => false));
// Execute the query and store it under the $cursor variable
$cursor = $collection->find($cond);
//Print the results
while($document = $cursor->getNext())
{
    print_r($document);
}
```

Similarly, the next example returns any contacts that have the Street field set:

```
// Connect to the database
$c = new MongoClient();
// Select the collection 'people' from the database 'contacts'
$collection = $c->contacts->people;
// Specify the conditional operator
$cond = array("Address.Street" => array('$exists' => true));
// Execute the query and store it under the $cursor variable
$cursor = $collection->find($cond);
//Print the results
while($document = $cursor->getNext())
{
    print_r($document);
}
```

Regular Expressions

Regular expressions are neat. You can use them for just about everything (except for making coffee, perhaps); and they can greatly simplify your life when searching for data. The PHP driver comes with its own class for regular expressions: the MongoRegex class. You can use this class to create regular expressions, and then use them to find data.

The MongoRegex class knows six regular expression flags that you can use to query your data. You may already be familiar with some of them:

- i: Triggers case insensitivity.

- m: Searches for content that is spread over multiple lines (line breaks).

- x: Allows your search to contain #comments.

- l: Specifies a locale.

- s: Also known as *dotall*, "." can be specified to match everything, including new lines.

- u: Matches Unicode.

Now let's take a closer look at how to use regular expressions in PHP to search for data in your collection. Obviously, this is best demonstrated with a simple example.

For example, assume you want to search for a contact about whom you have very little information. For example, you may vaguely recall the place where the person lives and that it contains something like *stradgynl* in the middle somewhere. Regular expressions give you a simple yet elegant way to search for such a person:

```
// Connect to the database
$c = new MongoClient();
// Select the collection 'people' from the database 'contacts'
```

```
$collection = $c->contacts->people;
// Specify the regular expression
$regex = new MongoRegex("/stradgynl/i");
// Execute the query and store it under the $cursor variable
$cursor = $collection->find(array("Address.Place" => $regex));
//Print the results
while($document = $cursor->getNext())
{
    print_r($document);
}
```

When creating a PHP application, you'll typically want to search for specific data. In the preceding example, you would probably replace the text ("stradgynl", in this case) with a $_POST variable.

Modifying Data with PHP

If we lived in a world where all data remained static and humans never made any typos, we would never need to update our documents. But the world is a little more flexible than that, and there are times when we make mistakes that we'd like to correct.

For such situations, you can use a set of modifier functions in MongoDB to update (and therefore change) your existing data. You can do this in several ways. For example, you might use the update() function to update existing information, and then use the save() function to save your changes. The following sections look at a handful of these and other modifier operators, illustrating how to use them effectively.

Updating via update()

As detailed in Chapter 4, you use the update() function to perform most document updates. Like the version of update() in the MongoDB shell, the update() function that comes with the PHP driver allows you to use an assortment of modifier operators to update your documents quickly and easily. PHP's version of the update() function operates almost identically; nevertheless, using the PHP version successfully requires a significantly different approach. The upcoming section will walk you through how to use the function successfully with PHP.

PHP's update() function takes a minimum of two parameters: the first describes the object(s) to update, and the second describes the object you want to update the matching record(s) with. Additionally, you can specify a third parameter for an expanded set of options.

The options parameter provides seven additional flags you can use with the update() function; this list explains what they are and how to use them:

- upsert: If set to true, this Boolean option causes a new document to be created if the search criteria are not matched.

- multiple: If set to true, this Boolean option causes all documents matching the search criteria to be updated.

- fsync: If set to true, this Boolean option causes the data to be synced to disk before returning a success. If this option is set to true, then it's implied that w is set to 0, even if it's set otherwise. Defaults to false.

- w: If set to 0, the update operation will not be acknowledged. When working with replica sets, w can also be set to n, ensuring that the primary server acknowledges the update operation when successfully replicated to n nodes. Can also be set to 'majority'—a reserved string—to ensure that the majority of replica nodes will acknowledge the update, or to a specific tag, ensuring that those nodes tagged will acknowledge the update. This option defaults to 1, acknowledging the update operation.

- j: If set to true, this Boolean option will force the data to be written to the journal before indicating the update was a success. Defaults to false.

- wtimeout: Used to specify how long the server is to wait for receiving acknowledgement (in milliseconds). Defaults to 10000.

- timeout: Used to specify how long (in milliseconds) the client needs to wait for a response from the database.

Now let's look at a common example that changes Victoria Wood's first name to "Vicky" without using any of the modifier operators (these will be discussed momentarily):

```
// Connect to the database
$c = new MongoClient();
// Select the collection 'people' from the database 'contacts'
$collection = $c->contacts->people;
// Specify the search criteria
$criteria = array("Last Name" => "Wood");
// Specify the information to be changed
$update = array(
        "First Name" => "Vicky",
        "Last Name" => "Wood",
        "Address" => array(
                        "Street" => "50 Ash lane",
                        "Place" => "Ystradgynlais",
                        "Postal Code" => "SA9 6XS",
                        "Country" => "UK"
        )
        ,
        "E-Mail" => array(
                "vw@example.com",
                "vw@office.com"
        ),
        "Phone" => "078-8727-8049",
        "Age" => 28
);
// Options
$options = array("upsert" => true);
// Perform the update
$collection->update($criteria,$update,$options);
// Show the result
print_r($collection->findOne($criteria));
```

The resulting output would look like this:

```
Array (
    [_id] => MongoId Object ()
    [First Name] => Vicky
    [Last Name] => Wood
    [Address] => Array (
        [Street] => 50 Ash lane
        [Place] => Ystradgynlais
```

```
            [Postal Code] => SA9 6XS
            [Country] => UK
        )
    [E-Mail] => Array (
            [0] => vw@example.com
            [1] => vw@office.com
        )
    [Phone] => 078-8727-8049
    [Age] => 28
)
```

This is a lot of work just to change one value—not exactly what you'd want to be doing to make a living. However, this is precisely what you would have to do if you didn't use PHP's modifier operators. Now let's look at how you can use these operators in PHP to make life easier and consume less time.

■ **Warning**   If you don't specify any of the conditional operators when applying the change, the data in the matching document(s) will be replaced by the information in the array. Generally, it's best to use $set if you want to change only one field.

Saving Time with Update Operators

The update operations are going to save you loads of typing. As you'll probably agree, the preceding example is just not feasible to work with. Fortunately, the PHP driver includes about half a dozen update operators for quickly modifying your data, without going through the trouble of writing it out fully. The purpose of each operator will be briefly summarized again, although you are probably familiar with most of them at this point (you can find more information about all the update operators discussed in this section in Chapter 4). However, the way you use them in PHP differs significantly, as do the options associated with them. We'll look at examples for each of these operators, not least so you can familiarize you with their syntax in PHP.

■ **Note**   None of the update operators that follow will include PHP code to review the changes made; rather, the examples that follow only apply the changes. It's suggested that you fire up the MongoDB shell alongside of the PHP code, so you can perform searches and confirm that the desired changes have applied. Alternatively, you can write additional PHP code to perform these checks.

Increasing the Value of a Specific Key with $inc

The $inc operator allows you to increase the value of a specific key by n, assuming that the key exists. If the key does not exist, it will be created instead. The following example increases the age of each person younger than 40 by three years:

```php
// Connect to the database
$c = new MongoClient();
// Select the collection 'people' from the database 'contacts'
$collection = $c->contacts->people;
// Search for anyone that's younger than 40
$criteria = array("Age" => array('$lt' => 40));
// Use $inc to increase their age by 3 years
$update = array('$inc' => array('Age' => 3));
```

```
// Options
$options = array("upsert" => true);
// Perform the update
$collection->update($criteria,$update,$options);
```

Changing the Value of a Key with $set

The $set operator lets you change the value of a key while ignoring any other fields. As noted previously, this would have been a much better choice for updating Victoria's first name to "Vicky" in the earlier example. The following example shows how to use the $set operator to change the contact's name to "Vicky":

```
// Connect to the database
$c = new MongoClient();
// Select the collection 'people' from the database 'contacts'
$collection = $c->contacts->people;
// Specify the search criteria
$criteria = array("Last Name" => "Wood");
// Specify the information to be changed
$update = array('$set' => array("First Name" => "Vicky"));
// Options
$options = array("upsert" => true);
// Perform the update
$collection->update($criteria,$update,$options);
```

You can also use $set to add a field for every occurrence found matching your query:

```
// Connect to the database
$c = new MongoClient();
// Select the collection 'people' from the database 'contacts'
$collection = $c->contacts->people;
// Specify the search criteria using regular expressions
$criteria = array("E-Mail" => new MongoRegex("/@office.com/i"));
// Add "Category => Work" into every occurrence found
$update = array('$set' => array('Category' => 'Work'));
// Options
$options = array('upsert' => true, 'multi' => true);
// Perform the upsert via save()
$collection->update($criteria,$update,$options);
```

Deleting a Field with $unset

The $unset operator works similarly to the $set operator. The difference is that $unset lets you delete a given field from a document. For instance, the following example removes the Phone field and its associated data from the contact information for Victoria Wood:

```
// Connect to the database
$c = new MongoClient();
// Select the collection 'people' from the database 'contacts'
$collection = $c->contacts->people;
```

```
// Specify the search criteria
$criteria = array("Last Name" => "Wood");
// Specify the information to be removed
$update = array('$unset' => array("Phone" => 1));
// Perform the update
$collection->update($criteria,$update);
```

Renaming a Field with $rename

The $rename operator can be used to rename a field. This can be helpful when you've accidently made a typo or simply wish to change its name to a more accurate one. The operator will search for the given field name within each document and its underlying arrays and subdocuments.

■ **Warning**   Be careful when using this operator. If the document already contains a field that has the new name, that field will be deleted, after which the old fieldname will be renamed to the new one as specified.

Let's look at an example where the First Name and Last Name fields will be renamed to Given Name and Family Name, respectively, for Vicky Wood:

```
// Connect to the database
$c = new MongoClient();
// Select the collection 'people' from the database 'contacts'
$collection = $c->contacts->people;
// Specify the search criteria
$criteria = array("Last Name" => "Wood");
// Specify the information to be changed
$update = array('$rename' => array("First Name" => "Given Name", "Last Name" => "Family Name"));
// Perform the update
$collection->update($criteria,$update);
```

Changing the Value of a Key during Upsert with $setOnInsert

PHP's $setOnInsert operator can be used to assign a specific value only in case the update function performs an insert when using the upsert operator. This might sound a bit confusing at first, but you can think of this operator as a conditional statement that only sets the given value when upsert *inserts* a document, rather than *updates* one. Let's look at an example to clarify how this work. First, we'll perform an upsert that matches an existing document, thus ignoring the $setOnInsert criteria specified:

```
// Connect to the database
$c = new MongoClient();
// Select the collection 'people' from the database 'contacts'
$collection = $c->contacts->people;
// Specify the search criteria
$criteria = array("Family Name" => "Wood");
// Specify the information to be set on upsert-inserts only
$update = array('$setOnInsert' => array("Country" => "Unknown"));
```

```
// Specify the upsert options
$options = array("upsert" => true);
// Perform the update
$collection->update($criteria,$update,$options);
```

Next, let's look at an example where an upsert performs an insert as the document does not exist yet. Here you'll find that the $setOnInsert criteria given will be successfully applied:

```
// Connect to the database
$c = new MongoClient();
// Select the collection 'people' from the database 'contacts'
$collection = $c->contacts->people;
// Specify the search criteria
$criteria = array("Family Name" => "Wallace");
// Specify the information to be set on upsert-inserts only
$update = array('$setOnInsert' => array("Country" => "Unknown"));
// Specify the upsert options
$options = array("upsert" => true);
// Perform the update
$collection->update($criteria,$update,$options);
```

This piece of code will search for any document where the Family Name-field (remember we renamed it previously) is set to "Wallace". If it's not found, an upsert will be done, as a result of which the Country field will be set to "Unknown", creating the following empty-looking document:

```
{
    "_id" : ObjectId("1"),
    "Country" : "Unknown",
    "Last Name" : "Wallace"
}
```

Appending a Value to a Specified Field with $push

PHP's $push operator lets you append a value to a specified field. If the field is an existing array, the data will be added; if the field does not exist, it will be created. If the field exists, but it is not an array, then an error condition will be raised. The following example shows how to use $push to add some data into an existing array:

```
// Connect to the database
$c = new MongoClient();
// Select the collection 'people' from the database 'contacts'
$collection = $c->contacts->people;
// Specify the search criteria
$criteria = array("Family Name" => "Wood");
// Specify the information to be added
$update = array('$push' => array("E-Mail" => "vw@mongo.db"));
// Perform the update
$collection->update($criteria,$update);
```

Adding Multiple Values to a Key with $push and $each

The $push operator also lets you append multiple values to a key. For this, the $each modifier needs to be added. The values, presented in an array, will be added in case they do not exist yet within the given field. As the $push operator is being used, the same general rules apply: if the field exists, and it is an array, then the data will be added; if it does not exist, then it will be created; if it exists, but it isn't an array, then an error condition will be raised. The following example illustrates how to use the $each modifier:

```
// Connect to the database
$c = new MongoClient();
// Select the collection 'people' from the database 'contacts'
$collection = $c->contacts->people;
// Specify the search criteria
$criteria = array("Family Name" => "Wood");
// Specify the information to be added
$update = array(
    '$push' => array(
        "E-Mail" => array(
            '$each' => array(
                "vicwo@mongo.db",
                "vicwo@example.com"
            )
        )
    )
);
// Perform the update
$collection->update($criteria,$update);
```

Adding Data to an Array with $addToSet

The $addToSet operator is similar to the $push operator, with one important difference: $addToSet ensures that data is added to an array only if the data is not in there. The $addToSet operator takes one array as a parameter:

```
// Connect to the database
$c = new MongoClient();
// Select the collection 'people' from the database 'contacts'
$collection = $c->contacts->people;
// Specify the search criteria
$criteria = array("Family Name" => "Wood");
// Specify the information to be added (successful because it doesn't exist yet)
$update = array('$addToSet' => array("E-Mail" => "vic@example.com"));
// Perform the update
$collection->update($criteria,$update);
```

Similarly, you can add a number of items that don't exist yet by combining the $addToSet operator with the $each operator:

```
// Connect to the database
$c = new MongoClient();
// Select the collection 'people' from the database 'contacts'
$collection = $c->contacts->people;
```

125

```
// Specify the search criteria
$criteria = array("Family Name" => "Wood");
// Specify the information to be added (partially successful; some
// examples were already there)
$update = array(
    '$addToSet' => array
        (
        "E-Mail" => array
            (
            '$each' => array
                (
                "vw@mongo.db",
                "vicky@mongo.db",
                "vicky@example.com"
                )
            )
        )
);
// Perform the update
$collection->update($criteria,$update);
```

Removing an Element from an Array with $pop

PHP's $pop operator lets you remove an element from an array. Keep in mind that you can remove only the first or last element in the array—and nothing in between. You remove the first element by specifying a value of -1; similarly, you remove the last element by specifying a value of 1:

```
// Connect to the database
$c = new MongoClient();
// Select the collection 'people' from the database 'contacts'
$collection = $c->contacts->people;
// Specify the search criteria
$criteria = array("Family Name" => "Wood");
// Pop out the first e-mail address found in the list
$update = array('$pop' => array("E-Mail" => -1));
// Perform the update
$collection->update($criteria,$update);
```

■ **Note** Specifying a value of -2 or 1000 wouldn't change which element is removed. Any negative number will remove the first element, whereas any positive number removes the last element. Using a value of 0 removes the last element from the array.

Removing Each Occurrence of a Value with $pull

You can use PHP's $pull operator to remove each occurrence of a given value from an array. For example, this is handy if you've accidentally added duplicates to an array when using $push or $pushAll. The following example removes any duplicate occurrence of an e-mail address:

```
// Connect to the database
$c = new MongoClient();
// Select the collection 'people' from the database 'contacts'
$collection = $c->contacts->people;
// Specify the search criteria
$criteria = array("Family Name" => "Wood");
// Pull out each occurrence of the e-mail address "vicky@example.com"
$update = array('$pull' => array("E-Mail" => "vicky@example.com"));
// Perform the update
$collection->update($criteria,$update);
```

Removing Each Occurrence of Multiple Elements

Similarly, you can use the $pullAll operator to remove each occurrence of multiple elements from your documents, as shown in the following example:

```
// Connect to the database
$c = new MongoClient();
// Select the collection 'people' from the database 'contacts'
$collection = $c->contacts->people;
// Specify the search criteria
$criteria = array("Family Name" => "Wood");
// Pull out each occurrence of the e-mail addresses below
$update = array(
        '$pullAll' => array(
                "E-Mail" => array("vw@mongo.db","vw@office.com")
        )
);
// Perform the update
$collection->update($criteria,$update);
```

Upserting Data with save()

Like the insert() function, the save() function allows you to insert data into your collection. The only difference is that you can also use save() to update a field that already holds data. As you might recall, this is called an *upsert*. The way you execute the save() function shouldn't come as a surprise at this point. Like the save() function in the MongoDB shell, PHP's save() takes two parameters: an array that contains the information you wish to save, and any options for the save. The following options can be used:

- fsync: If set to true, this Boolean option causes the data to be synced to disk before returning a success. If this option is set to true, then it's implied that w is set to 0, even if it's set otherwise.

- w: If set to 0, the save operation will not be acknowledged. When working with replica sets, w can also be set to *n*, ensuring that the primary server acknowledges the save operation when successfully replicated to *n* nodes. Can also be set to 'majority'—a reserved string—to ensure that the majority of replica nodes will acknowledge the save, or to a specific tag, ensuring that those nodes tagged will acknowledge the save. This option defaults to 1, acknowledging the save operation.

- j: If set to true, this Boolean option will force the data to be written to the journal before indicating the save was a success. Defaults to false.

- wtimeout: Used to specify how long the server is to wait for receiving acknowledgement (in milliseconds). Defaults to 10000.

- timeout: Used to specify how long (in milliseconds) the client needs to wait for a response from the database.

The syntax for PHP's save() version is similar to that in the MongoDB shell, as the following example illustrates:

```php
// Specify the document to be saved
$contact = array(
        "Given Name" => "Kenji",
        "Family Name" => "Kitahara",
        "Address" => array(
                        "Street" => "149 Bartlett Avenue",
                        "Place" => "Southfield",
                        "Postal Code" => "MI 48075",
                        "Country" => "USA"
        )
        ,
        "E-Mail" => array(
                "kk@example.com",
                "kk@office.com"
        ),
        "Phone" => "248-510-1562",
        "Age" => 34
);

// Connect to the database
$c = new MongoClient();
// Select the collection 'people'
$collection = $c->contacts->people;
// Save via the save() function
$options = array("fsync" => true);
// Specify the save() options
$collection->save($contact,$options);

// Realizing you forgot something, let's upsert this contact:
$contact['Category'] = 'Work';
// Perform the upsert
$collection->save($contact);
```

Modifying a Document Atomically

Like the save() and update() functions, the findAndModify() function can be invoked from the PHP driver. Remember that you can use the findAndModify() function to modify a document atomically and return the results after the update executes successfully. You use the findAndModify() function to update a single document—and nothing more. You may recall that, by default, the document returned will *not* show the modifications made— returning the document with the modifications made would require specifying an additional argument: the new parameter.

The findAndModify function takes four parameters; query, update, fields, and options. Some of these are optional, depending on your actions. For example, when specifying the update criteria, the fields and options are optional. However when you wish to use the remove option, the update and fields parameters need to be specified (using null, for example). The following list details the available parameters:

- query: Specifies a filter for the query. If this parameter isn't specified, then all documents in the collection will be seen as possible candidates, and the first document encountered will be updated or removed.

- update: Specifies the information to update the document. Note that any of the modifier operators specified previously can be used to accomplish this.

- fields: Specifies the fields you would like to see returned, rather than the entire document. This parameter behaves identically to the fields parameter in the find() function. Note that the _id field will always be returned, even if that field isn't included in your list of fields to return.

- options: Specifies the options to apply. The following options can be used:

  - sort: Sorts the matching documents in a specified order.

  - remove: If set to true, the first matching document will be removed.

  - update: If set to true, an update will be performed on the selected document.

  - new: If set to true, returns the updated document, rather than the selected document. Note that this parameter is not set by default, which might be a bit confusing in some circumstances.

  - upsert: If set to true, performs an upsert.

Now let's look at a set of examples that illustrate how to use these parameters. The first example searches for a contact with the last name "Kitahara" and adds an e-mail address to his contact card by combining an update() with the $push operator. The new parameter is not set in the following example, so the resulting output still displays the *old* information:

```
// Connect to the database
$c = new MongoClient();
// Specify the database and collection in which to work
$collection = $c->contacts->people;
// Specify the search criteria
$criteria = array("Family Name" => "Kitahara");
// Specify the update criteria
$update = array('$push' => array("E-Mail" => "kitahara@mongo.db"));
// Perform a findAndModify()
$collection->findAndModify($criteria,$update);
```

The result returned looks like this:

```
Array (
    [value] => Array (
        [Given Name] => Kenji
        [Family Name] => Kitahara
        [Address] => Array (
            [Street] => 149 Bartlett Avenue
            [Place] => Southfield
            [Postal Code] => MI 48075
            [Country] => USA
            )
        [E-Mail] => Array (
            [0] => kk@example.com
            [1] => kk@office.com
        )
        [Phone] => 248-510-1562
        [Age] => 34
        [_id] => MongoId Object ( )
        [Category] => Work
    )
    [ok] => 1
)
```

The following example shows how to use the remove and sort parameters:

```
// Connect to the database
$c = new MongoClient();
// Specify the database and collection in which to work
$collection = $c->contacts->people;
// Specify the search criteria
$criteria = array("Category" => "Work");
// Specify the options
$options = array("sort" => array("Age" => -1), "remove" => true);
// Perform a findAndModify()
$collection->findAndModify($criteria,null,null,$options);
```

Deleting Data

You can use the remove() function to remove a document like the one in the preceding example from the MongoDB shell. The PHP driver also includes a remove() function you can use to remove data. The PHP version of this function takes two parameters: one contains the description of the record or records to remove, while the other specifies additional options governing the removal process.

There are seven options available:

- justOne: If set to true, at most only one record matching the criteria must be removed.

- fsync: If set to true, this Boolean option causes the data to be synced to disk before returning a success. If this option is set to true, then it's implied that w is set to 0, even if it's set otherwise.

- w: If set to 0, the save operation will not be acknowledged. When working with replica sets, w can also be set to *n*, ensuring the primary server acknowledges the save operation when successfully replicated to *n* nodes. Can also be set to 'majority'—a reserved string—to ensure that the majority of replica nodes will acknowledge the save, or to a specific tag, ensuring those nodes tagged will acknowledge the save. This option defaults to 1, acknowledging the save operation.

- j: If set to true, this Boolean option will force the data to be written to the journal before indicating the save was a success. Defaults to false.

- wtimeout: Used to specify how long the server is to wait for receiving acknowledgement (in milliseconds). Defaults to 10000.

- timeout: Used to specify how long (in milliseconds) the client needs to wait for a response from the database.

Now let's look at a couple of code examples that illustrate how to remove a document:

```
// Connect to the database
$c = new MongoClient();
// Select the collection 'people' from the database 'contacts'
$collection = $c->contacts->people;
// Specify the search criteria
$criteria = array("Family Name" => "Wallace");
// Specify the options
$options = array('justOne' => true, 'w' => 0);
// Perform the removal
$collection->remove($criteria,$options);
```

Similarly, the next example removes multiple documents at the same time:

```
// Connect to the database
$c = new Mongo();
// Select the collection 'people' from the database 'contacts'
$collection = $c->contacts->people;
// Specify the search criteria using regular expressions
$criteria = array("E-Mail" => new MongoRegex("/@office.com/i"));
// Specify the options
$options = array("justOne" => false);
// Perform the removal
$collection->remove($criteria,$options);
```

■ **Warning** When you remove a document, remember that any reference to that document will remain in the database. Make sure that you also manually delete or update references to the deleted document; otherwise, these references will return null when evaluated.

Similarly, you can drop an entire collection using the drop() function. This following example returns an array with the removal results:

```
// Connect to the database
$c = new Mongo();
// Select the collection to remove
$collection = $c->contacts->people;
// Remove the collection and return the results
print_r($collection->drop());
```

The results returned look like this:

```
Array (
    [nIndexesWas] => 1
    [msg] => indexes dropped for collection
    [ns] => contacts.people
    [ok] => 1
)
```

Last but not least, you can use PHP to drop entire databases. You accomplish this by using the drop() function in the MongoDB class, as shown in the following example:

```
// Connect to the database
$c = new Mongo();
// Select the database to remove
$db = $c->contacts;
// Remove the database and return the results
print_r($db->drop());
```

The results returned show the name of the database dropped:

```
Array (
[dropped] => contacts
[ok] => 1
)
```

DBRef

DBRef enables you to create links between two documents stored in different locations; this functionality lets you implement behavior similar to that found in a relational database. This functionality can be particularly handy if you want to store the addresses from the people in an addresses collection, rather than include that information in your people collection.

There are two ways to do this. First, you can use a simple link (known as *manual referencing*); in this case, you include the _id of a document into another document. Second, you can use DBRef to create such links automatically.

First, let's look at how you implement manual referencing. In the following example, you add a contact and, under its address information, specify the _id of another document:

```
// Connect to the database
$c = new MongoClient();
$db = $c->contacts;
// Select the collections we want to store our contacts and addresses in
$people = $db->people;
```

```
$addresses = $db->addresses;
// Specify an address
$address = array(
    "Street" => "St. Annastraat 44",
    "Place" => "Monster",
    "Postal Code" => "2681 SR",
    "Country" => "Netherlands"
);
// Save the address
$addresses->insert($address);
// Add a contact living at the address
$contact = array(
    "First Name" => "Melvyn",
    "Last Name" => "Babel",
    "Age" => 35,
    "Address" => $address['_id']
);
$people->insert($contact);
```

Now assume you want to find the preceding contact's address information. To do this, simply query for the Object ID in the address field; you can find this information in the addresses collection (assuming you know the name of this collection).

This works, but the preferred method for referencing another document relies on DBRef. This is because DBRef relies on a common format that the database and all the drivers understand. We'll look at a DBRef version of the preceding example momentarily. Before doing so, however, let's take a look at the create() function of the DBRef class; you will use this class to create the desired reference.

The create() function takes three parameters:

- collection: Specifies the name of the collection where the information resides (without the database name).

- id: Specifies the ID of the document to link to.

- database: Specifies the name of the database in which the document resides.

The following example uses the create() function to create a reference to an address in another document:

```
// Connect to the database
$c = new Mongo();
$db = $c->contacts;

// Select the collections we want to store our contacts and addresses in
$people = $db->people;
$addresses = $db->addresses;

// Specify an address
$address = array(
    "Street" => "WA Visser het Hooftlaan 2621",
    "Place" => "Driebergen",
    "Postal Code" => "3972 SR",
    "Country" => "Netherlands"
);
```

```
// Save the address
$addresses->insert($address);

// Create a reference to the address
$addressRef = MongoDBRef::create($addresses->getName(), $address['_id']);

// Add a contact living at the address
$contact = array(
    "First Name" => "Ivo",
    "Last Name" => "Lauw",
    "Age" => 24,
    "Address" => $addressRef
);
$people->insert($contact);
```

■ **Note** The getName() function in this example is used to get the name of the collection.

Retrieving the Information

So far you've used DBRef to create a reference. Now it's time to look at how to retrieve the information referenced, so that you can display the contents again correctly. You do this using MongoDBRef's get() function.

MongoDBRef's get() function takes two parameters. The first parameter specifies the database to use, while the second provides the reference to fetch:

```
// Connect to the database
$c = new Mongo();
// Select the collection 'people' from the database 'contacts'
$people = $c->contacts->people;
// Define the search parameters
$lastname = array("Last Name" => "Lauw");
// Find our contact, and store under the $person variable
$person = $people->findOne(array("Last Name" => "Lauw"));
// Dereference the address
$address = MongoDBRef::get($people->db, $person['Address']);
// Print out the address from the matching contact
print_r($address);
```

The resulting output shows the document being referred to:

```
Array (
    [_id] => MongoId Object ( )
    [Street] => WA Visser het Hooftlaan 2621
    [Place] => Driebergen
    [Postal Code] => 3972 SR
    [Country] => Netherlands
)
```

DBRef provides a great way to store data you want to reference, not least because it permits flexibility in the collection and database names.

GridFS and the PHP Driver

The previous chapter elaborated on GridFS and its benefits. For example, it explained how to use this technology to store and retrieve data, in addition to other GridFS-related techniques. In this section, you'll learn how to use the PHP driver to store and retrieve files using GridFS.

The PHP driver contains its own classes for dealing with GridFS; here are three of its most important classes and what they do:

- MongoGridFS: Stores and retrieves files from the database. This class contains several methods, including delete(), find(), storeUpload(), and about a half dozen others.

- MongoGridFSFile: Works on a specific file in the database. It includes functions such as __construct(), getFilename(), getSize(), and write().

- MongoGridFSCursor: Works on the cursor. It contains a handful of functions, such as __construct(), current(), getNext(), and key().

Let's have a look at how we can use PHP to upload files into the database.

■ **Note**   The code in the following example will not work without an HTML form that uploads data. Such code is beyond the scope of this chapter, however, so it is not shown here.

Storing Files

You use the storeUpload() function to store files into your database with GridFS. This function takes two parameters: one indicates the fieldname of the file to be uploaded, and the other can optionally be used to specify the file's metadata. Once used, the function reports back the _id of the file stored.

The following simple code example shows how to use the storeUpload() function:

```
// Connect to the database
$c = new MongoClient();
// Select the name of the database
$db = $c->contacts;
// Define the GridFS class to ensure we can handle the files
$gridFS = $db->getGridFS();
// Specify the HTML field's name attribute
$file = 'fileField';
// Specify the file's metadata (optional)
$metadata = array('uploadDate' => date());
// Upload the file into the database
$id = $gridFS->storeUpload($file,$metadata);
```

And that's all there is to it. As you can see, $id is used as a parameter to store the file in the database. You might also use this parameter to reference the data with DBRef.

Adding More Metadata to Stored Files

Sometimes you may want to add more metadata to your stored files. By default, the only other data that's added is the _id field, which you might use to reference the data when you're storing a picture to a contact card. Unfortunately, that might prove to be more of a restriction than a benefit when you want to start searching for your data through these tags.

The following example shows how to store metadata for your uploaded data. This example builds on the previous code block and the $id parameter in particular. Obviously, you can customize this yourself, using any other desired search criteria:

```
// Specify the metadata to be added
$metadata = array('$set' => array("Tag" => "Avatar"));
// Specify the search criteria to which to apply the metadata
$criteria = array('_id' => $id);
// Insert the metadata
$db->grid->update($criteria, $metadata);
```

Retrieving Files

Of course, the ability to store your files in a database wouldn't do you any good if you weren't able to retrieve these files later. Retrieving files is about as hard (read: easy!) as storing them. Let's look at two examples: the first retrieves the filenames stored, while the second retrieves the files themselves.

The following example shows how to retrieve the filenames stored, which you accomplish using the getFilename() function:

```
// Connect to the database
$c = new MongoClient();
$db = $c->contacts;
// Initialize GridFS
$gridFS = $db->getGridFS();
// Find all files in the GridFS storage and store under the $cursor parameter
$cursor = $gridFS->find();
// Return all the names of the files
foreach ($cursor as $object) {
    echo "Filename:".$object->getFilename();
}
```

That was easy! Of course, this example assumes that you have some data stored in your database. You might also want to add more search parameters to the find() function after you've added a little more data or if you want to search for more specific data. Note that the find() function searches through the metadata added to each uploaded file (as detailed earlier in this chapter).

You might wonder how you go about retrieving the files themselves. After all, retrieving the data is probably what you'll be using the most in the end. You accomplish this by using the getBytes() function to send it to your browser. The next example uses the getBytes() function to retrieve a previously stored image. Note that you can retrieve the _id parameter by querying the database (the following example just makes up some parameters). Also, it's mandatory to specify the content type because, logically, this is not recognized by the browser when you build up the data again:

```
// Connect to the database
$c = new MongoClient();
// Specify the database name
$db = $c->contacts;
```

```
// Initialize the GridFS files collection
$gridFS = $db->getGridFS();
// Specify the search parameter for the file
$id = new MongoId('4c555c70be90968001080000');
// Retrieve the file
$file = $gridFS->findOne(array('_id' => $id));
// Specify the header for the file and write the data to it
header('Content-Type: image/jpeg');
echo $file->getBytes();
exit;
```

Deleting Data

You can ensure that any previously stored data is removed by using the delete() function. This function takes one parameter: the _id of the file itself. The following example illustrates how to use the delete() function to delete the file matching the Object ID 4c555c70be90968001080000:

```
// Connect to the database
$c = new MongoClient();
// Specify the database name
$db = $c->contacts;
// Initialize GridFS
$gridFS = $db->getGridFS();
// Specify the file via it's ID
$id = new MongoId('4c555c70be90968001080000');
$file = $gridFS->findOne(array('_id' => $id));
// Remove the file using the remove() function
$gridFS->delete($id);
```

Summary

In this chapter, you've taken an in-depth look at how to work with MongoDB's PHP driver. For example, you've seen how to use the most commonly used functions with the PHP driver, including the insert(), update(), and modify() functions. You've also learned how to search your documents by using the PHP driver's equivalent of the find() function. Finally, you've learned how to leverage DBRef's functionality, as well as how to store and retrieve files with GridFS.

One chapter couldn't possibly cover everything there is to know about using the PHP driver for MongoDB; nonetheless, this chapter should provide the necessary basics to perform most of the actions you'd want to accomplish with this driver. Along the way, you've also learned enough to use the server-side commands whenever the going gets a little more complicated.

In the next chapter, you'll explore the same concepts, but for the Python driver instead.

CHAPTER 7

■ ■ ■

Python and MongoDB

Python is one of the easier programming languages to learn and master. It's an especially great language to start with if you are relatively new to programming. And you'll pick it up that much more quickly if you're already quite familiar with programming.

Python can be used to develop an application quickly while ensuring that the code itself remains perfectly readable. With that in mind, this chapter will show you how to write simple yet elegant, clear, and powerful code that works with MongoDB through the Python driver (also called the PyMongo driver; this chapter will use both terms interchangeably).

First, you'll look at the Connection() function, which enables you to establish a connection to the database. Second, you'll learn how to write documents, or *dictionaries*, as well as how to insert them. Third, you'll learn how to use either the find() or the find_one() command to retrieve documents using the Python driver. Both of these commands optionally take a rich set of query modifiers to narrow down your search and make your query a little easier to implement. Fourth, you'll learn about the wide variety of operators that exist for performing updates. Finally, you'll take a look at how to use PyMongo to delete your data at the document or even the database level. As an added bonus, you'll learn how to use the DBRef module to refer to data stored elsewhere.

Let's get started.

■ **Note**   Throughout the chapter, you'll see many practical code examples that illustrate the concepts discussed. The code itself will be preceded by three greater-than (>>>) symbols to indicate that the command is written in the Python shell. The query code will be styled in **bold**, and the resulting output will be rendered in plaintext.

Working with Documents in Python

As mentioned in earlier chapters, MongoDB uses BSON-styled documents, and PHP uses associative arrays. In a similar vein, Python has what it calls *dictionaries*. If you've already played around with the MongoDB console, we're confident you are absolutely going to *love* Python. After all, the syntax is so similar that the learning curve for the language syntax will be negligible.

We've already covered the structure of a MongoDB document in the preceding chapter, so we won't repeat that information here. Instead, let's examine what a document looks like in the Python shell:

```
item = {
    "Type" : "Laptop",
    "ItemNumber" : "1234EXD",
    "Status" : "In use",
```

```
    "Location" : {
        "Department" : "Development",
    "Building" : "2B",
        "Floor" : 12,
        "Desk" : 120101,
        "Owner" : "Anderson, Thomas"
    },
    "Tags" : ["Laptop","Development","In Use"]
}
```

While you should keep the Python term *dictionary* in mind, in most cases this chapter will refer to its MongoDB equivalent, *document*. After all, most of the time, we will be working with MongoDB documents.

Using PyMongo Modules

The Python driver works with modules. You can treat these much as you treat the classes in the PHP driver. Each module within the PyMongo driver is responsible for a set of operations. There's an individual module for each of the following tasks (and quite a few more): establishing connections, working with databases, leveraging collections, manipulating the cursor, working with the DBRef module, converting the ObjectId, and running server-side JavaScript code.

This chapter will walk you through the most basic yet useful set of operations needed to work with the PyMongo driver. Step-by-step, you'll learn how to use commands with simple and easy-to-understand pieces of code that you can copy and paste directly into your Python shell (or script). From there, it's a short step to managing your MongoDB database.

Connecting and Disconnecting

Establishing a connection to the database requires that you first import the PyMongo driver's MongoClient module, which enables you to establish connections. Type the following statement in the shell to load the MongoClient module:

```
>>> from pymongo import MongoClient
```

Once your MongoDB service is up and running (this is mandatory if you wish to connect), you can establish a connection to the service by calling the MongoClient() function.

If no additional parameters are given, the function assumes that you want to connect to the service on the localhost (the default port number for the localhost is 27017). The following line establishes the connection:

```
>>> c = MongoClient()
```

You can see the connection coming in through the MongoDB service shell. Once you establish a connection, you can use the c dictionary to refer to the connection, just as you did in the shell with db and in PHP with $c. Next, select the database that you want to work with, storing that database under the db dictionary. You can do this just as you would in the MongoDB shell—in the following example, you use the inventory database:

```
>>> db = c.inventory
>>> db
Database(Connection('localhost', 27017), u'inventory')
```

The output in this example shows that you are connected to the localhost and that you are using the inventory database.

Now that the database has been selected, you can select your MongoDB collection in exactly the same way. Because you've already stored the database name under the db dictionary, you can use that to select the collection's name; it is called items in this case:

```
>>> collection = db.items
```

Inserting Data

All that remains is to define the document by storing it in a dictionary. Let's take the preceding example and insert that into the shell:

```
>>> item = {
...     "Type" : "Laptop",
...     "ItemNumber" : "1234EXD",
...     "Status" : "In use",
...     "Location" : {
...             "Department" : "Development",
...             "Building" : "2B",
...             "Floor" : 12,
...             "Desk" : 120101,
...             "Owner" : "Anderson, Thomas"
...     },
...     "Tags" : ["Laptop","Development","In Use"]
... }
```

Once you define the document, you can insert it using the same insert() function that is available in the MongoDB shell:

```
>>> collection.insert(item)
ObjectId('4c57207b4abffe0e0c000000')
```

That's all there is to it: you define the document and insert it using the insert() function.

There's one more interesting trick you can take advantage of when inserting documents: inserting multiple documents at the same time. You can do this by specifying both documents in a single dictionary, and then inserting that document. The result will return two ObjectId values; pay careful attention to how the brackets are used in the following example:

```
>>> two = [{
...     "Type" : "Laptop",
...     "ItemNumber" : "2345FDX",
...     "Status" : "In use",
...     "Location" : {
...             "Department" : "Development",
...             "Building" : "2B",
...             "Floor" : 12,
...             "Desk" : 120102,
...             "Owner" : "Smith, Simon"
...     },
...     "Tags" : ["Laptop","Development","In Use"]
... },
```

```
... {
...      "Type" : "Laptop",
...      "ItemNumber" : "3456TFS",
...      "Status" : "In use",
...      "Location" : {
...              "Department" : "Development",
...              "Building" : "2B",
...              "Floor" : 12,
...              "Desk" : 120103,
...              "Owner" : "Walker, Jan"
...      },
...      "Tags" : ["Laptop","Development","In Use"]
... }]
>>> collection.insert(two)
[ObjectId('4c57234c4abffe0e0c000001'), ObjectId('4c57234c4abffe0e0c000002')]
```

Finding Your Data

PyMongo provides two functions for finding your data: find_one(), which finds a single document in your collection that matches specified criteria; and find(), which can find multiple documents based on the supplied parameters (if you do not specify any parameters, find() matches all documents in the collection). Let's look at some examples.

Finding a Single Document

As just mentioned, you use the find_one() function to find a single document. The function is similar to the findOne() function in the MongoDB shell, so mastering how it works shouldn't present much of a challenge for you. By default, this function will return the first document in your collection if it is executed without any parameters, as in the following example:

```
>>> collection.find_one()
    {
    u'Status': u'In use',
    u'Tags': [u'Laptop', u'Development', u'In Use'],
    u'ItemNumber': u'1234EXD',
    u'Location':{
        u'Department': u'Development',
        u'Building': u'2B',
        u'Floor': 12,
        u'Owner': u'Anderson, Thomas',
        u'Desk': 120101
        },
    u'_id': ObjectId('4c57207b4abffe0e0c000000'),
    u'Type': u'Laptop'
    }
```

You can specify additional parameters to ensure that the first document returned matches your query. Every parameter used with the find() function can also be used for find_one() as well, although the limit parameter will be ignored. The query parameters need to be written just as they would if you were defining them in the shell; that is, you need to specify a key and its value (or a number of values). For instance, assume you want to find a document for which an ItemNumber has the value of 3456TFS, and you don't want to return the document's _id. The following query accomplishes that, returning the output as shown:

```
>>> collection.find_one({"ItemNumber" : "3456TFS"} ,fields={'_id' : False})
{
    u'Status': u'In use',
    u'Tags': [u'Laptop', u'Development', u'In Use'],
    u'ItemNumber': u'3456TFS',
    u'Location': {
        u'Department': u'Development',
        u'Building': u'2B',
        u'Floor': 12,
        u'Owner': u'Walker, Jan',
        u'Desk': 120103
    },
    u'Type': u'Laptop'
}
```

■ **Note**   Python is case-sensitive. Therefore, true and false are not the same as True and False.

If the search criteria are relatively common for a document, you can also specify additional query operators. For example, imagine querying for {"Department" : "Development"}, which would return more than one result. We'll look at such an example momentarily; however, first let's determine how to return multiple documents, rather than just one. This may be a little different than you suspect.

Finding Multiple Documents

You need to use the find() function to return more than a single document. You've probably used this command in MongoDB many times by this point in the book, so you're probably feeling rather comfortable with it. The concept is the same in Python: you specify the query parameters between the brackets to find the specified information.

Getting the results back to your screen, however, works a little differently. Just as when working with PHP and in the shell, querying for a set of documents will return a cursor instance to you. Unlike when typing in the shell, however, you can't simply type in db.items.find() to have all results presented to you. Instead, you need to retrieve all documents using the cursor. The following example shows how to display all documents from the items collection (note that you previously defined collection to match the collection's name; the results are left out for the sake of clarity):

```
>>> for doc in collection.find():
...             doc
...
```

Pay close attention to the indentation before the word doc. If this indentation is not used, then an error message will be displayed, stating that an expected indented block didn't occur. It's one of Python's strengths that it uses such an indentation method for block delimiters because this approach keeps the code well ordered. Rest assured, you'll get used to this *Pythonic* coding convention relatively quickly. If you do happen to forget about the indentation, however, you'll see an error message that looks something like this:

```
File "<stdin>", line 2
    doc
      ^
IndentationError: expected an indented block
```

Next, let's look at how to specify a query operator using the find() function. The methods used for this are identical to the ones seen previously in the book:

```
>>> for doc in collection.find({"Location.Owner" : "Walker, Jan"}):
...             doc
...
{
    u'Status': u'In use',
    u'Tags': [u'Laptop', u'Development', u'In Use'],
    u'ItemNumber': u'3456TFS',
    u'Location': {
        u'Department': u'Development',
        u'Building': u'2B',
        u'Floor': 12,
        u'Owner': u'Walker, Jan',
        u'Desk': 120103
    },
    u'_id': ObjectId('4c57234c4abffe0e0c000002'),
    u'Type': u'Laptop'
}
```

Using Dot Notation

Dot notation is used to search for matching elements in an embedded object. The preceding snippet shows an example of how to do this. When using this technique, you simply specify the key name for an item within the embedded object to search for it, as in the following example:

```
>>> for doc in collection.find({"Location.Department" : "Development"}):
...             doc
...
```

This example returns any document that has the Development department set. When searching for information in a simple array (for instance, the tags applied), you just need to fill in any of the matching tags:

```
>>> for doc in collection.find({"Tags" : "Laptop"}):
...             doc
...
```

Returning Fields

If your documents are relatively large, and you do not want to return all key/value information stored in a document, you can include an additional parameter in the find() function to specify that only a certain set of fields need to be returned using True, or kept hidden using False. You do this by providing the fields parameter, followed by a list of field names after the search criteria. Note that outside of the _id field, you cannot mix True and False in a query.

The following example returns only the current owner's name, the item number, and the object ID (this will always be returned, unless you explicitly tell MongoDB not to return it):

```
>>> for doc in collection.find({'Status' : 'In use'}, fields={'ItemNumber' : True, 'Location.Owner'
: True}):
...             doc
...
```

```
{
        u'ItemNumber': u'1234EXD',
        u'_id': ObjectId('4c57207b4abffe0e0c000000'),
        u'Location': {
                u'Owner': u'Anderson, Thomas'
        }
}
{
        u'ItemNumber': u'2345FDX',
        u'_id': ObjectId('4c57234c4abffe0e0c000001'),
        u'Location': {
                u'Owner': u'Smith, Simon'
        }
}
{
        u'ItemNumber': u'3456TFS',
        u'_id': ObjectId('4c57234c4abffe0e0c000002'),
        u'Location': {
                u'Owner': u'Walker, Jan'
        }
}
```

I suspect you'll agree that this approach to specifying criteria is quite handy.

Simplifying Queries with sort(), limit(), and skip()

The sort(), limit(), and skip() functions make implementing your queries much easier. Individually, each of these functions has its uses, but combining them makes them even better and more powerful. You can use the sort() function to sort the results by a specific key; the limit() function to limit the total number of results returned; and the skip() function to skip the first *n* items found before returning the remainder of the documents that match your query.

Let's look at a set of individual examples, beginning with the sort() function. To save some space, the following example includes another parameter to ensure that only a few fields are returned:

```
>>> for doc in collection.find ({'Status' : 'In use'},
...     fields={'ItemNumber' : True, 'Location.Owner' : True}).sort('ItemNumber'):
...         doc
...
{
        u'ItemNumber': u'1234EXD',
        u'_id': ObjectId('4c57207b4abffe0e0c000000'),
        u'Location': {
                u'Owner': u'Anderson, Thomas'
        }
}
{
        u'ItemNumber': u'2345FDX',
        u'_id': ObjectId('4c57234c4abffe0e0c000001'),
        u'Location': {
                u'Owner': u'Smith, Simon'
        }
}
```

```
{
        u'ItemNumber': u'3456TFS',
        u'_id': ObjectId('4c57234c4abffe0e0c000002'),
        u'Location': {
                u'Owner': u'Walker, Jan'
        }
}
```

Next, let's look at the limit() function in action. In this case, you tell the function to return only the ItemNumber from the first two items it finds in the collection (note that no search criteria are specified in this example):

```
>>> for doc in collection.find({}, {"ItemNumber" : "true"}).limit(2):
...        doc
...
{u'ItemNumber': u'1234EXD', u'_id': ObjectId('4c57207b4abffe0e0c000000')}
{u'ItemNumber': u'2345FDX', u'_id': ObjectId('4c57234c4abffe0e0c000001')}
```

You can use the skip() function to skip a few items before returning a set of documents, as in the following example:

```
>>> for doc in collection.find({}, {"ItemNumber" : "true"}).skip(2):
...        doc
...
{u'ItemNumber': u'3456TFS', u'_id': ObjectId('4c57234c4abffe0e0c000002')}
```

You can also combine the three functions to select only a certain number of items found, while simultaneously specifying a specific number of items to skip and sorting them:

```
>>> for doc in collection.find( {'Status' : 'In use'},
...        fields={'ItemNumber' : True, 'Location.Owner' : True}).limit(2).skip(1).sort 'ItemNumber'):
...            doc
...
{
        u'ItemNumber': u'2345FDX',
        u'_id': ObjectId('4c57234c4abffe0e0c000001'),
        u'Location': {
                u'Owner': u'Smith, Simon'
        }
}
{
        u'ItemNumber': u'3456TFS',
        u'_id': ObjectId('4c57234c4abffe0e0c000002'),
        u'Location': {
                u'Owner': u'Walker, Jan'
        }
}
```

What you just did—limiting the results returned and skipping a certain number of items—is generally known as *paging*. You can accomplish this in a slightly more simplistic way with the $slice operator, which will be covered later in this chapter.

Aggregating Queries

As previously noted, MongoDB comes with a powerful set of aggregation tools (see Chapter 4 for more information on these tools). You can use all these tools with the Python driver. These tools make it possible to using the count() function to perform a count on your data; using the distinct() function to get a list of distinct values with no duplicates; and, last but not least, use the map_reduce() function to group your data and batch-manipulate the results or simply to perform counts.

This set of commands, used separately or together, enables you to query effectively for the information you need to know—and nothing else.

Apart from these basic aggregation commands, the PyMongo driver also includes the aggregation framework. This powerful feature will allow you to calculate aggregated values without needing to use the—often overly complex—map/reduce (or MapReduce) framework.

Counting Items with count()

You can use the count() function if all you want is to count the total number of items matching your criteria. The function doesn't return all the information the way the find() function does; instead, it returns an integer value with the total of items found.

Let's look at some simple examples. We can begin by returning the total number of documents in the entire collection, without specifying any criteria:

```
>>> collection.count()
3
```

You can also specify these count queries more precisely, as in this example:

```
>>> collection.find({"Status" : "In use", "Location.Owner" : "Walker, Jan"}).count()
1
```

The count() function can be great when all you need is a quick count of the total number of documents that match your criteria.

Counting Unique Items with distinct()

The count() function is a great way to get the total number of items returned. However, sometimes you might accidentally add duplicates to your collection because you simply forget to remove or change an old document, and you want to get an accurate count that shows no duplicates. This is where the distinct() function can help you out. This function ensures that only unique items will be returned. Let's set up an example by adding another item to the collection, but with an ItemNumber used previously:

```
>>> dup = ( {
    "ItemNumber" : "2345FDX",
    "Status" : "Not used",
    "Type" : "Laptop",
    "Location" : {
        "Department" : "Storage",
        "Building" : "1A"
    },
    "Tags" : ["Not used","Laptop","Storage"]
} )
>>> collection.insert(dup)
ObjectId('4c592eb84abffe0e0c000004')
```

When you use the count() function at this juncture, the number of *unique* items won't be correct:

```
>>> collection.find({}).count()
4
```

Instead, you can use the distinct() function to ensure that any duplicates are ignored:

```
>>> collection.distinct("ItemNumber")
[u'1234EXD', u'2345FDX', u'3456TFS']
```

Grouping Data with the Aggregation Framework

The aggregation framework is a great tool for calculating aggregated values without needing to use MapReduce. Although MapReduce is very powerful—and available to the PyMongo driver—the aggregation framework can get most jobs done just as well, with better performance. To demonstrate this, one of the aggregate() function's most powerful pipeline operators, $group, will be used to group the previously added documents by their tags, and perform a count on it using the $sum aggregation expression. Let's look at an example:

```
>>> collection.aggregate([
...     {'$unwind' : '$Tags'},
...     {'$group' : {'_id' : '$Tags', 'Totals' : {'$sum' : 1}}}
... ])
```

First, the aggregate() function creates a stream of tag documents from the document's '$Tags' array (note the mandatory $ in its name) using the $unwind pipeline operator. Next, the $group pipeline operator is called, creating a separate row for every unique tag using its value as its '_id' and the total count—using the $group's $sum expression to calculate the 'Totals' value. The resulting output looks like this:

```
{
  u'ok': 1.0,
  u'result': [
    {u'_id': u'Laptop', u'Totals': 4},
    {u'_id': u'In Use', u'Totals': 3},
    {u'_id': u'Development', u'Totals': 3},
    {u'_id': u'Storage', u'Totals': 1},
    {u'_id': u'Not used', u'Totals': 1}
  ]
}
```

The output returns exactly the information that was requested. However, what if we wish to sort the output by its 'Totals'? This can be achieved by simply adding another pipeline operator, $sort. Before doing so, however, we need to import the SON module:

```
>>> from bson.son import SON
```

Now we can sort the results in descending order (-1) based on the 'Totals' value as shown here:

```
>>> collection.aggregate([
...     {'$unwind' : '$Tags'},
...     {'$group' : {'_id' : '$Tags', 'Totals' : {'$sum' : 1}}},
...     {'$sort' : SON([('Totals', -1)])}
... ])
```

This returns the following results, neatly presented in descending order:

```
{
  u'ok': 1.0,
  u'result': [
    {u'_id': u'Laptop', u'Totals': 4},
    {u'_id': u'In Use', u'Totals': 3},
    {u'_id': u'Development', u'Totals': 3},
    {u'_id': u'Storage', u'Totals': 1},
    {u'_id': u'Not used', u'Totals': 1}
  ]
}
```

In addition to the $sum pipeline expression, the $group pipeline operator also supports various others, some of which are listed below:

- $push: Creates and returns an array of all the values found in its group.

- $addToSet: Creates and returns an array of all the unique values found in its group.

- $first: Returns only the first value found in its group.

- $last: Returns only the last value found in its group.

- $max: Returns the highest value found in its group.

- $min: Returns the lowest value found in its group.

- $avg: Returns the average value found in its group.

In this example you've looked at the $group, $unwind, and $sort pipeline operators, but many more powerful pipeline operators exist, such, as the $geoNear operator. The aggregation framework and its operators are discussed in more detail in Chapters 4, 6, and 8.

Specifying an Index with hint()

You can use the hint() function to specify which index should be used when querying for data. Using this function can help you improve the query's performance. In Python, the hint() function also executes on the cursor. However, you should keep in mind that the hint name you specify in Python needs to be the same as the one you passed to the create_index() function.

In the next example, you will create an index first, and then search for the data that specifies the index. Before you can sort in ascending order, however, you will need to use the import() function to import the ASCENDING method. Finally, you need to execute the create_index() function:

```
>>> from pymongo import ASCENDING
>>> collection.create_index([("ItemNumber", ASCENDING)])
u'ItemNumber_1'

>>> for doc in collection.find({"Location.Owner" : "Walker, Jan"}) .hint([("ItemNumber",
ASCENDING)]):
...             doc
...
```

```
{
    u'Status': u'In use',
    u'Tags': [u'Laptop', u'Development', u'In Use'],
    u'ItemNumber': u'3456TFS',
    u'Location': {
        u'Department': u'Development',
        u'Building': u'2B',
        u'Floor': 12,
        u'Owner': u'Walker, Jan',
        u'Desk': 120103
    },
    u'_id': ObjectId('4c57234c4abffe0e0c000002'),
    u'Type': u'Laptop'
}
```

Using indexes can help you significantly increase performance speed when the size of your collections keeps growing (see Chapter 10 for more details on performance tuning).

Refining Queries with Conditional Operators

You can use conditional operators to refine your query. MongoDB includes more than half a dozen conditional operators accessible through PyMongo; these are identical to the conditional operators you've seen in the previous chapters. The following sections walk you through the conditional operators available in Python, as well as how you can use them to refine your MongoDB queries in Python.

Using the $lt, $gt, $lte, and $gte Operators

Let's begin by looking at the $lt, $gt, $lte, and $gte conditional operators. You can use the $lt operator to search for any numerical information that is less than n. The operator takes only one parameter: the number n, which specifies the limit. The following example finds any entries that have a desk number lower than 120102. Note that the comparison value itself is *not* included:

```
>>> for doc in collection.find({"Location.Desk" : {"$lt" : 120102} }):
...            doc
...
{
    u'Status': u'In use',
    u'Tags': [u'Laptop', u'Development', u'In Use'],
    u'ItemNumber': u'1234EXD',
    u'Location': {
        u'Department': u'Development',
        u'Building': u'2B',
        u'Floor': 12,
        u'Owner': u'Anderson, Thomas',
        u'Desk': 120101
    },
    u'_id': ObjectId('4c57207b4abffe0e0c000000'),
    u'Type': u'Laptop'
}
```

In a similar vein, you can use the $gt operator to find any items with a value *higher than* a provided comparison value. Again, note that the comparison value itself is not included:

```
>>> for doc in collection.find({"Location.Desk" : {"$gt" : 120102} }):
...             doc
...
{
    u'Status': u'In use',
    u'Tags': [u'Laptop', u'Development', u'In Use'],
    u'ItemNumber': u'3456TFS',
    u'Location': {
        u'Department': u'Development',
        u'Building': u'2B',
        u'Floor': 12,
        u'Owner': u'Walker, Jan',
        u'Desk': 120103
    },
    u'_id': ObjectId('4c57234c4abffe0e0c000002'),
    u'Type': u'Laptop'
}
```

If you want to include the comparison value in your results, then you can use either the $lte or $gte operators to find any values less than or equal to *n* or greater than or equal to *n*, respectively. The following examples illustrate how to use these operators:

```
>>> for doc in collection.find({"Location.Desk" : {"$lte" : 120102} }):
...             doc
...
{
    u'Status': u'In use',
    u'Tags': [u'Laptop', u'Development', u'In Use'],
    u'ItemNumber': u'1234EXD',
    u'Location': {
        u'Department': u'Development',
        u'Building': u'2B',
        u'Floor': 12,
        u'Owner': u'Anderson, Thomas',
        u'Desk': 120101
    },
    u'_id': ObjectId('4c57207b4abffe0e0c000000'),
    u'Type': u'Laptop'
}
{
    u'Status': u'In use',
    u'Tags': [u'Laptop', u'Development', u'In Use'],
    u'ItemNumber': u'2345FDX',
    u'Location': {
        u'Department': u'Development',
        u'Building': u'2B',
        u'Floor': 12,
```

```
        u'Owner': u'Smith, Simon',
        u'Desk': 120102
    },
    u'_id': ObjectId('4c57234c4abffe0e0c000001'),
    u'Type': u'Laptop'
}
```

```
>>> for doc in collection.find({"Location.Desk" : {"$gte" : 120102} }):
...             doc
...
{
    u'Status': u'In use',
    u'Tags': [u'Laptop', u'Development', u'In Use'],
    u'ItemNumber': u'2345FDX',
    u'Location': {
        u'Department': u'Development',
        u'Building': u'2B',
        u'Floor': 12,
        u'Owner': u'Smith, Simon',
        u'Desk': 120102
    },
    u'_id': ObjectId('4c57234c4abffe0e0c000001'),
    u'Type': u'Laptop'
}
{
    u'Status': u'In use',
    u'Tags': [u'Laptop', u'Development', u'In Use'],
    u'ItemNumber': u'3456TFS',
    u'Location': {
        u'Department': u'Development',
        u'Building': u'2B',
        u'Floor': 12,
        u'Owner': u'Walker, Jan',
        u'Desk': 120103
    },
    u'_id': ObjectId('4c57234c4abffe0e0c000002'),
    u'Type': u'Laptop'
}
```

Searching for Non-Matching Values with $ne

You can use the $ne (not equals) operator to search for any documents in a collection that do *not* match specified criteria. This operator requires one parameter, the key and value information that a document should *not* have for the result to return a match:

```
>>> collection.find({"Status" : {"$ne" : "In use"}}).count()
1
```

Specifying an Array of Matches with $in

The $in operator lets you specify an array of possible matches.

For instance, assume you're looking for only two kinds of development computers: not used or with Development. Also assume that you want to limit the results to two items, returning only the ItemNumber:

```
>>> for doc in collection.find({"Tags" : {"$in" : ["Not used","Development"]}} ,
fields={"ItemNumber":"true"}).limit(2):
...            doc
...
{u'ItemNumber': u'1234EXD', u'_id': ObjectId('4c57207b4abffe0e0c000000')}
{u'ItemNumber': u'2345FDX', u'_id': ObjectId('4c57234c4abffe0e0c000001')}
```

Specifying Against an Array of Matches with $nin

You use the $nin operator exactly as you use the $in operator; the difference is that this operator *excludes* any documents that match any of the values specified in the given array. For example, the following query finds any items that are currently *not* used in the Development department:

```
>>> for doc in collection.find({"Tags" : {"$nin" : ["Development"]}}, fields={"ItemNumber": True}):
...            doc
...
{u'ItemNumber': u'2345FDX', u'_id': ObjectId('4c592eb84abffe0e0c000004')}
```

Finding Documents that Match an Array's Values

Whereas the $in operator can be used to find any document that matches *any* of the values specified in an array, the $all operator lets you find any document that matches *all* of the values specified in an array. The syntax to accomplish this looks exactly the same:

```
>>> for doc in collection.find({"Tags" : {"$all" : ["Storage","Not used"]}},
fields={"ItemNumber":"true"}):
...            doc
...
{u'ItemNumber': u'2345FDX', u'_id': ObjectId('4c592eb84abffe0e0c000004')}
```

Specifying Multiple Expressions to Match with $or

You can use the $or operator to specify multiple values that a document can have, of which at least one must be true, to qualify as a match. This is roughly similar to the $in operator; the difference is that the $or operator lets you specify the key as well as the value. You can also combine the $or operator with another key/value pair. Let's look at a few examples.

This example returns all documents that have either the location set to Storage or the owner set, to Anderson, Thomas:

```
>>> for doc in collection.find({"$or" : [ { "Location.Department" : "Storage" },
...      { "Location.Owner" : "Anderson, Thomas"} ] } ):
...            doc
...
```

You can also combine the preceding code with another key/value pair, as in this example:

```
>>> for doc in collection.find({ "Location.Building" : "2B", "$or" : [ { "Location.Department" :
"Storage" },
...    { "Location.Owner" : "Anderson, Thomas"} ] } ):
...            doc
...
```

The $or operator basically allows you to conduct two searches simultaneously and combine the resulting output, even if the individual searches have nothing in common with each other. Also, the $or clauses are executed in parallel, and each clause may use a different index.

Retrieving Items from an Array with $slice

You can use the $slice operator to retrieve a certain number of items from a given array in your document. This operator provides functionality similar to the skip() and limit() functions; the difference is that those two functions work on full documents, whereas the $slice operator works on an array in a *single* document.

Before looking at an example, let's add a new document that will enable us to take a better look at this operator. Assume that your company is maniacally obsessed with tracking its chair inventory, tracking chairs wherever they might go. Naturally, every chair has its own history of desks to which it once belonged. The $slice example operator is great for tracking that kind of inventory.

Begin by adding the following document:

```
>>> chair = ({
...      "Status" : "Not used",
...      "Tags" : ["Chair","Not used","Storage"],
...      "ItemNumber" : "6789SID",
...      "Location" : {
...      "Department" : "Storage",
...      "Building" : "2B"
...      },
...      "PreviousLocation" :
...      [ "120100","120101","120102","120103","120104","120105",
...      "120106","120107","120108","120109","120110" ]
...      })
```

```
>>> collection.insert(chair)
ObjectId('4c5973554abffe0e0c000005')
```

Now assume you want to see all the information available for the chair returned in the preceding example, with one caveat: you don't want to see all the previous location information, but only the first three desks it belonged to:

```
>>> collection.find_one({'ItemNumber' : '6789SID'}, {'PreviousLocation' : {'$slice' : 3} })
{
    u'Status': u'Not used',
    u'PreviousLocation': [u'120100', u'120101', u'120102'],
    u'Tags': [u'Chair', u'Not used', u'Storage'],
    u'ItemNumber': u'6789SID',
    u'Location': {
```

```
        u'Department': u'Storage',
        u'Building': u'2B'
    },
    u'_id': ObjectId('4c5973554abffe0e0c000005')
}
```

Similarly, you can see its three most recent locations by making the integer value negative:

```
>>> collection.find_one({'ItemNumber' : '6789SID'}, {'PreviousLocation' : {'$slice' : -3} })
{
    u'Status': u'Not used',
    u'PreviousLocation': [u'120108', u'120109', u'120110'],
    u'Tags': [u'Chair', u'Not used', u'Storage'],
    u'ItemNumber': u'6789SID',
    u'Location': {
        u'Department': u'Storage',
        u'Building': u'2B'
    },
    u'_id': ObjectId('4c5973554abffe0e0c000005')
}
```

Or, you could skip the first five locations for the chair and limit the number of results returned to three (pay special attention to the brackets here):

```
>>> collection.find_one({'ItemNumber' : '6789SID'}, {'PreviousLocation' : {'$slice' : [5, 3] } })
{
    u'Status': u'Not used',
    u'PreviousLocation': [u'120105', u'120106', u'120107'],
    u'Tags': [u'Chair', u'Not used', u'Storage'],
    u'ItemNumber': u'6789SID',
    u'Location': {
        u'Department': u'Storage',
        u'Building': u'2B'
    },
    u'_id': ObjectId('4c5973554abffe0e0c000005')
}
```

You probably get the idea. This example might seem a tad unusual, but inventory control systems often veer into the unorthodox; and the $slice operator is intrinsically good at helping you account for unusual or complex circumstances. For example, the $slice operator might prove an especially effective tool for implementing the paging system for a website's Comments section.

Conducting Searches with Regular Expressions

One useful tool for conducting searches is the *regular expression*. The default regular expression module for Python is called re. Performing a search with the re module requires that you first load the module, as in this example:

```
>>> import re
```

After you load the module, you can specify the regular expression query in the value field of your search criteria. The following example shows how to search for any document where `ItemNumber` has a value that contains a 4 (for the sake of keeping things simple, this example returns only the values in `ItemNumber`):

```
>>> for doc in collection.find({'ItemNumber' : re.compile('4')}, {'ItemNumber' : True}):
...         doc
...
{u'ItemNumber': u'1234EXD', u'_id': ObjectId('4c57207b4abffe0e0c000000')}
{u'ItemNumber': u'2345FDX', u'_id': ObjectId('4c57234c4abffe0e0c000001')}
{u'ItemNumber': u'2345FDX', u'_id': ObjectId('4c592eb84abffe0e0c000004')}
{u'ItemNumber': u'3456TFS', u'_id': ObjectId('4c57234c4abffe0e0c000002')}
```

You can further define a regular expression. At this stage, your query is case-sensitive, and it will match any document that has a 4 in the value of `ItemNumber`, regardless of its position. However, assume you want to find a document where the value of `ItemNumber` ends with `FS`, is preceded by an unknown value, and can contain no additional data after the `FS`:

```
>>> for doc in collection.find({'ItemNumber' : re.compile('.FS$')},fields={'ItemNumber' : True}):
...         doc
...
{u'ItemNumber': u'3456TFS', u'_id': ObjectId('4c57234c4abffe0e0c000002')}
```

You can also use `find()` to search for information in a case-insensitive way, but first you must add another function, as in this example:

```
>>> for doc in collection.find({'Location.Owner' : re.compile('^anderson. ', re.IGNORECASE)},
...      fields={'ItemNumber' : True, 'Location.Owner' : True}):
...         doc
...
{
    u'ItemNumber': u'1234EXD',
    u'_id': ObjectId('4c57207b4abffe0e0c000000'),
    u'Location': {
        u'Owner': u'Anderson, Thomas'
    }
}
```

Regular expressions can be an extremely powerful tool, as long as you utilize them properly. For more details on how the `re` module works and the functions it includes, please refer to the module's official documentation at `http://docs.python.org/library/re.html`.

Modifying the Data

So far you've learned how to use conditional operators and regular expressions in Python to query for information in your database. In the next section, we'll examine how to use Python to modify the existing data in your collections. We can use Python to accomplish this task in several different ways. The upcoming sections will build on the previously used query operators to find the documents that should match your modifications. In a couple of cases, you may need to skip back to earlier parts of this chapter to brush up on particular aspects of using query operators—but that's a normal part of the learning process, and it will reinforce the lessons taught so far.

Updating Your Data

The way you use Python's `update()` function doesn't vary much from how you use the identically named function in the MongoDB shell or the PHP driver. In this case, you provide two mandatory parameters to update your data: `arg` and `doc`. The `arg` parameter specifies the key/value information used to match a document, and the `doc` parameter contains the updated information. You can also provide several optional parameter to specify your options. The following list covers Python's list of options to update information, including what they do:

- `upsert` *(optional)*: If set to `True`, performs an upsert.

- `manipulate` *(optional)*: If set to `True`, indicates the document will be manipulated *before* performing the update using all instances of the *SONManipulator*. For more information, refer to the son_manipulator documentation (`http://api.mongodb.org/python/current/api/pymongo/son_manipulator.html`).

- `check_keys` *(optional)*: If set to `True`, `update()` will check whether any of the keys in the document start with the restricted characters '$' or '.' when replacing *arg*.

- `multi` *(optional)*: If set to `True`, updates any matching document, rather than just the first document it finds (the default action). It is recommended that you always set this to `True` or `False`, rather than relying on the default behavior (which could always change in the future).

- `w` (optional): If set to 0, the update operation will not be acknowledged. When working with replica sets, `w` can also be set to *n*, ensuring that the primary server acknowledges the update operation when successfully replicated to *n* nodes. Can also be set to `majority`—a reserved string—to ensure that the majority of replica nodes will acknowledge the update, or to a specific tag, ensuring that the nodes tagged will acknowledge the update. This option defaults to 1, acknowledging the update operation.

- `wtimeout` (optional): Used to specify how long the server is to wait for receiving acknowledgement (in milliseconds). Defaults to 10000.

- `j` (optional): If set to `True`, this Boolean option will force the data to be written to the journal before indicating that the update was a success. Defaults to `False`.

- `fsync` (optional): If set to `True`, this Boolean option causes the data to be synced to disk before returning a success. If this option is set to `True`, then it's implied that `w` is set to 0, even if it's set otherwise.

If you do not specify any of the modifier operators when updating a document, then by default all information in the document will be replaced with whatever data you inserted in the doc parameter. It is best to avoid relying on the default behavior; instead, you should use the aforementioned operators to specify your desired updates explicitly (you'll learn how to do this momentarily).

You can see why it's best to use conditional operators with the `update()` command by looking at a case that doesn't use any conditional operators:

```
// Define the updated data
>>> update = ( {
    "Type" : "Chair",
    "Status" : "In use",
    "Tags" : ["Chair","In use","Marketing"],
    "ItemNumber" : "6789SID",
    "Location" : {
        "Department" : "Marketing",
        "Building" : "2B",
```

```
        "DeskNumber" : 131131,
        "Owner" : "Martin, Lisa"
    }
} )

// Now, perform the update
>>> collection.update({"ItemNumber" : "6789SID"}, update)

// Inspect the result of the update
>>> collection.find_one({"Type" : "Chair"})
{
    u'Status': u'In use',
    u'Tags': [u'Chair', u'In use', u'Marketing'],
    u'ItemNumber': u'6789SID',
    u'Location': {
        u'Department': u'Marketing',
        u'Building': u'2B',
        u'DeskNumber': 131131,
        u'Owner': u'Martin, Lisa'
    },
    u'_id': ObjectId('4c5973554abffe0e0c000005'),
    u'Type': u'Chair'
}
```

One big minus about this example is that it's somewhat lengthy, and it updates only a few fields. Next, we'll look at what the modifier operators can be used to accomplish.

Modifier Operators

Chapter 4 detailed how the MongoDB shell includes a large set of modifier operators that you can use to manipulate your data more easily, but without needing to rewrite an entire document to change a single field's value (as you had to do in the preceding example).

The modifier operators let you do everything from changing one existing value in a document, to inserting an entire array, to removing all entries from multiple items specified in an array. As a group, these operators make it easy to modify data. Now let's take a look at what the operators do and how you use them.

Increasing an Integer Value with $inc

You use the $inc operator to increase an integer value in a document by the given number, n. The following example shows how to increase the integer value of Location.Desknumber by 20:

```
>>> collection.update({"ItemNumber" : "6789SID"}, {"$inc" : {"Location.DeskNumber" : 20}})
```

Next, check to see whether the update worked as expected:

```
>>> collection.find_one({"Type" : "Chair"}, fields={"Location" : "True"})
{
    u'_id': ObjectId('4c5973554abffe0e0c000005'),
    u'Location': {
        u'Department': u'Marketing',
        u'Building': u'2B',
```

```
            u'Owner': u'Martin, Lisa',
            u'DeskNumber': 131151
        }
    }
}
```

Note that the $inc operator works only on integer values (that is, numeric values), but not on any string values or even numeric values added as a string (for example, "123" vs. 123).

Changing an Existing Value with $set

You use the $set operator to change an existing value in any matching document. This is an operator you'll use frequently. The next example changes the value from "Building" in any item currently matching the key/value "Location.Department / Development".

First use $set to perform the update, ensuring that all documents are updated:

```
>>> collection.update({"Location.Department" : "Development"},
...     {"$set" : {"Location.Building" : "3B"} },
...     multi = True )
```

Next, use the find_one() command to confirm that all went well:

```
>>> collection.find_one({"Location.Department" : "Development"}, fields={"Location.Building" :
True})
{
    u'_id': ObjectId('4c57207b4abffe0e0c000000'),
    u'Location': {u'Building': u'3B'}
}
```

Removing a Key/Value Field with $unset

Likewise, you use the $unset operator to remove a key/value field from a document, as shown in the following example:

```
>>> collection.update({"Status" : "Not used", "ItemNumber" : "2345FDX"},
...     {"$unset" : {"Location.Building" : 1 } } )
```

Next, use the find_one() command to confirm all went well:

```
>>> collection.find_one({"Status" : "Not used", "ItemNumber" : "2345FDX"}, fields={"Location" :
True})
{
    u'_id': ObjectId('4c592eb84abffe0e0c000004'),
    u'Location': {u'Department': u'Storage'}
}
```

Adding a Value to an Array with $push

The $push operator lets you add a value to an array, assuming the array exists. If the array does not exist, then it will be created with the value specified.

■ **Warning**   If you use $push to update an existing field that isn't an array, an error message will appear.

Now you're ready to add a value to an already existing array and confirm whether all went well. First, perform the update:

```
>>> collection.update({"Location.Owner" : "Anderson, Thomas"},
...    {"$push" : {"Tags" : "Anderson"} }, multi = True )
```

Now, execute find_one() to confirm whether the update(s) went well:

```
>>> collection.find_one({"Location.Owner" : "Anderson, Thomas"}, fields={"Tags" : "True"})
{
    u'_id': ObjectId('4c57207b4abffe0e0c000000'),
    u'Tags': [u'Laptop', u'Development', u'In Use', u'Anderson']
}
```

Adding Multiple Values to an Array with $push and $each

The $push operator can also be used to add multiple values at once to an existing array. This can be achieved by adding the $each modifier. Here, the same rule applies: the array must already exist, or you will receive an error. The following example uses the $each modifier in conjunction with the $ regular expression to perform a search; this enables you to apply a change to all matching queries:

```
>>> collection.update({ "Location.Owner" : re.compile("^Walker,") },
...    { '$push' : { 'Tags' : { '$each' : ['Walker','Warranty'] } } } )
```

Next, execute find_one() to see whether all went well:

```
>>> collection.find_one({"Location.Owner" : re.compile("^Walker,")}, fields={"Tags" : True})
{
    u'_id': ObjectId('4c57234c4abffe0e0c000002'),
    u'Tags': [u'Laptop', u'Development', u'In Use', u'Walker', u'Warranty']
}
```

Adding a Value to an Existing Array with $addToSet

The $addToSet operator also lets you add a value to an existing array. The difference is that this method checks whether the array already exists before attempting the update (the $push operator does not check for this condition).

This operator takes only one additional value; however, it's also good to know that you can combine $addToSet with the $each operator. Let's look at two examples. First, let's perform the update using the $addToSet operator on any object matching "Type : Chair" and then check whether all went well using the find_one() function:

```
>>> collection.update({"Type" : "Chair"}, {"$addToSet" : {"Tags" : "Warranty"} }, multi = True)

>>> collection.find_one({"Type" : "Chair"}, {"Tags" : "True"})
{
    u'_id': ObjectId('4c5973554abffe0e0c000005'),
    u'Tags': [u'Chair', u'In use', u'Marketing', u'Warranty']
}
```

You can also use the $each statement to add multiple tags. Note that you perform this search using a regular expression. Also, one of the tags in the list has been previously added; fortunately, it won't be added again, because this is what $addToSet specifically prevents:

```
// Use the $each operator to add multiple tags, including one that was already added
>>> collection.update({"Type" : "Chair", "Location.Owner" : re.compile("^Martin,")},
...     {"$addToSet" : { "Tags" : {"$each" : ["Martin","Warranty","Chair","In use"] } } } )
```

Now it's time to check whether all went well; specifically, you want to verify that the duplicate Warranty tag has not been added again:

```
>>> collection.find_one({"Type" : "Chair", "Location.Owner" : re.compile("^Martin,")},
fields={"Tags" : True})
{
    u'_id': ObjectId('4c5973554abffe0e0c000005'),
    u'Tags': [u'Chair', u'In use', u'Marketing', u'Warranty', u'Martin']
}
```

Removing an Element from an Array with $pop

So far, you've seen how to use the update() function to add values to an existing document. Now let's turn this around and look at how to remove data instead. We'll begin with the $pop operator.

This operator allows you to delete either the first or the last value from an array, but nothing in between. The following example removes the first value in the Tags array from the first document it finds that matches the "Type" : "Chair" criterion; the example then uses the find_one() command to confirm that all went well with the update:

```
>>> collection.update({"Type" : "Chair"}, {"$pop" : {"Tags" : -1}})

>>> collection.find_one({"Type" : "Chair"}, fields={"Tags" : True})
{
    u'_id': ObjectId('4c5973554abffe0e0c000005'),
    u'Tags': [u'In use', u'Marketing', u'Warranty', u'Martin']
}
```

Giving the Tags array a positive value instead removes the last occurrence in an array, as in the following example:

```
>>> collection.update({"Type" : "Chair"}, {"$pop" : {"Tags" :  1}})
```

Next, execute the find_one() function again to confirm that all went well:

```
>>> collection.find_one({"Type" : "Chair"}, fields={"Tags" : True})
{
    u'_id': ObjectId('4c5973554abffe0e0c000005'),
    u'Tags': [u'In use', u'Marketing', u'Warranty']
}
```

Removing a Specific Value with $pull

The $pull operator lets you remove each occurrence of a specific value from an array, regardless of how many times the value occurs; as long as the value is the same, it will be removed.

Let's look at an example. Begin by using the $push operator to add identical tags with the value Double to the Tags array:

```
>>> collection.update({"Type" : "Chair"}, {"$push" : {"Tags" : "Double"} }, multi = False )
>>> collection.update({"Type" : "Chair"}, {"$push" : {"Tags" : "Double"} }, multi = False )
```

Next, ensure that the tag was added twice, by executing the find_one() command. Once you confirm that the tag exists twice, use the $pull operator to remove both instances of the tag:

```
>>> collection.find_one({"Type" : "Chair"}, fields={"Tags" : True})
{
    u'_id': ObjectId('4c5973554abffe0e0c000005'),
    u'Tags': [u'In use', u'Marketing', u'Warranty', u'Double', u'Double']
}
```

```
>>> collection.update({"Type" : "Chair"}, {"$pull" : {"Tags" : "Double"} }, multi = False)
```

To confirm that all went well, execute the find_one() command again, this time making sure that the result no longer lists the Double tag:

```
>>> collection.find_one({"Type" : "Chair"}, fields={"Tags" : True})
{
    u'_id': ObjectId('4c5973554abffe0e0c000005'),
    u'Tags': [u'In use', u'Marketing', u'Warranty']
}
```

You can use the $pullAll operator to perform the same action; the difference from $pull is that $pullAll lets you remove multiple tags. Again, let's look at an example. First, you need to add multiple items into the Tags array again and confirm that they have been added:

```
>>> collection.update({"Type" : "Chair"}, {"$addToSet" : { "Tags" : {"$each" : ["Bacon","Spam"] } } } )
>>> collection.find_one({"Type" : "Chair"}, fields={"Tags" : True})
{
    u'_id': ObjectId('4c5973554abffe0e0c000005'),
    u'Tags': [u'In use', u'Marketing', u'Warranty', u'Bacon', u'Spam']
}
```

Now you can use the $pullAll operator to remove the multiple tags. The following example shows how to use this operator; the example also executes a find_one() command immediately afterward to confirm that the Bacon and Spam tags have been removed:

```
>>> collection.update({"Type" : "Chair"}, {"$pullAll" : {"Tags" : ["Bacon","Spam"] } },
multi = False)
>>> collection.find_one({"Type" : "Chair"}, fields={"Tags" : "True"})
{
    u'_id': ObjectId('4c5973554abffe0e0c000005'),
    u'Tags': [u'In use', u'Marketing', u'Warranty']
}
```

Saving Documents Quickly with save()

You can use the save() function to quickly add a document through the upsert method. For this to work, you must also define the value of the _id field. If the document you want to save already exists, it will be updated; if it does not exist already, it will be created.

Let's look at an example that saves a document called Desktop. Begin by specifying the document by typing it into the shell with an identifier, after which you can save it with the save() function. Executing the save() function returns the ObjectId from the document once the save is successful:

```
>>> Desktop = ( {
    "Status" : "In use",
    "Tags" : ["Desktop","In use","Marketing","Warranty"],
    "ItemNumber" : "4532FOO",
    "Location" : {
        "Department" : "Marketing",
        "Building" : "2B",
        "Desknumber" : 131131,
        "Owner" : "Martin, Lisa",
    }
} )
>>> collection.save(Desktop)
ObjectId('4c5ddbe24abffe0f34000001')
```

Now assume you realize that you forgot to specify a key/value pair in the document. You can easily add this information to the document by defining the document's name, followed by its key between brackets, and then including the desired contents. Once you do this, you can perform the upsert by simply saving the entire document again; doing so returns the ObjectId again from the document:

```
>>> Desktop[ "Type" ] = "Desktop"
>>> collection.save(Desktop)
ObjectId('4c5ddbe24abffe0f34000001')
```

As you can see, the value of the ObjectId returned is unchanged.

Modifying a Document Atomically

You can use the `find_and_modify()` function to modify a document atomically and return the results. The `find_and_modify()` function can be used to update only a single document—and nothing more. You should also keep in mind that the document returned will not by default include the modifications made; getting this information requires that you specify an additional argument, `new: True`.

The `find_and_modify()` function can be used with multiple parameters, and you must include either the `update` parameter or the `remove` parameter. The following list covers all the available parameters, explaining what they are and what they do:

- `query`: Specifies a filter for the query. If this isn't specified, then all documents in the collection will be seen as possible candidates, after which the first document it encounters will be updated or removed.

- `update`: Specifies the information to update the document with. Note that any of the modifying operators specified previously can be used for this.

- `upsert`: If set to `True`, performs an upsert.

- `sort`: Sorts the matching documents in a specified order.

- `full_response`: If set to `True`, returns the entire response object.

- `remove`: If set to `True`, removes the first matching document.

- `new`: If set to `True`, returns the updated document rather than the *selected* document. This is not set by default, however, which might be a bit confusing sometimes.

- `fields`: Specifies the fields you would like to see returned, rather than the entire document. This works identically to the `find()` function. Note that the `_id` field will always be returned unless explicitly disabled.

Putting the Parameters to Work

You know what the parameters do; now it's time to use them in a real-world example in conjunction with the `find_and_modify()` function. Begin by using `find_and_modify()`to search for any document that has a key/value pair of `"Type" : "Desktop"`—and then update each document that matches the query by setting an additional key/value pair of `"Status" : "In repair"`. Finally, you want to ensure that MongoDB returns the updated document(s), rather than the old document(s) matching the query:

```
>>> collection.find_and_modify(query={"Type" : "Desktop"},
...     update={'$set' : {'Status' : 'In repair'} }, new=True )
{
    u'ok': 1.0,
    u'value': {
        u'Status': u'In repair',
        u'Tags': [u'Desktop', u'In use', u'Marketing', u'Warranty'],
        u'ItemNumber': u'4532FOO',
        u'Location': {
            u'Department': u'Marketing',
            u'Building': u'2B',
            u'Owner': u'Martin, Lisa',
            u'Desknumber': 131131
        },
```

```
        u'_id': ObjectId('4c5dda114abffe0f34000000'),
        u'Type': u'Desktop'
    }
}
```

Let's look at another example. This time, you will use find_and_modify() to remove a document; in this case, the output will show which document was removed:

```
>>> collection.find_and_modify(query={'Type' : 'Desktop'},
...     sort={'ItemNumber' : -1}, remove=True){
    u'ok': 1.0,
    u'value': {
        u'Status': u'In use',
        u'Tags': [u'Desktop', u'In use', u'Marketing', u'Warranty'],
        u'ItemNumber': u'4532F00',
        u'Location': {
            u'Department': u'Marketing',
            u'Building': u'2B',
            u'Owner': u'Martin, Lisa',
            u'Desknumber': 131131
        },
        u'_id': ObjectId('4c5ddbe24abffe0f34000001'),
        u'Type': u'Desktop'
    }
}
```

Deleting Data

In most cases, you will use the Python driver to add or modify your data. However, it's also important to understand how to delete data. The Python driver provides several methods for deleting data. First, you can use the remove() function to delete a single document from a collection. Second, you can use the drop() or drop_collection() function to delete an entire collection. Finally, you can use the drop_database() function to drop an entire database. (It seems unlikely you'll be using this function frequently!)

Nevertheless, we will take a closer look at each of these functions, looking at examples for all of them.

Let's begin by looking at the remove() function. This function allows you to specify an argument as a parameter that will be used to find and delete any matching documents in your current collection. In this example, you use the remove() function to remove each document that has a key/value pair of "Status" : "In use"; afterward, you use the find_one() function to confirm the results:

```
>>> collection.remove({"Status" : "In use"})
>>> collection.find_one({"Status" : "In use"})
>>>
```

You need to be careful what kind of criteria you specify with this function. Usually, you should execute a find() first, so you can see exactly which documents will be removed. Alternatively, you can use the ObjectId to remove an item.

If you get tired of an entire collection, you can use either the drop() or the drop_collection() function to remove it. Both functions work the same way (one is just an alias for the other, really); specifically, both expect only one parameter, the collection's name:

```
>>> db.items.drop()
```

Last (and far from least because of its potential destructiveness), the drop_database() function enables you to delete an entire database. You call this function using the Connection module, as in the following example:

```
>>> c.drop_database("inventory")
```

Creating a Link Between Two Documents

Database references (DBRefs) are implemented in PyMongo via the DBRef() function as part of the DBRef module and can be used to create a link between two documents that reside in different locations. This is a field storage convention, which can be used for application logic. For example, you might create one collection for all employees and another collection for all the items—and then use the DBRef() function to create a reference between the employees and the location of the items, rather than typing them in manually for each item.

■ **Note**   MongoDB cannot ensure that DBRefs are valid. Caution should therefore be taken when deleting documents that may be linked by DBRefs.

As you may recall from the previous chapters, you can reference data in either of two ways. First, you can add a simple reference (*manual referencing*) that uses the _id field from one document to store a reference to it in another. Second, you can use the DBRef module, which brings a few more options with it than you get with manual referencing.

Let's create a manual reference first. Begin by saving a document. For example, assume you want to save the information for a person into a specific collection. The following example defines a jan dictionary and saves it into the people collection to get back an ObjectId:

```
>>> jan = {
...     "First Name" : "Jan",
...     "Last Name" : "Walker",
...     "Display Name" : "Walker, Jan",
...     "Department" : "Development",
...     "Building" : "2B",
...     "Floor" : 12,
...     "Desk" : 120103,
...     "E-Mail" : "jw@example.com"
... }

>>> people = db.people
>>> people.insert(jan)
ObjectId('4c5e5f104abffe0f34000002')
```

After you add an item and get its ID back, you can use this information to link the item to another document in another collection:

```
>>> laptop = {
...     "Type" : "Laptop",
...     "Status" : "In use",
...     "ItemNumber" : "12345ABC",
...     "Tags" : ["Warranty","In use","Laptop"],
...     "Owner" : jan[ "_id" ]
... }
>>> items = db.items
>>> items.insert(laptop)
ObjectId('4c5e6f6b4abffe0f34000003')
```

Now assume you want to find out the owner's information. In this case, all you have to do is query for the ObjectId given in the Owner field; obviously, this is possible only if you know which collection the data is stored in.

But assume that you don't know where this information is stored. It was for handling precisely such scenarios that the DBRef() function was created. You can use this function even when you do not know which collection holds the original data, so you don't have to worry so much about the collection names when searching for the information.

The DBRef() function takes three arguments; it can take a fourth argument that you can use to specify additional keyword arguments. Here's a list of the three main arguments and what they let you do:

- collection *(mandatory)*: Specifies the collection the original data resides in (for example, people).

- id *(mandatory)*: Specifies the _id value of the document that should be referred to.

- database *(optional)*: Specifies the name of the database to reference.

The DBRef module must be loaded before you can use the DBRef function, so let's load the module before going any further:

```
>>> from bson.dbref import DBRef
```

At this point, you're ready to look at a practical example of the DBRef() function. In the following example, you insert a person into the people collection and add an item to the items collection, using DBRef to reference the owner:

```
>>> mike = {
...     "First Name" : "Mike",
...     "Last Name" : "Wazowski",
...     "Display Name" : "Wazowski, Mike",
...     "Department" : "Entertainment",
...     "Building" : "2B",
...     "Floor" : 10,
...     "Desk" : 120789,
...     "E-Mail" : "mw@monsters.inc"
... }

>>> people.save(mike)
ObjectId('4c5e73714abffe0f34000004')
```

At this point, nothing interesting has happened. Yes, you added a document, but you did so without adding a reference to it. However, you do have the ObjectId of the document, so now you can add your next document to the collection, and then use DBRef() to point the owner field at the value of the previously inserted document. Pay special attention to the syntax of the DBRef() function; in particular, you should note how the first parameter given is the name of the collection where your previously specified document resides, while the second parameter is nothing more than a reference to the _id key in the mike dictionary:

```
>>> laptop = {
...     "Type" : "Laptop",
...     "Status" : "In use",
...     "ItemNumber" : "2345DEF",
...     "Tags" : ["Warranty","In use","Laptop"],
...     "Owner" : DBRef('people', mike[ "_id" ])
... }
```

```
>>> items.save(laptop)
ObjectId('4c5e740a4abffe0f34000005')
```

As you probably noticed, this code isn't very different from the code you used to create a manual reference. However, we recommend that you use DBRefs just in case you need to reference specific information, rather than embedding it. Adopting this approach also means you don't need to look up the collection's name whenever you query for the referenced information.

Retrieving the Information

You know how to reference information with DBRef(); now let's assume that you want to retrieve the previously referenced information. You can accomplish this using the Python driver's dereference() function. All you need to do is define the field previously specified that contains the referenced information as an argument, and then press the Return key.

To demonstrate, let's walk through the process of referencing and retrieving information from one document to another from start to finish. Let's begin by finding the document that contains the referenced data, and then retrieving that document for display. The first step is to create a query that finds a random document with the reference information in it:

```
>>> items.find_one({"ItemNumber" : "2345DEF"})
{
    u'Status': u'In use',
    u'Tags': [u'Warranty', u'In use', u'Laptop'],
    u'ItemNumber': u'2345DEF',
    u'Owner': DBRef(u'people', ObjectId('4c5e73714abffe0f34000004')),
    u'_id': ObjectId('4c5e740a4abffe0f34000005'),
    u'Type': u'Laptop'
}
```

Next, you want to store this item under a person dictionary:

```
>>> person = items.find_one({"ItemNumber" : "2345DEF"})
```

At this point, you can use the `dereference()` function to dereference the `Owner` field to the `person["Owner"]` field as an argument. This is possible because the `Owner` field is linked to the data you want to retrieve:

```
>>> db.dereference(person["Owner"])
{
    u'Building': u'2B',
    u'Floor': 10,
    u'Last Name': u'Wazowski',
    u'Desk': 120789,
    u'E-Mail': u'mw@monsters.inc',
    u'First Name': u'Mike',
    u'Display Name': u'Wazowski, Mike',
    u'Department': u'Entertainment',
    u'_id': ObjectId('4c5e73714abffe0f34000004')
}
```

That wasn't so bad! The point to take away from this example is that the DBRefs technique provides a great way for storing data you want to reference. Additionally, it permits some flexibility in how you specify the collection and database names. You'll find yourself using this feature frequently if you want to keep your database tidy, especially in cases where the data really shouldn't be embedded.

Summary

In this chapter, we've explored the basics of how MongoDB's Python driver (PyMongo) can be used for the most frequently used operations. Along the way, we've covered how to search for, store, update, and delete data.

We've also looked at how to reference documents contained in another collection using two methods: manual referencing and DBRefs. When looking at these approaches, we've seen how their syntax is remarkably similar, but the DBRefs approach provides a bit more robustness in terms of its functionality, so it is preferable in most circumstances.

The next chapter will delve into MongoDB's more advanced querying methods.

■ ■ ■

## CHAPTER 8

Advanced Queries

The chapters so far have covered most of the basic query mechanisms to find one or a series of documents by given criteria. There are a number of mechanisms for finding given documents to bring them back to your application so they can be processed. But sometimes these normal query mechanisms fall short and you want to perform complex operations over most or all documents in your collection. Many developers, when queries or operations of this kind are required, either iterate through all documents in the collection or write a series of queries to be executed in sequence to perform the necessary calculations. Although this is a valid way of doing things, it can be burdensome to write and maintain, as well as inefficient. It is for these reasons that MongoDB has some advanced query mechanics that you can use to drive the most from your data. The advanced MongoDB features we'll examine in this chapter are full-text search, the aggregation framework, and the MapReduce framework.

Full text search is one of the most-requested features to be added to MongoDB –. It represents the ability to create specialized text indexes in MongoDB and then perform text searches on those indexes to locate documents that contain matching text elements. The MongoDB full text search feature goes beyond simple string matching to include a full-stemmed approach based on the language you have selected for your documents, and it is an incredibly powerful tool for performing language queries on your documents. This recently introduced feature is marked as "experimental" in the 2.4 releases of MongoDB, because the development team is still working hard to improve it, which means you must manually activate it for use in your MongoDB environment.

The second feature this chapter will cover is the MongoDB aggregation framework. Introduced in chapters 4 and 6, this feature provides a whole host of query features that let you iterate over selected documents, or all of them, gathering or manipulating information. These query functions are then arranged into a pipeline of operations which are performed one after another on your collection to gather information from your queries.

The third and final feature we will cover is called MapReduce, which will sound familiar to those of you who have worked with Hadoop. MapReduce is a powerful mechanism that makes use of MongoDB's built-in JavaScript engine to perform abstract code executions in real time. It is an incredibly powerful tool that uses two JavaScript functions, one to map your data and another to transform and pull information out from the mapped data.

Probably the most important thing to remember throughout this chapter is that these are truly advanced features, and it is possible to cause serious performance problems for your MongoDB nodes if they are misused, so whenever possible you should test any of these features in a testing environment before deploying them to important systems.

Text Search

MongoDB's text search works by first creating a full text index and specifying the fields that you wish to be indexed to facilitate text searching. This text index will go over every document in your collection and tokenize and stem each string of text. This process of tokenizing and stemming involves breaking down the text into tokens, which conceptually are close to words. MongoDB then *stems* each token to find the root concept for the token. For example, suppose that breaking down a string reaches the token *fishing*. This token is then stemmed back to the root word *fish*, so MongoDB creates an index entry of *fish* for that document. This same process of tokenizing and stemming is applied to the search parameters a user enters to perform a given text search. The parameters are then compared against each document, and a relevance score is calculated. The documents are then returned to the user based on their score.

You are probably wondering how a word like *the* or *it* would be stemmed, and what happens if the documents aren't in English. The answer is that those and similar words would not be stemmed, and MongoDB text search supports many languages.

The MongoDB text search engine is a proprietary engine written for the MongoDB, Inc. team for text data retrieval. MongoDB text search also takes advantage of the Snowball string-processing language, which provides support for the stemming of words and for *stop words,* those words that aren't to be stemmed, as they don't represent any valuable concepts in terms of indexing or searching.

The thing to take away from this is that MongoDB's text search is incredibly complex and is designed to be as flexible and accurate as possible.

Text Search Costs and Limitations

As you can imagine from what you've learned about how text search functions, there are some costs associated with using MongoDB Text search. The first is that it changes the document storage allocation for future documents to the usePowerOf2Sizes option, which instructs MongoDB to allocate storage for more efficient re-use of free space. Second, text indexes are large and can grow very quickly depending on the number of documents you store and the number of tokens within each indexed field. The third limitation is that building a text index on existing documents is time-consuming, and it entails adding new entries to a field that has a text index, which is also more costly. Fourth, like everything in MongoDB, text indexes work better when in RAM. Finally, because of the complexity and size of text indexes they are currently limited to one per collection.

Enabling Text Search

As mentioned earlier, text search was introduced in MongoDB 2.4 as an experimental or beta feature. As such, you need to explicitly enable the text search functions on every MongoDB instance (and MongoS if you are sharding) that will be using this feature in your cluster. There are three ways you can enable text search; the first is to add the following option to the command you use to start or stop your MongoDB processes:

```
--setParameter textSearchEnabled=true
```

The second method is to add the following option to your MongoDB instance's configuration file:

```
setParameter = textSearchEnabled=true
```

The third and final method to get text search working on a MongoDB instance is to run the following command via the Mongo shell:

```
db.adminCommand({ setParameter: 1, textSearchEnabled : true }
```

With this set you can now work with the MongoDB full text search features on this node.

■ **Note** The fact that this feature is in beta does not mean it doesn't work. The MongoDB, Inc. team has put a considerable amount of effort into trying to get this feature right. By using the feature and reporting any issues you have on the MongoDB, Inc. JIRA (jira.mongodb.org), you can help them get this feature ready for full release.

By now you should have enabled the text search features on your MongoDB instance and are ready to take advantage of it! Let's look at how to create a text search index and perform text searches.

Using Text Search

Despite all the complexity we've described, MongoDB text search is surprisingly easy to use; you create a text index in the same way as any other index. For example, to create a text index on the "content" element of our theoretical blog collection, I would run the following

```
db.blog.ensureIndex( { content : "text" } );
```

And that's it. MongoDB will take care of the rest and insert a text index into your database, and all future documents that have a content field will be processed and have entries added to the text index to be searched. But really, just creating an index isn't quite enough data to work with. We need a suitable set of text data to work with and query.

Loading Text Data

Originally, we had planned to use a live stream of data from twitter, but the documents were too ungainly to work with. So we have instead created a small batch of eight documents mimicking twitter feeds to take text search out for a spin.

Go ahead and mongoimport the MongoDB data from the twitter.tgz into your database:

```
$ mongoimport test.json -d test -c texttest
connected to: 127.0.0.1
Sat Jul  6 17:52:19 imported 8 objects
```

Now that we have the data restored, go ahead and enable text indexing if it isn't already:

```
db.adminCommand({ setParameter: 1, textSearchEnabled : true });
{ "was" : false, "ok" : 1 }
```

Now that we have text indexing enabled, we should create a text index on the twitter data.

Creating a Text Index

In the case of twitter data, the portion we are concerned with is the textfield, which is the body text of the tweet. To set up the text index we run the following command:

```
use test;
db. texttest.ensureIndex( { body : "text" } );
```

If you see the error message "text search not enabled," you need to ensure that the text index is running, by using the commands just shown. Now if you review your logs you will see the following, which shows the text index being built:

```
Sat Jul  6 17:54:16.078 [conn41] build index test.texttest { _fts: "text", _ftsx: 1 }
Sat Jul  6 17:54:16.089 [conn41] build index done. scanned 8 total records. 0.01 secs
```

We can also check the indexes for the collection:

```
db.texttest.getIndexes()
[
    {
        "v" : 1,
        "key" : {
```

```
                    "_id" : 1
        },
        "ns" : "test.texttest",
        "name" : "_id_"
    },
    {
        "v" : 1,
        "key" : {
            "_fts" : "text",
            "_ftsx" : 1
        },
        "ns" : "test.texttest",
        "name" : "body_text",
        "weights" : {
            "body" : 1
        },
        "default_language" : "english",
        "language_override" : "language",
        "textIndexVersion" : 1
    }
]
```

Okay, we've enabled text search, created our index, and confirmed that it's there; now let's run our text search command.

Running the Text Search Command

In the version of MongoDB we are using there is no shell helper for the text command, so we execute it with the runCommand syntax as follows:

```
> db.texttest.runCommand( "text", { search :"fish" } )
```

This command will return any documents that match the query string of "fish". In this case it has returned two documents. The output shows quite a bit of debug information, along with a "results" array; this contains a number of documents. These include a combination of the score for the matching document and the returned, the matching document as the obj. You can see that the text portions of our matching documents both contain the word *fish* or *fishing* which both match our query! It's also worth noting that MongoDB text indexes are case-insensitive, which is an important consideration when performing your text queries.

■ **Note** Remember that all entries in Text Search are tokenized and stemmed. This means that words like fishy or fishing will be stemmed down to the word fish.

In addition, you can see the score, which was 0.75 or 0.666, indicating the relevance of that result to your query— the higher the value, the better the match. You can also see the stats for the query, including the number of objects returned (2) and the time taken, which was 112 microseconds.

```
{
        "queryDebugString" : "fish||||||",
        "language" : "english",
        "results" : [
                {
                        "score" : 0.75,
                        "obj" : {
                                "_id" : ObjectId("51d7ccb36bc6f959debe5514"),
                                "number" : 1,
                                "body" : "i like fish",
                                "about" : "food"
                        }
                },
                {
                        "score" : 0.6666666666666666,
                        "obj" : {
                                "_id" : ObjectId("51d7ccb36bc6f959debe5516"),
                                "number" : 3,
                                "body" : "i like to go fishing",
                                "about" : "recreation"
                        }
                }
        ],
        "stats" : {
                "nscanned" : 2,
                "nscannedObjects" : 0,
                "n" : 2,
                "nfound" : 2,
                "timeMicros" : 112
        },
        "ok" : 1
}
```

Now let's examine some other text search features that we can use to enhance our text queries.

Filtering Text Queries

The first thing we can do is to filter the text queries. To refine our fish query, let's say we only want documents that refer to fish as food, and not any that match "fishing" the activity. To add this additional parameter, we use the filter option and provide a document with a normal query. So in order to find our fish as food, we run the following:

```
> db.texttest.runCommand( "text", { search : "fish", filter : { about : "food" } })
{
        "queryDebugString" : "fish||||||",
        "language" : "english",
        "results" : [
                {
                        "score" : 0.75,
                        "obj" : {
                                "_id" : ObjectId("51d7ccb36bc6f959debe5514"),
                                "number" : 1,
```

```
                    "body" : "i like fish",
                    "about" : "food"
                }
            }
        ],
        "stats" : {
            "nscanned" : 2,
            "nscannedObjects" : 2,
            "n" : 1,
            "nfound" : 1,
            "timeMicros" : 101
        },
        "ok" : 1
}
```

That's perfect; we've returned only the one item as we wanted, without getting the unrelated "fishing" document. Notice that the nScanned and nscannedObjects values are 2, which denotes that this query scanned two documents from the index (nScanned) and then had to retrieve these two documents to review their contents (nScannedObjects) to return one matching document (n). Now let's look at another example.

More Involved Text Searching

First run the following query, which will return two documents. The results have been cut down to just the text fields for brevity.

db.texttest.runCommand("text", { search : "cook" })
```
"body" : "i want to cook dinner",
"body" : "i am to cooking lunch",
```

As you can see, we have two documents, both of which are about cooking a meal. Let's say we want to exclude lunch from our search and only return dinner. We can do this by adding –lunch to exclude the text lunch from our search.

```
> db.texttest.runCommand( "text", { search : "cook -lunch" })
{
    "queryDebugString" : "cook||lunch||||",
    "language" : "english",
    "results" : [
        {
            "score" : 0.6666666666666666,
            "obj" : {
                "_id" : ObjectId("51d7ccb36bc6f959debe5518"),
                "number" : 5,
                "body" : "i want to cook dinner",
                "about" : "activities"
            }
        }
    ],
    "stats" : {
        "nscanned" : 2,
        "nscannedObjects" : 0,
```

```
            "n" : 1,
            "nfound" : 1,
            "timeMicros" : 150
        },
        "ok" : 1
}
```

Notice first that the queryDebugString contains both cook and lunch, as these are the search terms we were using. Also note that two entries were scanned, but only one was returned. The search works by first finding all matches and then eliminating nonmatches.

The last search function that people may find valuable is *string literal searching*, which can be used to match specific words or phrases without stemming. As it stands, all the elements of our individual searches are being tokenized and then stemmed and each term evaluated. Take the following query:

```
> db.texttest.runCommand( "text", { search : "mongodb text search" })
{
    "queryDebugString" : "mongodb|search|text||||||",
    "language" : "english",
    "results" : [
        {
            "score" : 3.875,
            "obj" : {
                "_id" : ObjectId("51d7ccb36bc6f959debe551a"),
                "number" : 7,
                "body" : "i like mongodb text search",
                "about" : "food"
            }
        },
        {
            "score" : 3.8000000000000003,
            "obj" : {
                "_id" : ObjectId("51d7ccb36bc6f959debe551b"),
                "number" : 8,
                "body" : "mongodb has a new text search feature",
                "about" : "food"
            }
        }
    ],
    "stats" : {
        "nscanned" : 6,
        "nscannedObjects" : 0,
        "n" : 2,
        "nfound" : 2,
        "timeMicros" : 537
    },
    "ok" : 1
}
```

You can see in the queryDebugString that each element was evaluated and queried against. You can also see that this query evaluated and found two documents. Now notice the difference when we run the same query with escaped quote marks to make it a string literal:

```
> db.texttest.runCommand( "text", { search : "\"mongodb text search\"" })
{
     "queryDebugString" : "mongodb|search|text||||mongodb text search||",
     "language" : "english",
     "results" : [
          {
               "score" : 3.875,
               "obj" : {
                    "_id" : ObjectId("51d7ccb36bc6f959debe551a"),
                    "number" : 7,
                    "body" : "i like mongodb text search",
                    "about" : "food"
               }
          }
     ],
     "stats" : {
          "nscanned" : 6,
          "nscannedObjects" : 0,
          "n" : 1,
          "nfound" : 1,
          "timeMicros" : 134
     },
     "ok" : 1
}
```

You can see that only one document is returned, the document that actually contains the text in question. You can also see that in the queryDebugString the final element is the string itself rather than just the three tokenized and stemmed elements.

Additional Options

In addition to those we have discussed so far, there are three other options you can add into the text function. The first is limit, which limits the number of documents returned. It can be used as follows:

```
> db.texttest.runCommand( "text", { search :"fish", limit : 1 } )
```

The second option is project, which allows you to set the fields that will be displayed as the result of the query. This option takes a document describing which fields you wish to display, with 0 being off and 1 being on. By default when specifying this option all elements are off except for _id, which is on.

```
> db.texttest.runCommand( "text", { search :"fish", project :  { _id : 0, body : 1 } } )
```

The third and final option is language, which allows you to specify which language the text search will use. If no language is specified, then the index's default language is used. The language must be specified all in lower case. It can be invoked as follows:

```
> db.texttest.runCommand( "text", { search :"fish", lagnuage :  "french" } )
```

Currently text search supports the following languages.

- Danish
- Dutch
- English
- Finnish
- French
- German
- Hungarian
- Italian
- Norwegian
- Portuguese
- Romanian
- Russian
- Spanish
- Swedish
- Turkish

For more details on what is currently supported within MongoDB's text search, see the page `http://docs.mongodb.org/manual/reference/command/text/`.

Text Indexes in Other Languages

We originally created a simple text index earlier in order to get started with our text work. But there are a number of additional techniques you can use to make your text index better suited to your workload. You may recall from earlier that the logic for how words are stemmed will change based on the language that MongoDB uses to perform it. By default, all indexes are created in English, but this is not suitable for many people as their data may not be in English and thus the rules for language are different. You can specify the language to be used within each query, but that isn't exactly friendly when you know which language you are using. You can specify the default language by adding that option to the index creation:

```
db. texttest.ensureIndex( { content : "text" }, { default_language : "french" } );
```

This will create a text index with the French language as the default. Now remember that you can only have one text index per collection, so you will need to drop any other indexes before creating this one.

But what if we have multiple languages in one collection? The text index feature offers a solution, but it requires you to tag all your documents with the correct language. You may think it would be better for MongoDB to determine which language a given document is in, but there is no programmatic way to make an exact linguistic match. Instead, MongoDB allows you to work with documents that specify their own language. For example, take the following four documents:

```
{ _id : 1, content : "cheese", lingvo : "english" }
{ _id : 2, content : "fromage", lingvo: "french" }
{ _id : 3, content : "queso", lingvo : "spanish" }
{ _id : 4, content : "ost", lingvo : "swedish" }
```

They include four languages (in the `lingvo` fields), and if we keep any one default then we need to specify which language we will be searching within. Because we have specified the language the given content is in, we can use this field as a language override and the given language will be used rather than the default. We can create an index with this as follows:

```
db.texttest.ensureIndex( { content : "text" }, { language_override : "lingvo" } );
```

Thus the default language for those documents will be the one provided, and any documents lacking a `lingvo` field will use the default index, in this case English.

Compound Indexing with Text Indexes

Although it is true that you can only have one text index on a collection, you can have that text index cover a number of fields in a document or even all fields. You can specify extra fields just as you would for a normal index. Let's say we want to index both the content and any comments; we can do that as follows. Now we can make text searches on both fields.

```
db.texttest.ensureIndex( { content : "text", comments : "text" });
```

You may even want to create a text index on all the fields in a document. MongoDB has a wildcard specifier that can be used to reference all text elements of all documents; the notation is "$**". If you wish to specify this as the form for your text index, you will need to add the index option for a name to your document. This way, the automatically generated name will not be used and cause problems with the index by being too long a field. The maximum length of an index is 121 characters, which includes the names of the collection, the database, and the fields to be indexed.

■ **Note** It is strongly recommended that you specify a name with any compound index that has a text field to avoid running into issues caused by the name length.

This gives us the following syntax for creating a text index named `alltextindex` on all string elements of all documents in the `texttest` collection:

```
db.texttest.ensureIndex( { "$**": "text" }, { name: "alltextindex" } )
```

The next thing you can do with a compound text index is specifying weights for different text fields on that index. You do this by adding weight values above the default of one to each field that you will index. The values will then increase the importance of the given index's results in a ratio of N:1. Take the following example index:

```
db.texttest.ensureIndex( { content : "text", comments : "text"}, { weights : { content: 10,
comments: 5,                        } } );
```

This index will mean that the `content` portion of the document will be given 10:5 more precedence than the `comments` values. Any other field will have the default weight of 1, compared to the weight of 5 for comments and 10 for content. You can also combine weights and the wildcard text search parameters to weight specific fields.

■ **Note** Be aware that if you have too many text indexes, you will get a "too many text indexes" error. If that happens, you should drop one of your existing text indexes to allow you to create a new one.

In addition to creating compound indexes with other text fields, you can create compound indexes with other non-text fields. You can build these indexes just as you would add any other index, as in this example:

```
db.texttest.ensureIndex( { content : "text", username : 1 });
```

This command creates a text index on the content portion of the document and a normal index on the username portion. This can be especially useful when using the filter parameter, as the filter is effectively a query on all the subdocuments used. These, too, will need to be read either from the index or by reading the document itself. Let's look at our example from earlier:

```
db.texttest.runCommand( "text", { search : "fish", filter : { about : "food" } })
```

Given the filter on this query, we will need to index the about portion of the document; otherwise, every theoretically matched document would need to be fully read and then validated against, which is a costly process. However, if we index as follows we can avoid those reads by having an index like this, which includes the about element:

```
db.texttest.ensureIndex( { about : 1, content : "text" });
```

Now let's run the find command again:

```
> db.texttest.runCommand( "text", { search : "fish", filter : { about : "food" } })
{
    "queryDebugString" : "fish||||||",
    "language" : "english",
    "results" : [
        {
            "score" : 0.75,
            "obj" : {
                "_id" : ObjectId("51d7ccb36bc6f959debe5514"),
                "number" : 1,
                "body" : "i like fish",
                "about" : "food"
            }
        }
    ],
    "stats" : {
        "nscanned" : 1,
        "nscannedObjects" : 0,
        "n" : 1,
        "nfound" : 1,
        "timeMicros" : 95
    },
    "ok" : 1
}
```

You can see that there are no scanned objects, which should improve the overall efficiency of the query. With these options you should be able to drive some real flexibility and power into your text searching.

You should now see the enormous power of MongoDB's latest searching feature, and you should have the knowledge to drive some real power from text searching.

The Aggregation Framework

The *aggregation framework* in MongoDB represents the ability to perform a selection of operations on all of the data in your collection. This is done by creating a pipeline of aggregation operations that will be executed in order first on the data and then each subsequent operation will be on the results of the previous operation. Those of you familiar with the Linux or Unix shell will recognize this as forming a shell pipeline of operations.

Within the Aggregation framework there are a plethora of operators, which can be used as part of your aggregations to corral your data. Here we will cover off some of the high-level pipeline operators and run through some examples on how to use these. This means that we will be covering off the following operators:

- $group
- $limit
- $match
- $sort
- $unwind
- $project
- $skip

For further details about the full suite of operators, check out the aggregation documentation, available at http://docs.mongodb.org/manual/aggregation/. We've created an example collection you can use to test some of the aggregation commands. Extract the archive with the following command:

```
$ tar -xvf test.tgz
x test/
x test/aggregation.bson
x test/aggregation.metadata.json
x test/mapreduce.bson
x test/mapreduce.metadata.json
```

The next thing to do is to run the mongorestore command to restore the test database:

```
$ mongorestore test
connected to: 127.0.0.1
Sun Jul 21 19:26:21.342 test/aggregation.bson
Sun Jul 21 19:26:21.342        going into namespace [test.aggregation]
1000 objects found
Sun Jul 21 19:26:21.350        Creating index: { key: { _id: 1 }, ns: "test.aggregation", name: "_id_" }
Sun Jul 21 19:26:21.688 test/mapreduce.bson
Sun Jul 21 19:26:21.689        going into namespace [test.mapreduce]
1000 objects found
Sun Jul 21 19:26:21.695        Creating index: { key: { _id: 1 }, ns: "test.mapreduce", name: "_id_" }
```

Now that we have a collection of data to work with, we need to look at how to run an aggregation command and how to build an aggregation pipeline. To run an aggregation query we use the aggregate command and provide it a single document that contains the pipeline. For our tests we will run the following aggregation command with various pipeline documents:

```
> db.aggregation.aggregate({pipeline document})
```

So, without further ado, let's start working through our aggregation examples.

$group

The $group command does what its name suggests; it groups documents together so you can create an aggregate of the results. Let's start by creating a simple group command that will list out all the different colors within our "aggregation" collection. To begin, we create an _id document that will list all the elements from our collection that we want to group. So, we start our pipeline document with the $group command and add to it our _id document:

{ $group : { _id : "$color" } }

Now you can see we have the _id value of "$color". Note that there is a $ sign in front of the name color; this indicates that the element is a reference from a field in our documents. That gives us our basic document structure, so let's execute the aggregation:

```
> db.aggregation.aggregate( { $group : { _id : "$color" } } )
{
    "result" : [
        {
            "_id" : "red"
        },
        {
            "_id" : "maroon"
        },
...
        {
            "_id" : "grey"
        },
        {
            "_id" : "blue"
        }
    ],
    "ok" : 1
}
```

$sum

From the results of the $group operator you can see that we have a number of different colors in our result stack. The result is an array of elements, which contain a number of documents, each with an _id value of one of the colors in the "color" field from a document. This doesn't really tell us much, so let's expand what we do with our $group command. We can add a count to our group with the $sum operator, which can increment a value for each instance of the value found. To do this, we add an extra value to our $group command by providing a name for the new field and what its value should be. In this case, we want a field called "count", as it represents the number of times each color occurs; its value is to be {$sum : 1}, which means that we want to create a sum per document and increase it by 1 each time. This gives us the following document:

{ $group : { _id : "$color", count : { $sum : 1 } } }

Let's run our aggregation with this new document:

```
> db.aggregation.aggregate({ $group : { _id : "$color", count : { $sum : 1 } } }
{
    "result" : [
```

```
        {
                "_id" : "red",
                "count" : 90
        },
        {
                "_id" : "maroon",
                "count" : 91
        },
...
    {
                "_id" : "grey",
                "count" : 91
        },
        {
                "_id" : "blue",
                "count" : 91
        }
    ],
    "ok" : 1
}
```

Now you can see how often each color occurs. We can further expand what we are grouping by adding extra elements to the _id document. Let's say we want to find groups of "color" and "transport". To do that, we can change _id to be a document that contains a subdocument of items as follows:

{ $group : { _id : { color: "$color", transport: "$transport"} , count : { $sum : 1 } } }

If we run this we get a result that is about 50 elements long, far too long to display here. There is a solution to this, and that's the $limit operator.

$limit

The $limit operator is the next pipeline operator we will work with. As its name implies, $limit is used to limit the number of results returned. In our case we want to make the results of our existing pipeline more manageable, so let's add a limit of 5 to the results. To add this limit, we need to turn our one document into an array of pipeline documents.

```
[
        { $group : { _id : { color: "$color", transport: "$transport"} , count : { $sum : 1 } } },
        { $limit : 5 }
]
```

This will give us the following results:

```
> db.aggregation.aggregate( [ { $group : { _id : { color: "$color", transport: "$transport"} , count
: { $sum : 1 } } }, { $limit : 5 } ] )
{
    "result" : [
        {
                "_id" : {
                    "color" : "maroon",
                    "transport" : "motorbike"
```

```
        },
        "count" : 18
    },
    {
        "_id" : {
            "color" : "orange",
            "transport" : "autombile"
        },
        "count" : 18
    },
    {
        "_id" : {
            "color" : "green",
            "transport" : "train"
        },
        "count" : 18
    },
    {
        "_id" : {
            "color" : "purple",
            "transport" : "train"
        },
        "count" : 18
    },
    {
        "_id" : {
            "color" : "grey",
            "transport" : "plane"
        },
        "count" : 18
    }
    ],
    "ok" : 1
}
```

You can now see the extra fields from the transport element added to _id, and we have limited the results to only five. You should now see how we can build pipelines from multiple operators to draw data aggregated information from our collection.

$match

The next operator we will review is $match, which is used to effectively return the results of a normal MongoDB query within your aggregation pipeline. The $match operator is best used at the start of the pipeline to limit the number of documents that are initially put into the pipeline; by limiting the number of documents processed, we significantly reduce performance overhead. For example, suppose we want to perform our pipeline operations on only those documents that have a num value greater than 500. We can use the query { num : { $gt : 500 } } to return all documents matching this criterion. If we add this query as a $match to our to our existing aggregation, we get the following:

```
[
    { $match : { num : { $gt : 500 } } },
    { $group : { _id : { color: "$color", transport: "$transport"} , count : { $sum : 1 } } },
```

```
    { $limit : 5 }
]
```

This returns the following result:

```
{
    "result" : [
        {
            "_id" : {
                "color" : "white",
                "transport" : "boat"
            },
            "count" : 9
        },
        {
            "_id" : {
                "color" : "black",
                "transport" : "motorbike"
            },
            "count" : 9
        },
        {
            "_id" : {
                "color" : "maroon",
                "transport" : "train"
            },
            "count" : 9
        },
        {
            "_id" : {
                "color" : "blue",
                "transport" : "autombile"
            },
            "count" : 9
        },
        {
            "_id" : {
                "color" : "green",
                "transport" : "autombile"
            },
            "count" : 9
        }
    ],
    "ok" : 1
}
```

You will notice that the results returned are almost completely different from previous examples. This is because the order in which the documents were created has now changed. As such, when we run this query we limit the output, removing the original documents that had been our output earlier. You will also see that our counts are half the values of the earlier results. This is because we have cut our potential set of data to aggregate upon to about half the size it was before. If we want to have consistency among our return results, we need to invoke another pipeline operator, $sort.

$sort

As you've just seen, the $limit command can change which documents are returned in the result because it reflects the order in which the documents were originally output from the execution of the aggregation. This can be fixed with the advent of the $sort command. We simply need to apply a sort on a particular field before providing the limit in order to return the same set of limited results. The $sort syntax is the same as it is for a normal query; you specify documents that you wish to sort by, positive for ascending and negative for descending. To show how this works, let's run our query with and without the match and a limit of 1. You will see that with the $sort prior to the $limit we can return documents in the same order.

This gives us the first query of

```
[
        { $group : { _id : { color: "$color", transport: "$transport"} , count : { $sum : 1 } } },
        { $sort : { _id :1 } },
        { $limit : 5 }
]
```

The result of this query is:

```
{
    "result" : [
        {
            "_id" : {
                "color" : "black",
                "transport" : "autombile"
            },
            "count" : 18
        }
    ],
    "ok" : 1
}
```

The second query looks like this:

```
[
        { $match : { num : { $gt : 500 } } },
        { $group : { _id : { color: "$color", transport: "$transport"} , count : { $sum : 1 } } },
        { $sort : { _id :1 } },
        { $limit : 1 }
]
```

The result of this query is

```
{
    "result" : [
        {
            "_id" : {
                "color" : "black",
                "transport" : "autombile"
            },
            "count" : 9
        }
```

```
    ],
    "ok" : 1
}
```

You will notice that both queries now contain the same document, and they differ only in the count. This means that our sort has been applied before the limit and allows us to get a consistent result. These operators should give you an idea of the power you can drive by building a pipeline of operators to manipulate things until we get the desired result.

$unwind

The next operator we will look at is $unwind. This takes an array and splits each element into a new document (in memory and not added to your collection) for each array element. As with making a shell pipeline, the best way to understand what is output by the $unwind operator is simply to run it on its own and evaluate the output. Let's check out the results of $unwind:

db.aggregation.aggregate({ $unwind : "$vegetables" });
```
{
    "result" : [
        {
            "_id" : ObjectId("51de841747f3a410e3000001"),
            "num" : 1,
            "color" : "blue",
            "transport" : "train",
            "fruits" : [
                "orange",
                "banana",
                "kiwi"
            ],
            "vegetables" : "corn"
        },
        {
            "_id" : ObjectId("51de841747f3a410e3000001"),
            "num" : 1,
            "color" : "blue",
            "transport" : "train",
            "fruits" : [
                "orange",
                "banana",
                "kiwi"
            ],
            "vegetables" : "brocoli"
        },
        {
            "_id" : ObjectId("51de841747f3a410e3000001"),
            "num" : 1,
            "color" : "blue",
            "transport" : "train",
            "fruits" : [
                "orange",
                "banana",
                "kiwi"
```

```
        ],
            "vegetables" : "potato"
        },
...
    ],
    "ok" : 1
}
```

We now have 3000 documents in our result array, a version of each document that has its own vegetable and the rest of the original source document! You can see the power of what we can do with $unwind and how with a very large collection of giant documents you could get yourself in trouble. Always remember that if you run your match first, you can cut down the number of objects you want to work with before running the other, more intensive aggregation operations.

$project

Our next operator, $project, is used to limit the fields or to rename fields returned as part of a document. This is just like the field-limiting arguments that can be set on find commands. It's the perfect way to cut down on any excess fields returned by your aggregations. Let's say we want to see only the fruit and vegetables for each of our documents; we can provide a document that shows which elements we want to be displayed (or not) just as we would add to our find command. Take the following example:

```
[
{ $unwind : "$vegetables" },
{ $project : { _id: 0, fruits:1, vegetables:1 } }
]
```

This projection returns the following result:

```
{
    "result" : [
        {
            "fruits" : [
                "orange",
                "banana",
                "kiwi"
            ],
            "vegetables" : "corn"
        },
        {
            "fruits" : [
                "orange",
                "banana",
                "kiwi"
            ],
            "vegetables" : "brocoli"
        },
        {
            "fruits" : [
                "orange",
                "banana",
```

```
                    "kiwi"
                ],
                "vegetables" : "potato"
        },
...
    ],
    "ok" : 1
}
```

That's better than before, as now our documents are not as big. But still better would be to cut down on the number of documents returned. Our next operator will help with that.

$skip

$skip is a pipeline operator complementary to the $limit operator, but instead of limiting results to the first X documents, it skips over the first X documents and returns all other remaining documents. We can use it to cut down on the number of documents returned. If we add it to our previous query with a value of 2995, we will return only five results. This would give us the following query:

```
[
{ $unwind : "$vegetables" },
{ $project : { _id: 0, fruits:1, vegetables:1 } },
{ $skip : 2995 }
]
```

With a result of

```
{
    "result" : [
        {
                "fruits" : [
                    "kiwi",
                    "pear",
                    "lemon"
                ],
                "vegetables" : "pumpkin"
        },
        {
                "fruits" : [
                    "kiwi",
                    "pear",
                    "lemon"
                ],
                "vegetables" : "mushroom"
        },
        {
                "fruits" : [
                    "pear",
                    "lemon",
                    "cherry"
                ],
```

```
                    "vegetables" : "pumpkin"
            },
            {
                    "fruits" : [
                            "pear",
                            "lemon",
                            "cherry"
                    ],
                    "vegetables" : "mushroom"
            },
            {
                    "fruits" : [
                            "pear",
                            "lemon",
                            "cherry"
                    ],
                    "vegetables" : "capsicum"
            }
     ],
     "ok" : 1
}
```

And that's how you can use the $skip operator to reduce the number of entries returned. You can also use the complementary $limit operator to limit the number of results in the same manner and even combine them to pick out a set number of results in the middle of a collection. Let's say we wanted results 1500–1510 of our 3000-entry data set. We could provide a $skip value of 1500 and a $limit of 10, which would return only the 10 results we wanted.

We've reviewed just a few of the top-level pipeline operators available within the MongoDB aggregation framework. There are a whole host of smaller operators that can be used within the top-level pipeline operators as *pipeline expressions*. These include some geographic functions, mathematics functions such as average, first and last, and a number of date/time and other operations. And all of these can be used and combined to perform aggregation operations like the ones we have covered. Just remember that each operation in a pipeline will be performed on the results of the previous operation and that you can output and step through them to create your desired result.

MapReduce

MapReduce is one of the most complex query mechanisms within MongoDB. It works by taking two JavaScript functions, map and reduce. These two functions are completely user-defined, and this gives you an incredible amount of flexibility in what you can do! A few short examples will demonstrate some of the things you can do with MapReduce.

How MapReduce Works

Before we dive into the examples, it's a good idea to go over what Map/Reduce is and how it works. In MongoDB's implementation of MapReduce we issue a specialized query to a given collection, and all matching documents from that query are then input into our map function. This map function is designed to generate key/value pairs. Any set of keys that have multiple values are then input to the reduce function, which returns the aggregated result of the input data. After this there is one remaining optional step in which data can be finished for nice presentation by a finalize function.

Setting Up Testing Documents

To begin with, we need to set up some documents to test with. We've created a mapreduce collection that is part of the test database you restored earlier. If you haven't restored it yet, extract the archive with the following command:

```
$ tar -xvf test.tgz
x test/
x test/aggregation.bson
x test/aggregation.metadata.json
x test/mapreduce.bson
x test/mapreduce.metadata.json
```

Then run the mongorestore command to restore the test database:

```
$ mongorestore test
connected to: 127.0.0.1
Sun Jul 21 19:26:21.342 test/aggregation.bson
Sun Jul 21 19:26:21.342          going into namespace [test.aggregation]
1000 objects found
Sun Jul 21 19:26:21.350          Creating index: { key: { _id: 1 }, ns: "test.aggregation", name:
"_id_" }
Sun Jul 21 19:26:21.688 test/mapreduce.bson
Sun Jul 21 19:26:21.689          going into namespace [test.mapreduce]
1000 objects found
Sun Jul 21 19:26:21.695          Creating index: { key: { _id: 1 }, ns: "test.mapreduce", name: "_id_" }
```

This will give you a collection of documents to use in working with MapReduce. To begin, let's look at the world's simplest map function.

Working with Map functions

This function will "emit" the color and the num value from each document in the mapreduce collection. These two fields will be output in key/value form, with the first argument (color) as the key and the second argument (number) as the value. This is a lot to take in at first, so take a look at the simple map function that performs this emit:

```
var map = function() {
    emit(this.color, this.num);
};
```

In order to run a Map/Reduce we also need a reduce function, but before doing anything fancy let's see what's provided as the result of an empty reduce function to get an idea of what happens.

```
var reduce = function(color, numbers) { };
```

Enter both these commands into your shell, and you'll have just about all you need to run our MapReduce.

The last thing you will need to provide is an output string for the MapReduce to use. This string defines where the output for this MapReduce command should be put. The two most common options are

- To a collection
- To the console (inline)

For our current purposes, let's output to the screen so we can see exactly what is going on. To do this, we pass a document with the out option that has a value of { inline : 1 }, like this:

{ out : { inline : 1 } }

This gives us the following command:

db.mapreduce.mapReduce(map,reduce,{ out: { inline : 1 } });

The result looks like this:

```
{
    "results" : [
        {
            "_id" : "black",
            "value" : null
        },
        {
            "_id" : "blue",
            "value" : null
        },
        {
            "_id" : "brown",
            "value" : null
        },
        {
            "_id" : "green",
            "value" : null
        },
        {
            "_id" : "grey",
            "value" : null
        },
        {
            "_id" : "maroon",
            "value" : null
        },
        {
            "_id" : "orange",
            "value" : null
        },
        {
            "_id" : "purple",
            "value" : null
        },
        {
            "_id" : "red",
            "value" : null
        },
        {
            "_id" : "white",
            "value" : null
```

```
        },
        {
                "_id" : "yellow",
                "value" : null
        }
    ],
    "timeMillis" : 95,
    "counts" : {
        "input" : 1000,
        "emit" : 1000,
        "reduce" : 55,
        "output" : 11
    },
    "ok" : 1,
}
```

This shows that each "key" color value is split out individually and is the unique _id value for each document. Because we specified nothing for the value portion of each document, that is set to null. We can modify this by adding the output section for our desired MapReduce results. In this case we want a summary of what each functions takes. To do that we can use the function to modify what we want to return as the object in place of null. In this case, let's return the sum of all values for each of those colors. To do this we can create a function that will return the sum of all the array of numbers for each color that's passed into the reduce function. Thankfully, we can use a handy function called Array.sum to sum all values of an array. This gives us the following reduce function:

```
var reduce = function(color, numbers) {
    return Array.sum(numbers);
};
```

Perfect. In addition to our inline output we can also have MapReduce write to a collection; to do so, we simply have to replace that { inline : 1 } with the name of the collection we wish to output to. So let's output to a collection called mrresult. This gives us the following command:

```
db.mapreduce.mapReduce(map,reduce,{ out: "mrresult" });
```

When executed with our new reduce function, it gives us the following:

```
{
    "result" : "mrresult",
    "timeMillis" : 111,
    "counts" : {
        "input" : 1000,
        "emit" : 1000,
        "reduce" : 55,
        "output" : 11
    },
    "ok" : 1,
}
```

If you now want to see the document results, you need to query them from the mrresult collection, as follows:

```
> db.mrresult.findOne();
{ "_id" : "black", "value" : 45318 }
```

Now that we have a basic system working we can get more advanced!

Advanced MapReduce

Let's say that instead of the sum of all values we want the average! This becomes far harder, as we need to add another variable—the number of objects we have! But how can we pass two variables out from the map function? After all, the emit takes only two arguments. We can perform a "cheat" of sorts; we return a JSON document, which can have as many fields as we want! So let's expand our original map function to return a document that contains the color value and a counter value. First we define the document as a new variable, fill in the JSON document, and then emit that document.

```
var map = function() {
    var value = {
        num : this.num,
        count : 1
    };
    emit(this.color, value);
};
```

Notice that we set the counter value to 1, in order to count each document only once! Now for the reduce function. It will need to deal with an array of those value documents that we created earlier. One last thing to note is that we need to return the same values in our reduce function's return function that are created in our map function and sent to our emit.

■ **Note**   You could also accomplish all of the things we are doing here by using the length of the array containing all the numbers. But this way you get to see more of what you can do with MapReduce.

To deal with this array, we've created a simple for loop, the length of the array, and we iterate over each member and add the num and count for each document onto our new return variable, called reduceValue. Now we simply return this value and we have our result.

```
var reduce = function(color, val ) {
    reduceValue = { num : 0, count : 0};
    for (var i = 0; i < val.length; i++) {
        reduceValue.num += val[i].num;
        reduceValue.count += val[i].count;
    }
    return reduceValue;
};
```

At this point, you should be wondering how this gets us our average. We have the count and the number, but no actual average! If you run the MapReduce again you can see the results for yourself. Now, be warned that each time you output to a collection, MapReduce will drop that collection before writing to it! For us that's a good thing, as we only want this run's results but it could come back to haunt you in the future. If you want to merge the results of the two you can make an output document that looks like { out : { merge : "mrresult" } }.

```
db.mapreduce.mapReduce(map,reduce,{ out: "mrresult" });
```

Now Let's check those results quickly:

```
> db.mrresult.findOne();
{
    "_id" : "black",
    "value" : {
        "num" : 18381,
        "count" : 27028,
    }
}
```

No, there is not an average value. This means we have more work to do, but how do we make the average given that we have to return a document that matches the input of the emit? We need to a third function! MapRreduce provides one, called the `finalize` function. This allows you to do any final cleanup before returning your MapReduce results. Let's write a function that will take the result from `reduce` and calculate the average for us:

```
var finalize = function (key, value) {
    value.avg = value.num/value.count;
    return value;
};
```

Yes, it's that simple. So now with our `map`, `reduce`, and `finalize` functions ready, we simply add them to our call. The `finalize` option is set in the last document; along with the out, this gives us the following command:

```
db.mapreduce.mapReduce(map,reduce,{ out: "mrresult", finalize : finalize });
```

And from here let's query one of our example documents:

```
> db.mrresult.findOne();
{
    "_id" : "black",
    "value" : {
        "num" : 45318,
        "count" : 91,
        "avg" : 498
    }
}
```

Now that's better! We have our number, our count, and our average!

Debugging MapReduce

Debugging Map/Reduce is quite a time-consuming task, but there are a few little tricks to make your life easier. First let's look at debugging a `map`. You can debug a `map` by overloading the emit with a function, as shown here:

```
var emit = function(key, value) {
    print("emit results - key: " + key + "  value: " + tojson(value));
}
```

This emit function will return the key and value results the same as a map function would. You can test one using map.apply() and an example document from your collection as follows:

```
> map.apply(db.mapreduce.findOne());
emit results - key: blue   value: { "num" : 1, "count" : 1 }
```

Now that you know what to expect out of your map, you can look at debugging your reduce. You first need to confirm that your map and reduce are returning in the same format— that's critical. The next thing you can do is to create a short array with a few values just like the ones passed into your reduce, as shown here:

```
a = [{ "num" : 1, "count" : 1 },{ "num" : 2, "count" : 1 },{ "num" : 3, "count" : 1 }]
```

Now you can call reduce as follows. This will allow you to see the values returned by your emit:

```
>reduce("blue",a);
{ "num" : 6, "count" : 3 }
```

If all else fails and you're confused about what's going on inside your function, don't forget that you can use the printjson() function to print any JSON value out to the mongodb logfile to read. This is always a valuable tool when debugging software.

Summary

By now you should have an idea of exactly how much power and flexibility there is within MongoDB, using three of the most powerful and flexible query systems available. Through your reading of this chapter you should have an idea of how to use text indexes to perform highly powerful text searches in a number of languages. You should have the ability to create highly complex and flexible aggregations using the MongoDB aggregation framework. Finally you should now have the ability to use the powerful JavaScript-backed MapReduce which would allow you to write powerful groupings and transformations on your data.

PART 3

Advanced MongoDB with Big Data

CHAPTER 9

■ ■ ■

Database Administration

In this chapter, we will walk you through some of the basic administrative operations you can perform on a MongoDB server. We will also show how to automate some of those activities, such as backing up your server.

Because MongoDB is a nonrelational database system, many of the more traditional functions that a DB administrator would perform are not required. For example, it's not necessary to create new databases, collections, or fields on the server, because MongoDB will create these elements on the fly as you access them. Therefore, in the vast majority of cases you don't need to manage databases and schemas.

This freedom from having to predefine everything, however, can result in the unintended creation of elements, such as extraneous collections and fields in documents. Administrators and developers will occasionally need to clear out unused data elements from databases, particularly during the development phase of a project, when change is often rapid. They may have to try many approaches before finally settling on a solution and cleaning up the databases. MongoDB's ease of use encourages this explorative mode of development; however, it can also result in clutter in your datastores because the amount of effort required to create data structures has fallen almost to nothing.

A contributing factor to this clutter, and one of the more significant differences between MongoDB and SQL databases, is that all object and element names in MongoDB are case-sensitive on all platforms. Thus, the foo and Foo collection names refer to two completely different collections. Therefore, you need to be careful with your database and collection naming to avoid accidentally creating multiple databases that differ only in the case of the name. (There is, however, one exception to this, as of MongoDB 2.4: you can no longer create databases whose names differ only in case, as doing so will generate an error.)

The different versions of these databases will fill up your disk, and they can create a lot of confusion for developers and end users of the system by allowing them to connect to incomplete or unintended sets of data.

In this chapter, you will learn how to perform all the following tasks:

- Back up and restore your MongoDB system.

- Use the supplied MongoDB shell (invoked with the mongo command) to perform common tasks.

- Control access to your server with authentication.

- Monitor your database instances.

Before diving into those tasks, however, we'll begin by looking at the tools used to carry out many of them.

Using Administrative Tools

An administrator needs tools suitable for performing the day-to-day tasks of keeping the server running smoothly. There are some very good tools available in the MongoDB package, as well as an evolving collection of useful third-party tools. The following sections cover some of the most important tools available, as well as how to use them.

mongo, the MongoDB Console

The main tool you will use as an administrator is mongo, the MongoDB console tool. mongo is a command-line console utility based on JavaScript. It is similar to many of the query tools supplied with mainstream relational databases. However, mongo has one unique trick up its sleeve: it can run programs written in JavaScript that interact directly with the MongoDB database.

This console allows you to script all of your interactions with MongoDB in JavaScript, and then store those scripts in .js files to run as needed. In fact, many of the built-in commands in the mongo console are themselves written in JavaScript.

You can place any commands that you would type into the command shell into a file with a .js extension, and run them by simply adding the file name to the command line when starting up the shell or using the load() function from within the shell. The shell will execute the contents of the file and then exit. This is useful for running lists of repetitive commands.

In this chapter we will use the mongo console to demonstrate many of the administrative tasks that you can perform on a MongoDB server, and because it is distributed with the MongoDB server, we can guarantee it will be there.

Using Third-Party Administration Tools

Several third-party administration (admin) tools are available for MongoDB. MongoDB, Inc. maintains a page on the MongoDB website that lists currently available third-party tools. You can find this list at http://docs.mongodb.org/ecosystem/tools/administration-interfaces/.

Many of these tools are web-based and similar in principle to phpMyAdmin for MySQL, but some are also full-fledged desktop UIs.

Backing Up the MongoDB Server

The first skill a new MongoDB administrator should learn is how to back up and restore a MongoDB server. Arming yourself with this knowledge will make you feel more comfortable with exploring some of the more advanced administrative functions, because you know that your precious data is stored away safely somewhere.

Creating a Backup 101

Let's begin by performing a simple backup and then restoring it. Along the way, you will make sure the backup is intact, and you will look at some practical examples that illustrate how the backup and restoration features work. Once you have a solid understanding of how to use these features, you will be able to move on to exploring the more advanced administrative features of MongoDB.

In this simple backup example, we will assume the following:

- Your MongoDB server is running on the same machine that you are currently logged into.

- You have enough disk space for dump files that could be, at most, the same size as your database.

- Your backup will be made in your home directory. This means you won't have to deal with any issues related to permissions.

The MongoDB backup utility is called mongodump; this utility is supplied as part of the standard distribution. The following example performs a simple backup of the running MongoDB server to a designated disk directory:

```
$> cd ~
$> mkdir testmongobackup
$> cd testmongobackup
$> mongodump
```

When mongodump is running, you should see it output something that looks like the following:

```
$ mongodump
connected to: 127.0.0.1
Tue May 21 20:52:58.639 all dbs
Tue May 21 20:52:58.640 DATABASE: blog          to       dump/blog
Tue May 21 20:52:58.640        blog.system.indexes to dump/blog/system.indexes.bson
Tue May 21 20:52:58.641          4 objects
Tue May 21 20:52:58.641        blog.system.profile to dump/blog/system.profile.bson
Tue May 21 20:52:58.645          3688 objects
Tue May 21 20:52:58.645        Metadata for blog.system.profile to dump/blog/system.profile.metadata.
json
Tue May 21 20:52:58.645        blog.authors to dump/blog/authors.bson
Tue May 21 20:52:58.646          1 objects
Tue May 21 20:52:58.646        Metadata for blog.authors to dump/blog/authors.metadata.json
Tue May 21 20:52:58.646        blog.posts to dump/blog/posts.bson
Tue May 21 20:52:58.686          29997 objects
Tue May 21 20:52:58.709        Metadata for blog.posts to dump/blog/posts.metadata.json
Tue May 21 20:52:58.710        blog.tagcloud to dump/blog/tagcloud.bson
Tue May 21 20:52:58.710          1 objects
Tue May 21 20:52:58.710        Metadata for blog.tagcloud to dump/blog/tagcloud.metadata.json
```

If your output doesn't look very similar to this, you should double-check that your environment matches up with the assumptions stated previously.

If you do see the correct output, then your database has been backed up to the testmongobackup/dump directory. The following snippet restores your database to its state at the time you performed the backup:

```
$> cd ~/testmongobackup
$> mongorestore --drop
connected to: 127.0.0.1
Tue May 21 20:53:46.337 dump/blog/authors.bson
Tue May 21 20:53:46.337        going into namespace [blog.authors]
Tue May 21 20:53:46.337         dropping
1 objects found
Tue May 21 20:53:46.338        Creating index: { key: { _id: 1 }, ns: "blog.authors", name: "_id_" }
Tue May 21 20:53:46.339 dump/blog/posts.bson
Tue May 21 20:53:46.339        going into namespace [blog.posts]
Tue May 21 20:53:46.339         dropping
29997 objects found
Tue May 21 20:53:47.284        Creating index: { key: { _id: 1 }, ns: "blog.posts", name: "_id_" }
Tue May 21 20:53:47.375        Creating index: { key: { Tags: 1 }, ns: "blog.posts", name: "Tags_1" }
Tue May 21 20:53:47.804 dump/blog/system.profile.bson
Tue May 21 20:53:47.804         skipping
Tue May 21 20:53:47.804 dump/blog/tagcloud.bson
Tue May 21 20:53:47.804        going into namespace [blog.tagcloud]
Tue May 21 20:53:47.804         dropping
1 objects found
Tue May 21 20:53:47.821        Creating index: { key: { _id: 1 }, ns: "blog.tagcloud", name: "_id_" }
```

The --drop option tells the mongorestore utility to discard each collection in the database before restoring it. Consequently, the backed-up data replaces the data currently in the database. If you were to choose not to use the --drop option, the restored data would be appended to the end of each collection, which would result in duplicated items.

Let's examine what happened in this example more closely.

By default, the mongodump utility connects to the local database using the default port, and pulls out all of the data associated with each database and collection and stores them in a predefined folder structure.

The default folder structure created by mongodump takes this form:

```
./dump/[databasename]/[collectionname].bson
```

The database system used in the example consists of a single database called blog. The blog database contains three collections: authors, posts, and tagcloud.

The mongodump saves the data it retrieves from the database server in .bson files that are just a copy of the internal BSON format that MongoDB uses internally to store documents. You can also see the indexes on each collection being restored in the preceding example. The MongoDB server maintains indexes, and it records index definitions for each collection, which are stored in the metadata.json files. It is these metadata files that allow you to rebuild the indexes when restoring from a backup.

Once you have dumped the database, you can archive and store the folder on any online or offline media, such as CD, USB drive, tape, or S3 format.

■ **Note** The mongodump utility does not empty the contents of the output directory before it writes the backup files to it. If you have existing contents in this directory, they won't be removed unless they match the name of a file (*collectionname*.bson) that mongodump has been instructed to back up. This is good if you want to add multiple collection dumps to the same dump directory; however, it could cause problems if you use the same dump directory each time you back up data but don't clear it out. For example, assume you have a database that you back up regularly, and at some point you decide to delete a collection from this database. Unless you either clear out the directory where you are performing your backup or manually remove the file associated with the deleted collection, then the next time you restore the data, the deleted collection will reappear. Unless you want to overlay data in your backups, you should make sure you clear out the destination directory before you use mongodump.

Backing Up a Single Database

When you have multiple applications running on the same server, often you may find yourself wanting to back up each database individually, rather than all at once, as in the preceding example.

With mongodump, you can do this by adding the -d *database_name* option to the command line. This causes mongodump to create the ./dump folder; however, this folder will contain only the backup files for a single database.

Backing Up a Single Collection

Imagine you have a blog site where the contents of the authors collection do not change much. Instead, the rapidly changing content of the blog site is contained in the posts and tagcloud collections. You might back up the entire database only once a day but want to back up these two collections once per hour. Fortunately, you can do that easily with mongodump by using the -c option to specify the collection you wish to back up.

The mongodump utility does not clear its destination directories. This means that, for each collection you want to back up, you can call mongodump successively to add a given collection to your backup, as shown in the following example:

```
$mkdir ~/backuptemp
$cd ~/backuptemp
$mongodump -d blog -c posts
$mongodump -d blog -c tagcloud
...
    archive the dump folder ~/backuptemp away as a tar file
...
$ cd ~
$ rm -rf backuptemp
```

Digging Deeper into Backups

At this point, you know how to perform the rudimentary tasks of backing up and subsequently restoring your data. Now you're ready to look at some of the powerful options that allow you to tailor MongoDB's backup and restore functionality to suit your particular needs.

The mongodump utility includes the options shown in Figure 9-1, captured by running help in MongoDB 2.5.3.

```
$mongodump --help
Export MongoDB data to BSON files.

Options:
  --help                                produce help message
  -v [ --verbose ]                      be more verbose (include multiple times
                                        for more verbosity e.g. -vvvvv)
  --quiet                               silence all non error diagnostic
                                        messages
  --version                             print the program's version and exit
  -h [ --host ] arg                     mongo host to connect to ( <set
                                        name>/s1,s2 for sets)
  --port arg                            server port. Can also use --host
                                        hostname:port
  --ipv6                                enable IPv6 support (disabled by
                                        default)
  -u [ --username ] arg                 username
  -p [ --password ] arg                 password
  --authenticationDatabase arg          user source (defaults to dbname)
  --authenticationMechanism arg (=MONGODB-CR)
                                        authentication mechanism
  --dbpath arg                          directly access mongod database files
                                        in the given path, instead of
                                        connecting to a mongod  server - needs
                                        to lock the data directory, so cannot
                                        be used if a mongod is currently
                                        accessing the same path
  --directoryperdb                      each db is in a separate directory
                                        (relevant only if dbpath specified)
  --journal                             enable journaling (relevant only if
                                        dbpath specified)
  -d [ --db ] arg                       database to use
  -c [ --collection ] arg               collection to use (some commands)
  -o [ --out ] arg (=dump)              output directory or "-" for stdout
  -q [ --query ] arg                    json query
  --oplog                               Use oplog for point-in-time
                                        snapshotting
  --repair                              try to recover a crashed database
  --forceTableScan                      force a table scan (do not use
                                        $snapshot)

Auditing Options:
  --auditLog arg          turn on auditing and specify output for log: textfile,
                          bsonfile, syslog, console
  --auditPath arg         full filespec for audit log file
  --auditFilter arg       filter spec to screen audit records
```

Figure 9-1. *The mongodump utility help display showing its options*

Most of the options listed here are self-explanatory, with the following exceptions:

- --dbpath *arg*: If you have a large amount of data to back up and fast drives, and you aren't concerned with backing up your indexes, it may be preferable to back up the database by copying the datafiles that the MongoDB server uses directly to the backup medium. This option allows you to back up directly from the server's datafiles, but it can only be used if the server is offline or otherwise *write-frozen* (see the "Backing Up Large Databases" section later in this chapter for more information).

- --directoryperdb: You use this command-line option in conjunction with the --dbpath option to specify that the MongoDB server being backed up was configured to place its datafiles for each database in a separate directory. By default, MongoDB places all of its datafiles in a single directory. You should use this option only if you have configured your server to operate in this mode.

- -o [--out] *arg*: You use this option to specify the directory where you want the database dumps to be placed. By default, the mongodump utility creates a folder called /dump in the current directory and writes the dumps into that. You can use the -o/--out option to choose an alternative path to place the output dumps.

- --authenticationDatabase *arg*: Specifies the database that holds the user's credentials. Mongodump will default to using the databases specified with –db without this option.

- --authenticationMechanism *arg*: Defaults to MongoDB's challenge/response (username/ password) mechanism. This command is used to switch to MongoDB Enterprise edition's Kerberos authentication.

Restoring Individual Databases or Collections

You've just seen how the mongodump utility can back up a single database or collection; the mongorestore utility has the same flexibility. You can use mongorestore to restore an item if the dump directory it is restoring from has the backup files for the required collection or database in it; you don't need to restore all the items present in the backup. If you wish, you can restore them individually.

Let's begin by looking at the options available in mongorestore, shown in Figure 9-2.

```
$mongorestore --help
Import BSON files into MongoDB.

usage: mongorestore [options] [directory or filename to restore from]
Options:
  --help                        produce help message
  -v [ --verbose ]              be more verbose (include multiple times
                                for more verbosity e.g. -vvvvv)
  --quiet                       silence all non error diagnostic
                                messages
  --version                     print the program's version and exit
  -h [ --host ] arg             mongo host to connect to ( <set
                                name>/s1,s2 for sets)
  --port arg                    server port. Can also use --host
                                hostname:port
  --ipv6                        enable IPv6 support (disabled by
                                default)
  -u [ --username ] arg         username
  -p [ --password ] arg         password
  --authenticationDatabase arg  user source (defaults to dbname)
  --authenticationMechanism arg (=MONGODB-CR)
                                authentication mechanism
  --dbpath arg                  directly access mongod database files
                                in the given path, instead of
                                connecting to a mongod  server - needs
                                to lock the data directory, so cannot
                                be used if a mongod is currently
                                accessing the same path
  --directoryperdb              each db is in a separate directory
                                (relevant only if dbpath specified)
  --journal                     enable journaling (relevant only if
                                dbpath specified)
  -d [ --db ] arg               database to use
  -c [ --collection ] arg       collection to use (some commands)
  --objcheck                    validate object before inserting
                                (default)
  --noobjcheck                  don't validate object before inserting
  --filter arg                  filter to apply before inserting
  --drop                        drop each collection before import
  --oplogReplay                 replay oplog for point-in-time restore
  --oplogLimit arg              include oplog entries before the
                                provided Timestamp (seconds[:ordinal])
                                during the oplog replay; the ordinal
                                value is optional
  --keepIndexVersion            don't upgrade indexes to newest version
  --noOptionsRestore            don't restore collection options
  --noIndexRestore              don't restore indexes
  --w arg (=0)                  minimum number of replicas per write

Auditing Options:
  --auditLog arg        turn on auditing and specify output for log: textfile,
                        bsonfile, syslog, console
  --auditPath arg       full filespec for audit log file
  --auditFilter arg     filter spec to screen audit records
```

Figure 9-2. *The mongorestore help display showing its options*

You probably recognize most of these options from the discussion of mongodump; however, the following two options are worthy of special mention:

- **--drop**: This option instructs mongorestore to drop the existing collection before restoring it. This helps ensure that there are no duplicates. If this option is not used, the restored data is appended (inserted) into the target collection.

- **--noobjcheck**: This option instructs mongorestore to ignore the step of validating the object before inserting it into the destination collection.

Restoring a Single Database

You can use the mongorestore utility's -d option to restore a single database. As before, don't forget to use the --drop option if the database already exists in your MongoDB server:

```
$cd ~/testmongobackup
$mongorestore -d blog --drop
```

Restoring a Single Collection

You use similar syntax to restore a single collection to a database; the difference is that you also specify a collection name with the -c option, as shown in the following example:

```
$cd ~/testmongobackup
$mongorestore -d blog -c posts --drop
```

Automating Backups

For small installations or developer setups, the simple act of running the mongodump utility and saving the results is a perfectly adequate method of performing ad-hoc backups. For example, a common practice on a Mac OS X workstation is to let Time Machine (the Mac backup utility) store the backups.

For any kind of production setup, you will want to back up the server automatically; regular backups can help you prevent or recover from trouble if you encounter any problems. This holds true not only with your installation (for example, if you have corrupted databases), but also if your users inadvertently damage or destroy data.

Let's look at some simple scripts that you can use to automate your backups.

Using a Local Datastore

A simple backup script that creates archives in a specified directory will suffice if you have a large backup drive attached to your system or you can mount an external filesystem through NFS or SMB. The following backup script is easy to set up; simply edit the variables at the top of the script to match those of your local system:

```
#!/bin/bash
#######################################
# Edit these to define source and destinations

MONGO_DBS=""
BACKUP_TMP=~/tmp
BACKUP_DEST=~/backups
```

```
MONGODUMP_BIN=/usr/bin/mongodump
TAR_BIN=/usr/bin/tar

#########################################

BACKUPFILE_DATE=`date +%Y%m%d-%H%M`


# _do_store_archive <Database> <Dump_dir> <Dest_Dir> <Dest_file>

function _do_store_archive {
        mkdir -p $3
        cd $2
        tar -cvzf $3/$4 dump
}

# _do_backup <Database name>

function _do_backup {
        UNIQ_DIR="$BACKUP_TMP/$1"`date "+%s"`
        mkdir -p $UNIQ_DIR/dump
        echo "dumping Mongo Database $1"
        if [ "all" = "$1" ]; then
                $MONGODUMP_BIN -o $UNIQ_DIR/dump
        else
                $MONGODUMP_BIN -d $1 -o $UNIQ_DIR/dump
        fi
        KEY="database-$BACKUPFILE_DATE.tgz"
        echo "Archiving Mongo database to $BACKUP_DEST/$1/$KEY"
        DEST_DIR=$BACKUP_DEST/$1

        _do_store_archive  $1 $UNIQ_DIR $DEST_DIR $KEY

        rm -rf $UNIQ_DIR
}

# check to see if individual databases have been specified, otherwise backup the whole server
#  to "all"

if [ "" = "$MONGO_DBS"  ]; then
        MONGO_DB="all"
        _do_backup $MONGO_DB
else
        for MONGO_DB in $MONGO_DBS; do
                _do_backup $MONGO_DB
        done
fi
```

Table 9-1 lists the variables you have to change to make this simple backup script work with your system.

Table 9-1. *The Variables Used in the Local Datastore Backup Script*

Variable	Description
MONGO_DBS	Leave this variable empty ("") to back up all databases on the local server. Or you can place a list of databases into it to back up selected databases ("db1 db2 db3").
BACKUP_TMP	Set this variable to a temporary directory suitable for holding the dump files for the backup. After the archive has been created, the temporary data used in this directory is deleted. Be sure to choose a suitable directory that is relevant to using your script. For example, if you are using the script to create backups in your local account, use ~/tmp; if you are using it as a system cronjob that runs under a system account, use /tmp. On an Amazon EC2 instance, you should probably use /mnt/tmp, so that the folder is not created on the system root partition, which is quite small.
BACKUP_DEST	This variable holds the destination folder for the backups, and individual folders will be created below this folder. Again, place this directory at a point relevant to the way you use your backup script.
MONGODUMP_BIN	Because your backup script may be running under an account that does not have a full set of paths set up, it's wise to use this variable to specify the full path to this binary. You can determine the appropriate path on your system by typing **which mongodump** into a terminal window.
TAR_BIN	You use this variable to set the full path for the tar binary; use **which tar** in a terminal window to determine this path.

You can now use this script to back up your databases; doing so will create a set of archival backups in the specified BACKUP_DEST directory. The files created follow this naming format:

Database Name/database-YYYYMMDD-HHMM.tgz

For example, the following snippet shows the backup names for this chapter's test database:

Backups:$ tree

```
.
|-- blog
|   |-- database-20100611-1144.tgz
|   `-- database-20100611-1145.tgz
`-- all
    |-- database-20100611-1210.tgz
    |-- database-20100611-1221.tgz
    |-- database-20100611-1222.tgz
    |-- database-20100611-1224.tgz
    `-- database-20100611-1233.tgz
```

Of course, you also need to install the script. If you want to run this script daily, just put it into /etc/cron.daily and restart the cron service to make it active. This approach will work on most Linux distributions, such as Ubuntu, Fedora, CentOS, and RedHat. If you want less frequent backups, just move the script to /etc/cron.weekly or /etc/cron.monthly. For more frequent backups, you can use /etc/cron.hourly.

Using a Remote (Cloud-Based) Datastore

The script described in the previous section has a separate function for creating and storing the archive. This makes it relatively easy to modify the script so that it uses an external datastore to store the backup archive. Table 9-2 provides a couple of examples, but many more other mechanisms are possible.

Table 9-2. *Remote (Cloud-Based) Backup Storage Options*

Method	Description
rsync/ftp/tftp or scp to another server	You can use rsync to move the archive to a backup storage machine.
s3 storage	S3 storage is a good place to put your backups if you run your system on EC2 because storage costs are low and Amazon makes redundant copies.

We will examine the S3 method of storing your backup; however, the same principles apply to any of the other mechanisms.

This example uses the s3cmd utility (written in python) available from http://s3tools.org. On Ubuntu, you can install this script using the sudo apt-get install s3cmd command; on Mac OSX, this script is available from the MacPorts collection. On Fedora, CentOS, and RedHat, you can acquire the yum package from http://s3tools.org, and then install it using yum.

Once you have installed the package, run s3cmd –configure to set your Amazon S3 credentials. Note that you only need to supply two keys: AWS_ACCESS_KEY and AWS_SECRET_ACCESS_KEY. The s3cmd utility will create a config file that contains the information you need in this file: ~/.s3cfg.

Here are the changes that you need to make for your backup script to work with S3:

```
# _do_store_archive <Database> <Dump_dir> <Dest_Dir> <Dest_file>

BACKUP_S3_CONFIG=~/.s3cfg
BACKUP_S3_BUCKET=somecompany.somebucket
S3CMD_BIN=/usr/bin/s3cmd

function _do_store_archive {
        UNIQ_FILE="aws"`date "+%s"`
        cd $2
        tar -cvzf $BACKUP_TMP/$UNIQ_FILE dump
        $S3CMD_BIN --config $BACKUP_S3_CONFIG put $BACKUP_TMP/$UNIQ_FILE \
        s3://$BACKUP_S3_BUCKET/$1/$4
        rm -f $BACKUP_TMP/$UNIQ_FILE
}
```

Table 9-3 lists some variables that you need to configure to make this adapted script work.

Table 9-3. *Configuring the Variables of Your Adapted Backup Script*

Variable	Description
BACKUP_S3_CONFIG	The path to the s3cmd configuration file that was created when you ran s3cmd –configure to save the details of your S3 account.
BACKUP_S3_BUCKET	The name of the bucket where that you want the script to store backups.
S3CMD_BIN	The path to the s3cmd executable program, again use **which s3cmd** to find it on your system.

Backing Up Large Databases

Creating effective backup solutions can become a problem when working with large database systems. Often the time taken to make a copy of the database is significant; it may even require hours to complete. During that time, you have to maintain the database in a consistent state, so the backup does not contain files that were copied at different points in time. The holy grail of a database backup system is a *point-in-time* snapshot, which can be done very quickly. The faster the snapshot can be done, the smaller the window of time during which the database server must be *frozen*.

Using a Hidden Secondary Server for Backups

One technique used to perform large backups is to make the backup from a *hidden secondary* that can be frozen while the backup is taken. This secondary server is then restarted to catch up with the application after the backup is complete.

MongoDB makes it very simple to set up a hidden secondary and have it track the *primary* server using MongoDB's replication mechanism. It's also relatively easy to configure (see Chapter 11 for more details on how to set up a hidden secondary).

Creating Snapshots with a Journaling Filesystem

Many modern volume managers have the ability to create snapshots of the state of the drive at any particular point in time. Using a filesystem snapshot is one of the fastest and most efficient methods of creating a backup of your MongoDB instance. While setting up one of these systems is beyond the scope of this book, we can show you how to place the MongoDB server in a state where all of its data is in a consistent state on the disk. We also show you how to block writes so that further changes are not written to the disk, but are instead buffered in memory.

A snapshot allows you to read the drive exactly as it was when the snapshot was taken. A system's volume or filesystem manager makes sure that any blocks of data on the disk that are changed after the snapshot is taken are not written back to the same place on the drive; this preserves all the data on the disk to be read. Generally, the procedure for using a snapshot goes something like this:

1. Create a snapshot.

2. Copy data from the snapshot or restore the snapshot to another volume, depending on your volume manager.

3. Release the snapshot; doing so releases all preserved disk blocks that are no longer needed back into the free space chain on the drive.

4. Back up the data from the copied data while the server is still running.

The great thing about the method just described is that reads against the data can continue unhindered while the snapshot is taken.

Some volume managers that have this capability include:

- Linux and the LVM volume management system

- Sun ZFS

- Amazon EBS volumes

- Windows Server using shadow copies

Most of those volume managers have the ability to perform a snapshot in a very short time—often just a few seconds—even on very large amounts of data. The volume managers don't actually copy the data out at this point; instead, they effectively insert a bookmark onto the drive, so that you can read the drive in the state it existed at the point in time the snapshot was taken.

Once the backup system has read the drive from the snapshot, then the old blocks that have been subsequently changed can be released back to the drive's free space chain (or whatever mechanism the filesystem uses to mark free space).

To make this an effective method of creating a backup, we must either have the MongoDB journal files existing on this same device or get MongoDB to flush all outstanding disk writes to the disk so we can take a snapshot. The feature that forces MongoDB to do this flushing is called *fsync*; the function that blocks further writes is called a *lock*. MongoDB has the ability to perform both operations at the same time, so that after the fsync, no further writes are done to the disk until the lock is released. By having the journal on the same device or performing an fsync and lock, we make the image of the database on the disk *consistent* and ensure that it stays consistent until we have completed the snapshot.

You use the following commands to make MongoDB enter the fsync and lock state:

```
$mongo
>use admin
>db.fsyncLock()
{
    "info" : "now locked against writes",
    "ok" : 1
}
```

You use these commands to check the current state of the lock:

```
$mongo
>use admin
>db.currentOp()
{
    "inprog" : [
    ],
    "fsyncLock" : 1
}
```

The "fsyncLock": 1 status indicates that MongoDB's fsync process, which is responsible for writing changes to the disk, is currently blocked from performing writes.

At this point, you can issue whatever commands are required to make your volume manager create the snapshot of the folders where MongoDB has its datafiles stored. Once the snapshot is completed, you can use the following commands to release the lock:

```
$mongo
>db.fsyncUnlock();
{ "ok" : 1, "info" : "unlock requested" }
```

Note that there may be a small delay before the lock is released; however, you can use the db.currentOp() function to check the result.

When the lock is finally cleared, db.currentOp() will return the following:

```
$mongo
>use admin
>db.currentOp()
{ "inprog" : [] }
```

The { "inprog" : [] } line means that the lock has been released and MongoDB can start writing to the disk again.

Now that you have the snapshot bookmark inserted, you can use the utilities associated with your volume manager to copy the contents of the snapshot to a suitable place so you can store your backup. Don't forget to release the snapshot once your backup is complete.

You can visit the following links for more information about snapshots:

- `http://docs.mongodb.org/manual/tutorial/backup-databases-with-filesystem-snapshots/`

- `http://tldp.org/HOWTO/LVM-HOWTO/snapshots_backup.html`

- `http://docs.huihoo.com/opensolaris/solaris-zfs-administration-guide/html/ch06.html`

- `http://support.rightscale.com/09-Clouds/AWS/02-Amazon_EC2/EBS/Create_an_EBS_Snapshot`

Disk Layout to Use with Volume Managers

Some volume managers can take a snapshot of subdirectories on a partition, but most can't, so it is a good idea to mount the volume you are planning to store your MongoDB data on in a suitable place on your filesystem (for example, /mnt/mongodb) and use the server configuration options to place the data directories, the configuration file, and any other MongoDB-related files (for example, journal) solely on that mount.

This means that when you take a snapshot of the volume, you capture the complete state of the server, including its configuration. It may even be a good idea to place the binaries of the server distribution directly on that volume, so that your backup contains a completely coordinated set of components.

Importing Data into MongoDB

Sometimes, you need to load lots of bulk data into MongoDB for use as reference data. Such data might include Zip code tables, IP geolocation tables, parts catalogs, and so on.

MongoDB includes a bulk "loader," mongoimport, designed to import data directly into a particular collection on the server; this differs from mongorestore, which is designed to restore MongoDB binary from backups.

The mongoimport utility can load data from any of three file formats:

1. *CSV*: In this file format, each line represents a document, and fields are separated by commas.

2. *TSV*: This file format is similar to CSV; however, it uses a tab character as the delimiter. This format is popular because it does not require the escaping of any text characters other than those for new lines.

3. *JSON*: This format contains one block of JSON per line that represents a document. Unlike the other formats, JSON can support documents with variable schemas.

The use of this utility is fairly intuitive. For input, it takes a file in one of the three formats, a string or a file with a set of column header names (these form the element names in a MongoDB document), and several options that are used to control how the data is interpreted. Figure 9-3 shows how to use the mongoimport utility.

```
$mongoimport --help
Import CSV, TSV or JSON data into MongoDB.

When importing JSON documents, each document must be a separate line of the input file.

Example:
  mongoimport --host myhost --db my_cms --collection docs < mydocfile.json

Options:
  --help                                produce help message
  -v [ --verbose ]                      be more verbose (include multiple times
                                        for more verbosity e.g. -vvvvv)
  --quiet                               silence all non error diagnostic
                                        messages
  --version                             print the program's version and exit
  -h [ --host ] arg                     mongo host to connect to ( <set
                                        name>/s1,s2 for sets)
  --port arg                            server port. Can also use --host
                                        hostname:port
  --ipv6                                enable IPv6 support (disabled by
                                        default)
  -u [ --username ] arg                 username
  -p [ --password ] arg                 password
  --authenticationDatabase arg          user source (defaults to dbname)
  --authenticationMechanism arg (=MONGODB-CR)
                                        authentication mechanism
  --dbpath arg                          directly access mongod database files
                                        in the given path, instead of
                                        connecting to a mongod  server - needs
                                        to lock the data directory, so cannot
                                        be used if a mongod is currently
                                        accessing the same path
  --directoryperdb                      each db is in a separate directory
                                        (relevant only if dbpath specified)
  --journal                             enable journaling (relevant only if
                                        dbpath specified)
  -d [ --db ] arg                       database to use
  -c [ --collection ] arg               collection to use (some commands)
  -f [ --fields ] arg                   comma separated list of field names
                                        e.g. -f name,age
  --fieldFile arg                       file with field names - 1 per line
  --ignoreBlanks                        if given, empty fields in csv and tsv
                                        will be ignored
  --type arg                            type of file to import.  default: json
                                        (json,csv,tsv)
  --file arg                            file to import from; if not specified
                                        stdin is used
  --drop                                drop collection first
  --headerline                          first line in input file is a header
                                        (CSV and TSV only)
  --upsert                              insert or update objects that already
                                        exist
  --upsertFields arg                    comma-separated fields for the query
                                        part of the upsert. You should make
                                        sure this is indexed
  --stopOnError                         stop importing at first error rather
                                        than continuing
  --jsonArray                           load a json array, not one item per
                                        line. Currently limited to 16MB.

Auditing Options:
  --auditLog arg          turn on auditing and specify output for log: textfile,
                          bsonfile, syslog, console
  --auditPath arg         full filespec for audit log file
  --auditFilter arg       filter spec to screen audit records
```

Figure 9-3. *The mongoimport help display showing its options*

The following options deserve more explanation:

- --headerline: Uses the first line of the file as the list of field names. Note that this applies only to CSV and TSV formats.

- --ignoreblanks: Does *not* import empty fields. If a field is empty, then a corresponding element will not be created in the document for that row; if you don't invoke this option, then an empty element with the column name is created.

- --drop: Drops a collection and then re-creates it with data only from this import; otherwise, the data is appended to the collection.

You also have to specify the database name and the collection name when you use mongoimport to import data with the -d and -c options, as in the following example:

```
$mongoimport -d blog -c tagcloud --type csv --headerline < csvimportfile.csv
```

Exporting Data from MongoDB

The mongoexport utility is similar to mongoimport, but mongoexport, as its name implies, creates export files from an existing MongoDB collection instead. This is one of the best ways to extract data from your MongoDB instance in a format that can be read by other databases or spreadsheet applications. Figure 9-4 shows how to use the mongoexport utility.

```
$mongoexport --help
Export MongoDB data to CSV, TSV or JSON files.

Options:
  --help                              produce help message
  -v [ --verbose ]                    be more verbose (include multiple times
                                      for more verbosity e.g. -vvvvv)
  --quiet                             silence all non error diagnostic
                                      messages
  --version                           print the program's version and exit
  -h [ --host ] arg                   mongo host to connect to ( <set
                                      name>/s1,s2 for sets)
  --port arg                          server port. Can also use --host
                                      hostname:port
  --ipv6                              enable IPv6 support (disabled by
                                      default)
  -u [ --username ] arg               username
  -p [ --password ] arg               password
  --authenticationDatabase arg        user source (defaults to dbname)
  --authenticationMechanism arg (=MONGODB-CR)
                                      authentication mechanism
  --dbpath arg                        directly access mongod database files
                                      in the given path, instead of
                                      connecting to a mongod  server - needs
                                      to lock the data directory, so cannot
                                      be used if a mongod is currently
                                      accessing the same path
  --directoryperdb                    each db is in a separate directory
                                      (relevant only if dbpath specified)
  --journal                           enable journaling (relevant only if
                                      dbpath specified)
  -d [ --db ] arg                     database to use
  -c [ --collection ] arg             collection to use (some commands)
  -f [ --fields ] arg                 comma separated list of field names
                                      e.g. -f name,age
  --fieldFile arg                     file with field names - 1 per line
  -q [ --query ] arg                  query filter, as a JSON string
  --csv                               export to csv instead of json
  -o [ --out ] arg                    output file; if not specified, stdout
                                      is used
  --jsonArray                         output to a json array rather than one
                                      object per line
  -k [ --slaveOk ] arg (=1)           use secondaries for export if
                                      available, default true
  --forceTableScan                    force a table scan (do not use
                                      $snapshot)
  --skip arg (=0)                     documents to skip, default 0
  --limit arg (=0)                    limit the numbers of documents
                                      returned, default all

Auditing Options:
  --auditLog arg          turn on auditing and specify output for log: textfile,
                          bsonfile, syslog, console
  --auditPath arg         full filespec for audit log file
  --auditFilter arg       filter spec to screen audit records
```

Figure 9-4. *The mongoexport help display showing its options*

Notable options from the mongoexport utility include the following:

- -q: Specifies the query used to locate the records tooutput. This query can be any JSON query string (but not a JavaScript query string, as this often doesn't work as expected) that you might use with the db.collection.find() function to select a subset of records. If you don't specify this option or you set it to {}, the mongoexport utility will output all records.

- -f: Lists the database element names to be exported.

The following example illustrates how to use the options for the mongoexport utility:

```
$mongoexport -d blog -c posts -q {} -f _id,Title,Message,Author --csv >blogposts.csv
connected to: 127.0.0.1
exported 1 records
```

Securing Your Data by Restricting Access to a MongoDB Server

In some cases, your applications may be dealing with sensitive data, such as user records in social networks or payment details in ecommerce applications. In many cases, there are rules mandating that you have to ensure restricted access to sensitive data in your database systems.

MongoDB supports a simple role-based authentication system that allows you to control who has access to each database, and the level of access they are granted.

Most of the commands that change the configuration of data or make major alterations to its structure on a MongoDB server are restricted to running only inside the special admin database that is created automatically during each new MongoDB installation.

Before you can issue these commands, you have to switch to the admin database with the use admin command. Upcoming sections will note any command that is admin-only, so you will always know when you need to be in the admin database before you can use it. This chapter assumes that you can select the database and authenticate against it, if necessary.

By default, MongoDB does not use any authentication methods. Anybody with access to the network connection can connect and issue commands to the server. However, you can add *users* to any database, and MongoDB can be configured to require both connection and console authentication to access the relevant database. This is the recommended mechanism for restricting access to admin functions.

Protecting Your Server with Authentication

MongoDB supports a simple authentication model that allows the administrator to restrict access to databases on a per user basis.

MongoDB supports individual access control records on each database; these records are stored in a special system.users collection. For normal users to have access to two databases (for example, db1 and db2), their credentials and rights must be added to both databases.

If you create individual logins and access rights for the same user on different databases, there is no synchronization between those records. In other words, changing a user password on one database does not change the password on any other database. However, the MongoDB team introduced a new mechanism in the 2.4 release to allow delegated credentials. Using these credentials in this manner, you can create one master user with a password. Then create users on other databases and specify that this user already exists on the master database and its credentials should be used for authentication.

There is also one final (and critical) exception to this rule: any users added to the special admin database will have the same access rights on all databases; you do not need to assign rights to such users individually.

■ **Note** If you enable authentication before adding the admin users, you will only be able to access your database via localhost, meaning a connection made from the machine hosting the MongoDB instance. This is a security feature designed to allow administrators to create users after having enabled authentication.

Adding an Admin User

Adding the admin user is as simple as changing to the admin database and using the addUser() function:

```
$mongo
> use admin
> db.addUser({user : "admin", pwd: "pass", roles: [ "readWrite", "dbAdmin" ] })
{
    "user" : "admin",
    "pwd" : "e4e538f5dcb52537cad02bbf8491693c",
    "roles" : [
        "readWrite",
        "dbAdmin"
    ],
    "_id" : ObjectId("5239915b1ce3dc1efebb3c84")
}
```

You only need to add a single admin user at this point; once that user is defined, you can use it to add other admin users to the admin database or normal users to any other database.

Enabling Authentication

Now you need to alter your server's configuration to enable authentication. Do so by stopping your server and adding --auth to the startup parameters.

If you installed MongoDB with a packaged installer such as yum or Aptitude, then typically you can edit /etc/mongodb.conf to enable auth=true. Next, you can use the following command to restart the server and enable authentication:

```
$sudo service mongodb restart
```

In addition to auth you can also use a *keyfile*, a file that contains a preshared key of some description, which is used to confirm communication between MongoDB nodes. To create a keyfile, just create a simple file with a phrase or string in it to be used. Then add the option keyfile=/path/to/keyfile just as you did with auth. You can even remove the old auth=true option, as running with keyfile implies auth.

Authenticating in the mongo Console

Before you can run restricted commands in the admin database, you will need to be authenticated as an admin user, as in the following example:

```
$mongo
> use admin
switched to db admin
>show collections
```

```
Sun May 26 17:22:26.132 JavaScript execution failed: error: {
    "$err" : "not authorized for query on admin.system.namespaces",
    "code" : 16550
} at src/mongo/shell/query.js:L131 }
>db.auth("admin", "pass");
1
```

At this point, the mongo console will print either 1 (successful authentication) or 0 (a failed authentication):

```
1
>show collections
system.indexes
system.users
```

If your authentication was successful, you will be able to perform any operations available based on your user permissions.

If your authentication was unsuccessful, then you need to check whether your username/password is correct and whether the admin user has been correctly added to the admin database. Reset your server so it has no authentication, and then use the following command to list the contents of the system.users collection in the admin database:

```
$mongo
>use admin
> db.system.users.find()
{ "_id" : ObjectId("5239915b1ce3dc1efebb3c84"), "user" : "admin", "pwd" :
"e4e538f5dcb52537cad02bbf8491693c", "roles" : [  "readWrite",  "dbAdmin" ] }
```

■ **Note** If you are using an admin credential to access databases other than admin, then you must first authenticate against the admin database. Otherwise, you will not be able to access any other databases in the system.

The mongo console shows the contents of the user collection, enabling you to see what the userid is, while the password is shown as an MD5 hash of the original password you supplied:

```
$ mongo
> use blog
switched to db blog
> show collections
Wed Sep 18 21:42:51.855 JavaScript execution failed: error: {
    "$err" : "not authorized for query on blog.system.namespaces",
    "code" : 13
} at src/mongo/shell/query.js:L128
> db.auth("admin","pass")
Error: 18 { code: 18, ok: 0.0, errmsg: "auth fails" }
0
> use admin
switched to db admin
> db.auth("admin","pass")
1
```

```
> use blog
switched to db blog
> show collections
system.indexes
system.users
authors
posts
tagcloud
```

MongoDB User Roles

Currently MongoDB supports the following roles that users can have within its permissions framework:

- read—Allows the user to read from the given database.

- readWrite—Grants the user read and write access to the given database.

- dbAdmin—Allows the user to perform administrative functions within the given database such as creating or removing indexes, viewing statistics or accessing the system.profile collection.

- userAdmin—Allows the user to write to the system.users collection. With this permission you can create, delete, and administer the users for this database.

- clusterAdmin—Available only within the admin database. Confers full administrative access to all sharding and replica set–related functions.

- readAnyDatabase—Available only within the admin database. Grants the read permission on all databases.

- readWriteAnyDatabase—Available only within the admin database. Grants the readWrite permission on all databases.

- userAdminAnyDatabase—Available only within the admin database. Grants the userAdmin permission on all databases.

- dbAdminAnyDatabase—Available only within the admin database. Grants the dbAdmin permission on all databases.

Delegated Credentials

As mentioned earlier, beginning with the 2.4 release of MongoDB it is possible to have one master user and then create subsequent users that use the master user's credentials for authentication, a feature called creating *delegated credentials*. Let's say we create the user test on our foo database as follows:

```
> use foo
> db.addUser(user : "test", pwd: "password", roles: ["readWrite" ])
```

Now, let's say we want to create that same test user on the bar database. We can run the following command (as a user with userAdmin permissions on that database, of course) to create our test user that will use the **foo** database's definition for its password:

```
>use bar
> db.system.users.insert{ user: "test", roles: ["read"], userSource: "foo"}
```

Notice that this user is granted only the read-only permission "read." This is because the access granted to the test user on bar are still based on this bar users credentials. We are simply sourcing the rest of the details we need (namely the password) from the foo database. By using delegated credentials, you can create a single place from which to update the username and password for all of your users.

Changing a User's Credentials

It's easy to change a user's access rights or password. You do this by executing the addUser() function again, which causes MongoDB to update the existing user record. Technically, you can use any normal data-manipulation command to change a user's record; however, only the addUser() function can create the password field.

Regardless, you can see how addUser() works by listing its contents:

```
$mongo
>use admin
> db.addUser
function () {
    if (arguments.length == 0) {
        throw Error("No arguments provided to addUser");
    }
    if (typeof arguments[0] == "object") {
        this._addUser.apply(this, arguments);
    } else {
        this._addUserV22.apply(this, arguments);
    }
}
```

addUser() is just a function defined in JavaScript. Knowing how the password is constructed is useful if you want to create a web form that allows you to add users to the database or you want to import users into the system en masse from another credential source.

Most mongo console functions can be listed in this fashion, enabling you to inspect the details of how they work.

Adding a Read-Only User

The addUser() function includes an additional parameter that allows you to create a user who has only read-only permissions. The MongoDB client will throw an exception if a process authenticated as the newly created user attempts to do anything that would result in a change to the contents of the database. The following example gives a user access to the database for status monitoring or reporting purposes:

```
$mongo
>use admin
switched to db admin
>db.addUser(user : "admin", pwd: "pass", roles: [ "read" ])
1
```

```
>use blog
switched to db blog
>db.addUser("shadycharacter","shadypassword", true)
```

Deleting a User

To remove a user from a database, simply use the normal remove() function for a collection. The following example removes the user just added; note that you have to authenticate against the admin database before you can remove the user:

```
$mongo
>use admin
switched to db admin
> db.auth("admin","pass")
1
>use blog
switched to db blog
>db.removeUser("shadycharacter")
```

Using Authenticated Connections in a PHP Application

In Chapter 4, you saw how to create a connection with PHP to a MongoDB server. Once you have enabled authentication on your server, PHP applications will also have to supply credentials before they can execute commands against the server. The following simple example shows how to open an authenticated connection to a database:

```php
<?php

// Establish the database connection
$connection = new Mongo();
$db = $connection->selectDB("admin");
$result = $db->authenticate("admin", "pass");
if(!$result['ok']){
    // Your Error handling here
    die("Authentication Error: {$result['errmsg']}");
}

// Your code here

// Close the database connection
$connection->close();

?>
```

Managing Servers

As an administrator, you must ensure the smooth and reliable running of your MongoDB servers.

You will periodically have to tune the servers to achieve maximum performance or reconfigure them to better match the environment you are operating in. To that end, you need to familiarize yourself with a number of procedures that enable you to manage and control your servers.

Starting a Server

Most modern Linux distributions now include a set of /etc/init.d scripts that are used to manage services. If you installed your MongoDB server using one of the distribution packages from the MongoDB site (see Chapter 2 for more information on these packages), the init.d scripts for managing your server will already be installed.

You can use the service command on Ubuntu, Fedora, CentOS, and RedHat to start, stop, and restart your server, as shown in the following examples:

```
$sudo service mongodb start
mongodb start/running, process 3474
$sudo service mongodb stop
mongodb stop/waiting

$sudo service mongodb restart
mongodb start/running, process 3474
```

If you don't have an initialization script available, you can start the MongoDB server manually by opening a terminal window and then typing the following:

```
$ mongod
Fri May 24 15:06:20.475 [initandlisten] MongoDB starting : pid=97163 port=27017
dbpath=/var/lib/mongodb 64-bit host=Pixl.local
Fri May 24 15:06:20.475 [initandlisten] db version v2.5.1-pre
Fri May 24 15:06:20.475 [initandlisten] git version: 704dc4fdf5248077c53271f249260478d6c56cd3
Fri May 24 15:06:20.475 [initandlisten] build info: Darwin bs-osx-106-x86-64-1.local 10.8.0
Darwin Kernel Version 10.8.0: Tue Jun  7 16:33:36 PDT 2011; root:xnu-1504.15.3~1/RELEASE_I386
i386 BOOST_LIB_VERSION=1_49
Fri May 24 15:06:20.475 [initandlisten] allocator: system
Fri May 24 15:06:20.475 [initandlisten] options: {}
Fri May 24 15:06:20.479 [initandlisten] journal dir=/data/db/journal
Fri May 24 15:06:20.479 [initandlisten] recover : no journal files present, no recovery needed
Fri May 24 15:06:20.547 [websvr] admin web console waiting for connections on port 28017
```

The server will show all connections being made, as well as other information you can use to monitor how the server is working.

To terminate the server in manual mode, just type ^C; this causes the server to shut down cleanly.

If you don't supply a configuration file, then MongoDB will start up with a default database path of /data/db and bind to all network IPs using the default ports of 27017 (mongodb) and 28017 (admin interface), as in the following example:

```
$ mkdir -p /data/db
$ mongod
mongod --help for help and startup options
...
Sun Jun 13 13:38:00 waiting for connections on port 27017
Sun Jun 13 13:38:00 web admin interface listening on port 28017
```

```
^C

Sun Jun 13 13:40:26 got kill or ctrl c signal 2 (Interrupt), will terminate after current cmd ends
...
Sun Jun 13 13:40:26  dbexit: really exiting now
```

Reconfiguring a Server

MongoDB supplies three main methods for configuring the server. First, you can use command-line options in conjunction with the mongod server daemon. Second, you can do so by loading a configuration file. And third, you can change most of these settings using the setParameter command. For example, we can change the logLevel back to the default of 0 with the following command:

> db.adminCommand({setParameter:1, logLevel:0 })

Most of the prepackaged MongoDB installers use the latter method, using a file that is normally stored in /etc/ mongodb.conf on Unix/Linux systems.

You can change the configuration of your server by editing this file and restarting your server. The contents of this file look like this:

```
# mongodb.conf
dbpath=/var/lib/mongodb
logpath=/var/log/mongodb/mongodb.log
logappend=true
auth = false
#enable the rest interface
rest =true
```

You enable an option by removing the # code from the front of the option and setting its value as you require it, as any line starting with # is considered to be a "comment" and is thus ignored.

Placing any of the following option values in the configuration file is the same as specifying

```
--<optionname> <optionvalue>
```

on the command line when starting up MongoDB:

- dbpath: Indicates where MongoDB will store your data; you should make sure it is on a fast storage volume that is large enough to support your database size.

- logpath: Indicates the file that MongoDB will store its logs in. The standard place to put this is /var/logs/mongodb/mongodb.log; you need to use logrotate to rotate this logfile and prevent it from filling up your server's drive.

- logappend: Setting this option to false causes the logfile to be cleared each time MongoDB is started up. Setting this option to true causes all log entries to be appended to the end of any existing logfile.

- auth: Enables or disables the authentication mode on MongoDB server; see the discussion earlier in this chapter for more information on authentication.

- rest: Enables or disables the rest interface to MongoDB. You must enable this interface if you want to use the links from the web-based status display to show additional information, but this is not advised for production servers, as all of this information should be available via the Mongo shell.

Getting the Server's Version

You can use the db.version() function to get the build and version information for a server. This information is useful for determining whether upgrades are required or when reporting an issue to a support forum. The following snippet shows how to use this command:

```
$mongo
> use admin
switched to db admin
> db.version()
version: 2.5.1-pre-
```

Getting the Server's Status

MongoDB provides a simple method for determining the status of a server.

■ **Note** Remember that your user will need permissions to run these commands if you are using auth.

The following example shows the information returned, including such things as server uptime, the maximum number of connections, and so on:

```
$mongo
> db.serverStatus()
{
    "host" : "Pixl.local",
    "version" : "2.5.1-pre-",
    "process" : "mongod",
    "pid" : 3737,
    "uptime" : 44,
    "uptimeMillis" : NumberLong(43035),
    "uptimeEstimate" : 39,
    "localTime" : ISODate("2013-05-25T12:38:34.015Z"),
    "asserts" : {
        "regular" : 0,
        "warning" : 0,
        "msg" : 0,
        "user" : 1,
        "rollovers" : 0
    },
    "connections" : {
        "current" : 1,
        "available" : 2047,
        "totalCreated" : NumberLong(1)
    },
    "cursors" : {
        "totalOpen" : 0,
        "clientCursors_size" : 0,
        "timedOut" : 0
    },
```

```
        "globalLock" : {
            "totalTime" : NumberLong(43035000),
            "lockTime" : NumberLong(48184),
            "currentQueue" : {
                "total" : 0,
                "readers" : 0,
                "writers" : 0
            },
        },
        "locks" : {
            "admin" : {
                "timeLockedMicros" : {
                    "r" : NumberLong(54),
                    "w" : NumberLong(0)
                },
                "timeAcquiringMicros" : {
                    "r" : NumberLong(2190),
                    "w" : NumberLong(0)
                }
            },
            "local" : {
                "timeLockedMicros" : {
                    "r" : NumberLong(45),
                    "w" : NumberLong(6)
                },
                "timeAcquiringMicros" : {
                    "r" : NumberLong(7),
                    "w" : NumberLong(1)
                }
            },
            ...
        },
        "network" : {
            "bytesIn" : 437,
            "bytesOut" : 6850,
            "numRequests" : 7
        },
        "opcounters" : {
            "insert" : 1,
            "query" : 6,
            "update" : 0,
            "delete" : 0,
            "getmore" : 0,
            "command" : 7
        },
    ...
        "mem" : {
            "bits" : 64,
            "resident" : 37,
            "virtual" : 3109,
            "supported" : true,
```

```
            "mapped" : 320,
            "mappedWithJournal" : 640
      },
            "ttl" : {
                "deletedDocuments" : NumberLong(0),
                "passes" : NumberLong(0)
            }
      },
      "ok" : 1
}
```

As you can see, serverStatus outputs quite a lot of detail and the above is the truncated! You can find the two most important sections of the information returned by this function in the opcounters and asserts sections.

The opcounters section shows the number of operations of each type that have been performed against the database server. You should have a good idea about what constitutes a normal balance for these counters for your particular application. If these counters start to move out of the normal ratio, then it may be an early warning that your application has a problem.

For example, the profile illustrated has an extremely high ratio of inserts to reads. This could be normal for a logging application; however, for a blogging application, it could indicate that either a spambot was hitting your "comments" section or a URL pattern that caused writes to the database was being repeatedly crawled by a search engine spider. In this case, it would be time to either put a captcha on your comments form or to block the particular URL pattern in your robots.tx file.

The asserts section shows the number of server and client exceptions or warnings that have been thrown. If such exceptions or warnings start to rise rapidly, then it's time to take a good look through your server's logfiles to see whether a problem is developing. A high number of asserts may also indicate a problem with the data in the database, and you should review your MongoDB instance's logfile to confirm the nature of these asserts and if they indicate normal "user asserts," which represent things like duplicate key violations, or more pressing issues.

Shutting Down a Server

If you have installed your MongoDB server from a package, you can use the operating system's service management scripts to shut down the server. For example, Ubuntu, Fedora, CentOS, and RedHat let you shut down the server by issuing the following command:

$sudo service mongod stop

You can also shut down the server from the mongo console:

$mongo
>use admin
>db.shutdownServer()

You can use the Posix process management commands to terminate a server, or you can use the SIG_TERM(-15) or SIG_INT(-2) signal to shut down the server.

If—and only if—the server fails to respond to those two methods, you can use the following command:

$sudo killall -15 mongod

■ **Warning**   You must *not* use the SIG_KILL(-9) signal to terminate a server, because this could result in a corrupted database, and you will probably have to repair the server.

It might be that you have a particularly active server with a lot of write activity, and you have reconfigured the server so it has a large sync delay. If that's the case, then the server may not respond immediately to a termination request, because it is writing out all the in-memory changes to the disk. A little patience goes a long way here.

Using MongoDB Logfiles

By default, MongoDB writes its entire log output to stdout; however, you can use the logpath option described previously to redirect the log output to a file instead.

You can use the contents of the logfile to spot problems such as excessive connections from individual machines and other error messages that may indicate problems with your application logic or data.

Validating and Repairing Your Data

It is possible that your data will be left in a damaged or incomplete state if your server unexpectedly reboots or your MongoDB server crashes for any reason.

Here are some indications that your data has been compromised:

- Your database server refuses to start, stating that the datafiles are corrupted.

- You start seeing *asserts* in your server log files or a high assert count when using the db. serverStatus() command.

- You get strange or unexpected results from queries.

- The record counts on collections don't match up with your expectations.

Any of these signs may indicate problems with your application or, more worryingly, corruption or inconsistency in your data.

Fortunately, MongoDB ships with tools to assist you in repairing or recovering your database server. Nevertheless, you might still suffer the loss of some data, so please remember the golden rule of making sure you have either a good backup of your data or a replication slave.

Repairing a Server

Before you initiate the server repair process, you must be aware that running the repair command is a costly operation that can take significant time, and it requires up to twice the space taken by your MongoDB data files as all your data is cloned out to new files and fully re-created, this is effectively a rebuild of all your datafiles. This is one of the best arguments for using replica sets: you don't have to fully stop your replica set from servicing your clients if you have to take one machine offline to repair it.

To initiate the repair process, just use the manual server startup process (as described previously in this chapter). However, this time you need to add the --repair option to the end of the command, as in the following example:

```
$ mongod --dbpath /data/db --repair
Wed Sep 18 21:21:21.364 [initandlisten] MongoDB starting : pid=5973 port=27017 dbpath=/data/db
64-bit host=Pixl.local
Wed Sep 18 21:21:21.364 [initandlisten]
```

```
Wed Sep 18 21:21:21.364 [initandlisten] ** WARNING: soft rlimits too low. Number of files is 256,
should be at least 1000
Wed Sep 18 21:21:21.364 [initandlisten] db version 2.5.1-pre-
Wed Sep 18 21:21:21.364 [initandlisten] git version: 704dc4fdf5248077c53271f249260478d6c56cd3
Wed Sep 18 21:21:21.364 [initandlisten] build info: Darwin bs-osx-106-x86-64-2.10gen.cc 10.8.0
Darwin Kernel Version 10.8.0: Tue Jun  7 16:32:41 PDT 2011; root:xnu-1504.15.3~1/RELEASE_X86_64
x86_64 BOOST_LIB_VERSION=1_49
Wed Sep 18 21:21:21.364 [initandlisten] allocator: system
Wed Sep 18 21:21:21.364 [initandlisten] options: { dbpath: "/data/db", repair: true }
Wed Sep 18 21:21:21.367 [initandlisten] build index test.system.users { user: 1, userSource: 1 }
Wed Sep 18 21:21:21.368 [initandlisten] build index done.  scanned 1 total records. 0.001 secs
Wed Sep 18 21:21:21.368 [initandlisten] ****
Wed Sep 18 21:21:21.368 [initandlisten] ****
Wed Sep 18 21:21:21.368 [initandlisten] need to upgrade database test with pdfile version 4.5,
new version: 4.5
Wed Sep 18 21:21:21.368 [initandlisten]         starting upgrade
Wed Sep 18 21:21:21.368 [initandlisten]   test repairDatabase test
Wed Sep 18 21:21:21.369 [FileAllocator] allocating new datafile /data/db/_tmp_repairDatabase_0/test.
ns, filling with zeroes...
Wed Sep 18 21:21:21.369 [FileAllocator] creating directory /data/db/_tmp_repairDatabase_0/_tmp
Wed Sep 18 21:21:21.389 [FileAllocator] done allocating datafile /data/db/_tmp_repairDatabase_0/
test.ns, size: 16MB,  took 0.02 secs
Wed Sep 18 21:21:21.389 [FileAllocator] allocating new datafile /data/db/_tmp_repairDatabase_0/
test.0, filling with zeroes...
Wed Sep 18 21:21:21.583 [FileAllocator] done allocating datafile /data/db/_tmp_repairDatabase_0/
test.0, size: 64MB,  took 0.193 secs
Wed Sep 18 21:21:21.583 [FileAllocator] allocating new datafile /data/db/_tmp_repairDatabase_0/
test.1, filling with zeroes...
Wed Sep 18 21:21:21.586 [initandlisten] build index test.foo { _id: 1 }
Wed Sep 18 21:21:21.661 [initandlisten]         fastBuildIndex dupsToDrop:0
Wed Sep 18 21:21:21.661 [initandlisten] build index done.  scanned 1 total records. 0.074 secs
Wed Sep 18 21:21:21.661 [initandlisten] build index test.system.users { user: 1, userSource: 1 }
Wed Sep 18 21:21:21.662 [initandlisten]         fastBuildIndex dupsToDrop:0
Wed Sep 18 21:21:21.662 [initandlisten] build index done.  scanned 0 total records. 0 secs
Wed Sep 18 21:21:21.662 [initandlisten] build index test.system.users { _id: 1 }
Wed Sep 18 21:21:21.663 [initandlisten]         fastBuildIndex dupsToDrop:0
Wed Sep 18 21:21:21.663 [initandlisten] build index done.  scanned 1 total records. 0 secs
Wed Sep 18 21:21:22.002 [FileAllocator] done allocating datafile /data/db/_tmp_repairDatabase_0/
test.1, size: 128MB,  took 0.418 secs
Wed Sep 18 21:21:22.018 [initandlisten] finished checking dbs
Wed Sep 18 21:21:22.018 dbexit:
Wed Sep 18 21:21:22.018 [initandlisten] shutdown: going to close listening sockets...
Wed Sep 18 21:21:22.018 [initandlisten] shutdown: going to flush diaglog...
Wed Sep 18 21:21:22.018 [initandlisten] shutdown: going to close sockets...
Wed Sep 18 21:21:22.018 [initandlisten] shutdown: waiting for fs preallocator...
Wed Sep 18 21:21:22.018 [initandlisten] shutdown: closing all files...
Wed Sep 18 21:21:22.018 [initandlisten] closeAllFiles() finished
Wed Sep 18 21:21:22.018 [initandlisten] shutdown: removing fs lock...
Wed Sep 18 21:21:22.018 dbexit: really exiting now
```

In this example, `repair` detected that the `admin` database was probably created under an older version of MongoDB and that it required an upgrade of its storage format to match the currently running server.

■ **Note** It is normal for the server to exit after running the `mongod` utility with the `--repair` option; to bring it back online, just start it up again without specifying the `--repair` option.

Once the repair process finishes, you should be able to start up the server as usual, and then restore any missing data from your backups.

If you're trying to repair a large database, you may find that your drive runs out of disk space because MongoDB may need to make a temporary copy of the database files on the same drive as the data (see the `.../$tmp_repairDatabase_0/..` directory in the preceding example).

To overcome this potential issue, the MongoDB repair utility supports an additional command-line parameter called `--repairpath`. You can use this parameter to specify a drive with enough space to hold the temporary files it creates during the rebuild process, as in the following example:

```
$ mongod -f /etc/mongodb.conf --repair --repairpath /mnt/bigdrive/tempdir
```

Validating a Single Collection

Occasionally, you may suspect there is a problem with the data on a running server. In this case, you can use a handful of tools that ship with MongoDB to help you determine whether the server in question is corrupted or damaged.

You can use the `validate` option to validate the contents of a collection in a database. The next example shows how to run the `validate` option against a collection with one million records in it:

```
$mongo
> use blog
switched to db blog
>db.posts.ensureIndex({Author:1})
> db.posts.validate()
{
    "ns" : "blog.posts",
    "firstExtent" : "0:f000 ns:blog.posts",
    "lastExtent" : "0:2b9000 ns:blog.posts",
    "extentCount" : 6,
    "datasize" : 6717520,
    "nrecords" : 29997,
    "lastExtentSize" : 8388608,
    "padding" : 1,
    "firstExtentDetails" : {
        "loc" : "0:f000",
        "xnext" : "0:11000",
        "xprev" : "null",
        "nsdiag" : "blog.posts",
        "size" : 8192,
        "firstRecord" : "0:f0b0",
        "lastRecord" : "0:10e50"
    },
```

```
    "lastExtentDetails" : {
        "loc" : "0:2b9000",
        "xnext" : "null",
        "xprev" : "0:b9000",
        "nsdiag" : "blog.posts",
        "size" : 8388608,
        "firstRecord" : "0:2b90b0",
        "lastRecord" : "0:6ec830"
    },
    "deletedCount" : 4,
    "deletedSize" : 3983552,
    "nIndexes" : 2,
    "keysPerIndex" : {
        "blog.posts.$_id_" : 29997,
        "blog.posts.$Author_1" : 29997
    },
    "valid" : true,
    "errors" : [ ],
    "warning" : "Some checks omitted for speed. use {full:true} option to do more thorough scan.",
    "ok" : 1
}
```

The preceding example takes about 30 seconds to complete. By default, the validate option checks both the datafiles and the indexes, and it provides some statistics about the collection when it completes. The option will tell you if there are any problems with either the datafiles or the indexes, but it will not examine every document for correctness. If examining every document is what you want, then you can run (as suggested in the output) validate with the {full: true} option, which is invoked by adding the true argument to the function call, as shown here: db.posts.validate(true).

You can also use the validate option if you have a very large database and you want only to validate the indexes. There is no shell helper command for this in the current version (2.6.0). But that isn't an impediment, as you can readily accomplish this index validation using the runCommand option:

```
$mongo
>use blog
>db.runCommand({validate:"posts", scandata:false})
```

In this case, the server does not scan the datafiles; instead, it merely reports the information stored about the collection.

Repairing Collection Validation Faults

If running validation on your collections turns up an error, which would be noted in the errors section of the validate document, you have several options for repairing the data. Again, it's impossible to overstress the importance of having good backups. Before jumping straight into restoring your backup, you should look into the MongoDB instance's logs to see if there is any additional information about the nature of the error; if so, this should inform the next steps you take.

Repairing a Collection's Indexes

If the validation process shows that the indexes are damaged, use the reIndex() function to reindex the affected collection. In the example that follows, you use the reIndex() function to reindex the blog's posts collection to which you added the author index previously:

```
$mongo
>use blog
> db.posts.reIndex()
{
    "nIndexesWas" : 2,
    "msg" : "indexes dropped for collection",
    "nIndexes" : 2,
    "indexes" : [
        {
            "key" : {
                "_id" : 1
            },
            "ns" : "blog.posts",
            "name" : "_id_"
        },
        {
            "key" : {
                "Author" : 1
            },
            "ns" : "blog.posts",
            "name" : "Author_1"
        }
    ],
    "ok" : 1
}
```

The MongoDB server will drop all the current indexes on the collection and rebuild them; however, if you use the database repair option, it will also run the reIndex() function on all the collections in the database.

Repairing a Collection's Datafiles

The best—and most dangerous—way to repair all of the datafiles in a database is to use either the server's --repair option or the db.repairDatabase() command in the shell. The latter repairs all the collection files in an individual database, and then reindexes all of the defined indexes. However, repairDatabase() is not a suitable function to run on a live server, because it will block any requests to the data while the datafiles are being rebuilt. This results in blocking all reads and writes while the database repair completes. The following snippet shows the syntax for using the repairDatabase() function:

```
$mongo
>use blog
>db.repairDatabase()
{ "ok" : 1 }
```

> ■ **Warning** MongoDB's repair is a brute-force option. It attempts to repair and rebuild your data structures and indexes. It does this by attempting to read and then rebuild the entire data structure from disk. If possible, you should attempt to recover from backup; `repairDatabase()` should only be used as a last resort.

Compacting a Collection's Datafiles

Because of the way MongoDB allocates datafiles internally, you can run into what's colloquially known as "Swiss cheese," meaning that small empty sections of data storage space are left in the on-disk data structure. This can be a problem as it means there are large sections of your datafiles being unused. While a repair to rebuild your entire data structure may help, there can be other unintended consequences. The `compact` command will defragment and restructure the data structure for a given collection within the existing datafiles, but it will not recover disk space.

```
$mongo
>use blog
>db.runCommand({compact:"posts"})
{ "ok" : 1 }
```

Upgrading MongoDB

Occasionally, new versions of MongoDB require you to upgrade the format of the database files. The team at MongoDB, Inc. are aware of the impact (including the resulting downtime) caused by running an upgrade on a running production service; however, there are times when the need to support heavily demanded new features requires that an upgrade take place.

> ■ **Warning** It is *essential* that you make a complete backup of your data before attempting any upgrade process. In addition to this, you should *always* review the release notes, which are available at
> `http://docs.mongodb.org/manual/release-notes/`.

MongoDB's developers try to anticipate every possible problem that will present itself during an upgrade; nevertheless, you must take steps to protect yourself as well. Upgrades will typically rewrite every piece of data in your system in a new format, which means that even the slightest problem with the process can have disastrous consequences.

The following list walks you through the proper steps required to upgrade a database server:

1. Back up your data and make sure that the backup is viable. If possible, restore the backup to another server and verify that it's OK.

2. Stop your application or divert it to another server.

3. Stop your MongoDB server.

4. Upgrade the code of your MongoDB server to the desired version.

5. Use the shell to perform initial sanity checks on the data.

6. If anything looks suspicious, use the validation tools to check the data.

7. Re-enable your application when you are satisfied that everything looks OK.

8. Test your application carefully before reopening the service or diverting traffic back to this server.

Rolling Upgrade of MongoDB

One of the great features of having a replica set is that it can be used to perform a rolling upgrade. This is a method designed to minimize the potential downtime and impacts involved with large changes like this. In addition to following the process outlined below you should always take a backup and be testing in your non-production environment. Once you have performed due diligence to ensure that your system is recoverable, you can follow this process:

1. Stop and perform an upgrade for each secondary one at a time.

2. Run the rs.stepDown() command on the primary. One of the upgraded secondaries will step into place as primary.

3. Upgrade the primary.

Monitoring MongoDB

The MongoDB distribution contains a simple status-monitoring tool called mongostat. This tool is designed mainly to provide a simple overview of what is happening on your server (see Figure 9-5).

```
$mongostat
connected to: 127.0.0.1
insert query update delete getmore command flushes mapped vsize   res faults  locked db  idx miss %  qr|qw  ar|aw  netIn netOut  conn     time
   *0   *0    *0    *0      0     110      0  320m 3.04g   37m      0 local:0.0%          0    0|0    0|0   62b    3k     1  17:34:34
   *0   *0    *0    *0      0     110      0  320m 3.04g   37m      0 local:0.0%          0    0|0    0|0   62b    3k     1  17:34:35
   *0   *0    *0    *0      0     110      0  320m 3.04g   37m      0 local:0.0%          0    0|0    0|0   62b    3k     1  17:34:36
   *0   *0    *0    *0      0     110      0  320m 3.04g   37m      0 local:0.0%          0    0|0    0|0   62b    3k     1  17:34:37
   *0   *0    *0    *0      0     110      0  320m 3.04g   37m      0 local:0.0%          0    0|0    0|0   62b    3k     1  17:34:38
   *0   *0    *0    *0      0     110      0  320m 3.04g   37m      0 local:0.0%          0    0|0    0|0   62b    3k     1  17:34:39
   *0   *0    *0    *0      0     110      0  320m 3.04g   37m      0 local:0.0%          0    0|0    0|0   62b    3k     1  17:34:40
   *0   *0    *0    *0      0     110      0  320m 3.04g   37m      0 local:0.0%          0    0|0    0|0   62b    3k     1  17:34:41
   *0   *0    *0    *0      0     110      0  320m 3.04g   37m      0 local:0.0%          0    0|0    0|0   62b    3k     1  17:34:42
   *0   *0    *0    *0      0     110      0  320m 3.04g   37m      0      .:0.0%          0    0|0    0|0   62b    3k     1  17:34:43
insert query update delete getmore command flushes mapped vsize   res faults  locked db  idx miss %  qr|qw  ar|aw  netIn netOut  conn     time
   *0   *0    *0    *0      0     110      0  320m 3.04g   37m      0 local:0.0%          0    0|0    0|0   62b    3k     1  17:34:44
   *0   *0    *0    *0      0     110      0  320m 3.04g   37m      0 local:0.0%          0    0|0    0|0   62b    3k     1  17:34:45
   *0   *0    *0    *0      0     110      0  320m 3.04g   37m      0 local:0.0%          0    0|0    0|0   62b    3k     1  17:34:46
   *0   *0    *0    *0      0     110      0  320m 3.04g   37m      0 local:0.0%          0    0|0    0|0   62b    3k     1  17:34:47
   *0   *0    *0    *0      0     110      0  320m 3.04g   37m      0 local:0.0%          0    0|0    0|0   62b    3k     1  17:34:48
   *0   *0    *0    *0      0     110      0  320m 3.04g   37m      0 local:0.0%          0    0|0    0|0   62b    3k     1  17:34:49
   *0   *0    *0    *0      0     110      0  320m 3.04g   37m      0 local:0.0%          0    0|0    0|0   62b    3k     1  17:34:50
   *0   *0    *0    *0      0     110      0  320m 3.04g   37m      0 local:0.0%          0    0|0    0|0   62b    3k     1  17:34:51
   *0   *0    *0    *0      0     110      0  320m 3.04g   37m      0 local:0.0%          0    0|0    0|0   62b    3k     1  17:34:52
```

***Figure 9-5.** Monitoring the status of MongoDB with the mongostat utility*

The statistics produced by this tool are not extensive, but they do provide a good overview of what is going on in your MongoDB installation. For example, this display lets you see how frequently database operations are being performed, the rate at which the index is hit, and how much time your application spends blocked as it waits for locks on the database to be released.

The main columns of interest are the first six columns, which show the rate at which the mongod server is handling certain operations (for example, insert or query). Other columns worth keeping an eye on when diagnosing problems with your installation include the following:

- Pagefaults: Represents when your MongoDB instance needs to read data from disk in order to fulfill queries. This is normally an indicator of suboptimal performance and that all the data you normally need for your day-to-day operations can't be held within the RAM available to MongoDB. You should check to see if there are any queries that may be scanning all your documents and not using indexes, or you may need to move to a server with more available RAM.

- queues: Represents the number of operations queued up waiting for their turn to execute. As MongoDB allows one writer (inserts, updates and deletes) and many readers (finds), this can lead to a situation where read queries are being blocked by poorly performing writes. Worse still, you can wind up in situations where you have a number of reads and writes blocked by one poorly performing write. Check to see which queries may be blocking the others from executing.

- % locked: Shows the percentage of time a given collection had its write lock taken out. A very high number here indicates that you are performing one or more write operations running for nearly the whole time window. A high % locked will likely impact the performance of all queries. Check to see if you have poorly performing writes or if your system is page-faulting, which may indicate the need for more RAM. This could also be related to schema issues such as very large arrays in documents, and remember that prior to MongoDB 2.2 locking was done at the per-instance level, so upgrading may help lower this value with the more recent concurrency improvements.

ROLLING YOUR OWN STAT MONITORING TOOL

Much of the information provided by mongostat is the same information that you can get from the db.serverStatus() call. It would not be a big task to create a service that uses this API to poll the server every few seconds and then places the results into a MongoDB collection.

The application of a few indexes, some carefully crafted queries, and a graphing package would enable you to use such a simple real-time monitor to produce historical logs.

There are also many third-party adapters available for MongoDB that let you use common open source or commercial monitoring systems, including tools such as Nagios, Ganglia, and Cacti. As mentioned previously, the MongoDB manual includes a page on its website that shares the latest information about monitoring interfaces available for MongoDB (for more information on this topic, see http://docs.mongodb.org/manual/administration/monitoring/).

Using the MongoDB Management Service (MMS)

Most of the statistical information discussed so far is also available via the MongoDB Management Service, also known as MMS. MMS is a monitoring service provided by MongoDB, Inc. It provides an agent you can install on a local machine. Once it is installed, you can add your servers via the MMS web page in order to instruct the agent to monitor them. Once monitoring has begun, you can then dive into specific hosts to see graphs of the performance statistics for that MongoDB instance. You can monitor everything from individual MongoDB instances to replica sets, right up to full sharded clusters, including config servers and MongoS. MMS also has facilities to view all the individual members of these groups or to view aggregated statistics for each. You can then configure alerts to be sent to you based on your particular performance requirements or if events occur within your MongoDB instances. You can sign up for MMS at mms.mongodb.com, and we highly recommend you do so. There is nothing more powerful than being able to dive into exactly how each of your MongoDB nodes is performing (see Figure 9-6 for an example).

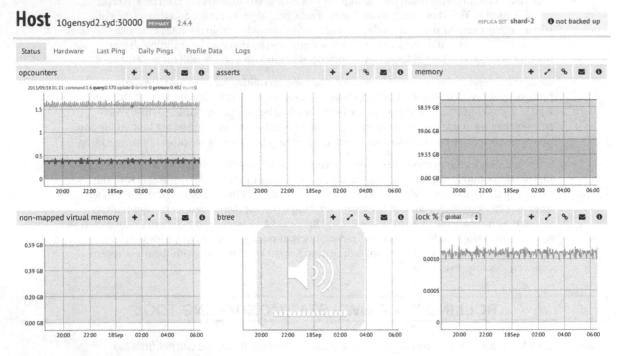

Figure 9-6. *Viewing statistics via MMS*

Summary

Keeping your MongoDB installation running smoothly typically requires very little effort. In this chapter, you have seen how you can use the tools provided with the MongoDB distribution to manage and maintain your system, as well as to stay on top of any problems that may develop.

By working through this chapter you should now have the skills to backup, restore, upgrade and monitor your MongoDB instance. You should be familiar with tools such as mongodump and mongorestore, know how to import and export data from only certain collections and be familiar with a number of administrative commands that you can use to derivce performance and usage statistics from your MongoDB instance.

Lastly, it must be stressed (and you've probably grasped that from everything that has been said) that the most important lesson to take away from this chapter is this: as the administrator of a database system, your first responsibility is to ensure that a reliable backup and restoration scheme for your data is available.

CHAPTER 10

■ ■ ■

Optimization

There is a tongue-in-cheek statement attributed to an unknown Twitter user: "If a MongoDB query runs for longer than 0ms, then something is wrong." This is typical of the kind of buzz that surrounded the product when it first burst onto the scene in 2009.

The reality is that MongoDB is extraordinarily fast. But if you give it the wrong data structures, or you don't set up collections with the right indexes, MongoDB can slow down dramatically, like any data storage system.

MongoDB also contains advanced features, which require some tuning to get them running with optimal efficiency.

The design of your data schemas can also have a big impact on performance; in this chapter, we will look at some techniques to shape your data into a form that makes maximum use of MongoDB's strengths and minimizes its weaknesses.

Before we look at improving the performance of the queries being run on the server or the ways of optimizing the structure of the data, we'll begin with a look at how MongoDB interacts with the hardware it runs on and the factors that affect performance. We then look at indexes and how they can be used to improve the performance of your queries and how to profile your MongoDB instance to determine which, if any, of your queries are not performing well.

Optimizing Your Server Hardware for Performance

Often the quickest and cheapest optimization you can make to a database server is to right-size the hardware it runs on. If a database server has too little memory or uses slow drives, it can impact database performance significantly. And while some of these constraints may be acceptable for a development environment, where the server may be running on a developer's local workstation, they may not be acceptable for production applications, where care must be used in calculating the correct hardware configuration to achieve the best performance.

Understanding How MongoDB Uses Memory

MongoDB uses memory-mapped file I/O to access its underlying data storage. This method of file I/O has some characteristics that you should be aware of, because they can affect both the type of operating system (OS) you run it under and the amount of memory you install.

The first notable characteristic of memory-mapped files is that, on modern 64-bit operating systems, the maximum file size that can be managed is around of 128TB on Linux (the Linux virtual memory address limit) or 8TB (4TB with Journaling enabled) on Windows because of its limitation for memory-mapped files. On 32-bit operating systems, you are limited to only 2GB worth of data, so it is not recommended that you use a 32-bit OS unless running a small development environment.

The second notable characteristic is that memory-mapped files use the operating system's virtual memory system to map the required parts of the database files into RAM as needed. This can result in the slightly alarming impression that MongoDB is using up all your system's RAM. That is not really the case, because MongoDB will share the virtual address space with other applications. And the OS will release memory to the other processes as it is needed. Using the free memory total as an indicator of excessive memory consumption is not a good practice, because a good OS will ensure that there is little or no "free" memory. All of your expensive memory is pressed into good use through caching or buffering disk I/O. Free memory is wasted memory.

By providing a suitable amount of memory, MongoDB can keep more of the data it needs mapped into memory, which reduces the need for expensive disk I/O.

In general, the more memory you give to MongoDB, the faster it will run. However, if you have a 2GB database, then adding more than 2–3GB of memory will not make much difference, because the whole database will sit in RAM anyway.

Understanding Working Set Size

Now we need to talk about one of the more complex things involved with performance tuning your MongoDB instance, working-set size. This size represents the amount of data stored in your MongoDB instance that will be accessed "in the course of regular usage." That phrase alone should tell you that this is a subjective measure and something that is hard to get an exact value for.

Despite being hard to quantify, understanding the impact of working set size will help you better optimize your MongoDB instance. The main precept is that for most installations, only a portion of the data will need to be accessed as part of regular operations. Understanding what portion of your data you will be working with regularly allows you to size your hardware correctly and thus improves your performance.

Choosing the Right Database Server Hardware

There is a general pressure to move to lower-power (energy) systems for hosting services. However, many of the lower-power servers use laptop or notebook components to achieve the lower power consumption. Unfortunately, lower-quality server hardware can use less expensive disk drives in particular. Such drives are not suited for heavy-duty server applications because of their disks' low rotation speed, which slows the rate at which data can be transferred to and from the drive. Also, make sure you use a reputable supplier, one you trust to assemble a system that has been optimized for server operation. It's also worth mentioning that faster and more modern drives such as SSDs are available, which will provide a significant performance boost. If you can arrange it, the MongoDB, Inc. team recommends the use of RAID10 for both performance and redundancy. For those of you in the cloud, getting things like Provisioned IOPS from Amazon is a great way to improve the performance and reliability of your disks.

If you plan to use replication or any kind of frequent backup system that would have to read across the network connections, you should consider putting in an extra network card and forming a separate network so the servers can talk with each other. This reduces the amount of data being transmitted and received on the network interface used to connect the application to the server, which also affects an application's performance.

Probably the biggest thing to be aware of when purchasing hardware is RAM. Because MongoDB uses memory-mapped files, having sufficient space to keep necessary data somewhere that it can be accessed quickly is a great way to ensure high performance. This is where you can link in the working-set concept discussed earlier. Having an idea of how much data you need to allocate for is the key when looking to purchase hardware. Finally, remember that you don't need to go out and buy 512GB of RAM and install it on one server; you can spread the data load out using sharding (discussed in Chapter 12).

Evaluating Query Performance

MongoDB has two main tools for optimizing query performance: explain() and the MongoDB Profiler (the profiler). The profiler is a good tool for finding those queries that are not performing well and selecting candidate queries for further inspection, while explain() is good for investigating a single query, so you can determine how well it is performing.

Those of you familiar with MySQL will probably also be familiar with the use of the slow query log, which helps you find queries that are consuming a lot of time; MongoDB uses the profiler to provide this capability.

The MongoDB Profiler

The MongoDB profiler is a tool that records statistical information and execution plan details for every query that meets the trigger criteria. You can enable this tool separately on each database or for all databases by using the --profile and --slowms options to start your MongoD process (more on what these values mean shortly). These options can also be added to your mongodb.conf file, if that is how you are starting your MongoD process.

Once the profiler is enabled, MongoDB inserts a document with information about the performance and execution details of each query submitted by your application into a special *capped* collection called system.profile. You can use this collection to inspect the details of each query logged using standard collection querying commands.

The system.profile collection is limited to a maximum of 1024KB of data, so that the profiler will not fill the disk with logging information. This limit should be enough to capture a few thousand profiles of even the most complex queries.

■ **Warning** When the profiler is enabled, it will impact the performance of your server, so it is not a good idea to leave it running on a production server unless you are performing an analysis for some observed issue. Don't be tempted to leave it running permanently to provide a window on recently executed queries.

Enabling and Disabling the DB Profiler

It's a simple matter to turn on the MongoDB profiler:

```
$mongo
>use blog
>db.setProfilingLevel(1)
```

It is an equally simple matter to disable the profiler:

```
$mongo
>use blog
>db.setProfilingLevel(0)
```

MongoDB can also enable the profiler only for queries that exceed a specified execution time. The following example logs only queries that take more than half a second to execute:

```
$mongo
>use blog
>db.setProfilingLevel(1,500)
```

As shown here, for profiling level 1, you can supply a maximum query execution time value in milliseconds (ms). If the query runs for longer than this amount of time, it is profiled and logged; otherwise, it is ignored. This provides the same functionality seen in MySQL's slow query log.

Finally, you can enable profiling for all queries by setting the profiler level to 2.

```
$mongo
>use blog
>db.setProfilingLevel(2)
```

Finding Slow Queries

A typical record in the system.profile collection looks like this:

```
> db.system.profile.find()
{
    "op" : "query",
    "ns" : "blog.system.profile",
    "query" : {

    },
    "ntoreturn" : 0,
    "ntoskip" : 0,
    "nscanned" : 1,
    "keyUpdates" : 0,
    "numYield" : 0,
    "lockStats" : {
        "timeLockedMicros" : {
            "r" : NumberLong(60),
            "w" : NumberLong(0)
        },
        "timeAcquiringMicros" : {
            "r" : NumberLong(4),
            "w" : NumberLong(3)
        }
    },
    "nreturned" : 1,
    "responseLength" : 370,
    "millis" : 12,
    "ts" : ISODate("2013-05-18T05:40:27.106Z"),
    "client" : "127.0.0.1",
    "user" : ""
}
```

Each record contains fields, and the following list outlines what they are and what they do:

- op: Displays the type of operation; it can be either query, insert, update, command, or delete.

- query: The query being run.

- ns: The full namespace this query was run against.

- ntoreturn: The number of documents to return,

- nscanned: The number of index entries scanned to return this document.

- ntoskip: The number of documents skipped.

- keyUpdates: The number of index keys updated by this query.

- numYields: The number of times this query yielded its lock to another query.

- lockStats: The number of microseconds spent acquiring or in the read and write locks for this database.

- nreturned: The number of documents returned.

- responseLength: The length in bytes of the response.

- millis: The number of milliseconds it took to execute the query.

- ts: Displays a timestamp in UTC that indicates when the query was executed.

- client: The connection details of the client who ran this query.

- user: The user who ran this operation.

Because the system.profile collection is just a normal collection, you can use MongoDB's query tools to home in quickly on problematic queries.

The next example finds all the queries that are taking longer than 10ms to execute. In this case, you can just query for cases where millis >10 in the system.profile collection, and then sort the results by the execution time in descending order:

```
> db.system.profile.find({millis:{$gt:10}}).sort({millis:-1})
{ "op" : "query", "ns" : "blog.system.profile", "query" : { }, "ntoreturn" : 0, "ntoskip" : 0,
"nscanned" : 1, "keyUpdates" : 0, "numYield" : 0, "lockStats" : { "timeLockedMicros" : { "r"
: NumberLong(60), "w" : NumberLong(0) }, "timeAcquiringMicros" : { "r" : NumberLong(4), "w" :
NumberLong(3) } }, "nreturned" : 1, "responseLength" : 370, "millis" : 12, "ts" : ISODate("2013-05-
18T05:40:27.106Z"), "client" : "127.0.0.1", "allUsers" : [ ], "user" : "" }
```

If you also know your problem occurred during a specific time range, then you can use the ts field to add query terms that restrict the range to the required slice.

Increase the Size of Your Profile Collection

If you find that for whatever reason your profile collection is just too small, you can increase its size.

First you need to disable profiling on the database whose profile collection size you wish to increase, to ensure that nothing writes to it while you are doing this operation:

```
$mongo
>use blog
>db.setProfilingLevel(0)
```

Next you need to delete the existing system.profile collection:

```
>db.system.profile.drop()
```

With the collection dropped, you can now create your new profiler collection with the createCollection command and specifying the desired size in bytes. The following example creates a collection capped at 50MB. It uses notation that converts 50 bytes into kilobytes and then into megabytes by multiplying it by 1024 for each increase in scale:

```
>db.createCollection( "system.profile", { capped: true, size: 50 * 1024 * 1024 } )
{ "ok" : 1 }
```

With your new larger capped collection in place, you can now re-enable profiling:

```
>db.setProfilingLevel(2)
```

Analyzing a Specific Query with explain()

If you suspect a query is not performing as well as expected, you can use the explain() modifier to see exactly how MongoDB is executing the query.

When you add the explain() modifier to a query, on execution MongoDB returns a document that describes how the query was handled, rather than a cursor to the results. The following query runs against a database of blog posts and indicates that the query had to scan 13,325 records to form a cursor to return all the posts:

```
$mongo
>use blog
> db.posts.find().explain()
{
    "cursor" : "BasicCursor",
    "isMultiKey" : false,
     "n" : 13235,
     "nscannedObjects" : 13235,
     "nscanned" : 13235,
     "nscannedObjectsAllPlans" : 13235,
     "nscannedAllPlans" : 13235,
     "scanAndOrder" : false,
     "indexOnly" : false,
     "nYields" : 0,
     "nChunkSkips" : 0,
     "millis" : 0,
     "indexBounds" : {

     },
     "server" : "Pixl.local:27017"
}
```

You can see the fields returned by explain() listed in Table 10-1.

Table 10-1. *Elements Returned by explain()*

Element	Description
Cursor	Indicates the type of cursor created to enumerate the results. Typically, this is one of the following: BasicCursor, a natural-order reading cursor; a BtreeCursor, which is an index cursor; or a GeoSearchCursor, which is a query using a geospatial index.
indexBounds	Indicates the min/max values used on an indexed lookup.
nScanned	Indicates the number of index entries scanned to find all the objects in the query.
nScannedObjects	Indicates the number of actual objects that were scanned, rather than just their index entries.
n	Indicates the number of items on the cursor (that is, the number of items to be returned).
millis	Indicates the number of milliseconds it took to execute the query.
nscannedAllPlans	Indicates the nscanned value of all the attempted plans.
nscannedObjectsAllPlans	Indicates the nScannedObjects value of all the attempted plans.

(*continued*)

Table 10-1. (*continued*)

Element	Description
scanAndOrder	A true/false value indicating whether the documents need to read in order to be sorted, rather than taking advantage of an index.
indexOnly	Indicates that no documents needed to be scanned in order to return the results for the query; all the fields being queried and being returned are on one index.
nYields	The number of times this query yielded its read lock to allow writes to execute.
nChunkSkips	The number of documents skipped because of an active chunk migration.
server	The server on which this query was executed.

Using the Profiler and explain() to Optimize a Query

Now let's walk through a real-world optimization scenario and look at how we can use MongoDB's profiler and explain()tools to fix a problem with a real application.

The example discussed in this chapter is based on a small sample blog application. This database has a function to get the posts associated with a particular tag; in this case it's the even tag. Let's assume you have noticed that this function runs slowly, so you want to determine whether there is a problem.

Let's begin by writing a little program to fill the aforementioned database with data so that we have something to run queries against, to demonstrate the optimization process.

```php
<?php

// Get a connection to the database

$mongo = new MongoClient();
$db=$mongo->blog;

// First let's get the first AuthorsID
// We are going to use this to fake a author

$author = $db->authors->findOne();

if(!$author){
        die("There are no authors in the database");
}

for( $i = 1; $i < 10000; $i++){
        $blogpost=array();
        $blogpost['author'] = $author['_id'];
        $blogpost['Title']   = "Completely fake blogpost number {$i}";
        $blogpost['Message'] = "Some fake text to create a database of blog posts";
        $blogpost['Tags'] = array();
        if($i%2){
                // Odd numbered blogs
                $blogpost['Tags'] = array("blog", "post", "odd", "tag{$i}");
        } else {
```

```
                   // Even numbered blogs
                   $blogpost['Tags'] = array("blog", "post", "even", "tag{$i}");
             }
             $db->posts->insert($blogpost);
      }
?>
```

This program finds the first author in the blog database's authors collection, and then pretends that the author has been extraordinarily productive. It creates 10,000 fake blog postings in the author's name, all in the blink of an eye. The posts are not very interesting to read; nevertheless, they are alternatively assigned odd and even tags. These tags will serve to demonstrate how to optimize a simple query.

The next step is to save the program as fastblogger.php and then run it using the command-line PHP tool:

```
$php fastblogger.php
```

Next, you need to enable the database profiler, which you will use to determine whether you can improve the example's queries:

```
$ mongo
> use blog
switched to db blog
> show collections
authors
posts
...
system.profile
tagcloud
...
users
> db.setProfilingLevel(2)
{ "was" : 0, "slowms" : 100, "ok" : 1 }
```

Now wait a few moments for the command to take effect, open the required collections, and then perform its other tasks. Next, you want to simulate having the blog website access all of the blog posts with the even tag. Do so by executing a query that the site can use to implement this function:

```
$Mongo
use blog
$db.posts.find({Tags:"even"})
...
```

If you query the profiler collection for results that exceed 5ms, you should see something like this:

```
>db.system.profile.find({millis:{$gt:5}}).sort({millis:-1})
{ "op" : "query", "ns" : "blog.posts", "query" : { "tags" : "even" }, "ntoreturn" : 0, "ntoskip" :
0, "nscanned" : 19998, "keyUpdates" : 0, "numYield" : 0, "lockStats" : { "timeLockedMicros" : { "r"
: NumberLong(12869), "w" : NumberLong(0) }, "timeAcquiringMicros" : { "r" : NumberLong(5), "w" :
NumberLong(3) } }, "nreturned" : 0, "responseLength" : 20, "millis" : 12, "ts" : ISODate("2013-05-
18T09:04:32.974Z"), "client" : "127.0.0.1", "allUsers" : [ ], "user" : "" }...
```

The results returned here show that some queries are taking longer than 0ms (remember the quote at the beginning of the chapter).

Next, you want to reconstruct the query for the first (and worst-performing) query, so you can see what is being returned. The preceding output indicates that the poorly performing query is querying blog.posts and that the query term is {Tags:"even"}. Finally, you can see that this query is taking a whopping 15ms to execute.

The reconstructed query looks like this:

```
>db.posts.find({Tags:"even"})
{ "_id" : ObjectId("4c727cbd91a01b2a14010000"), "author" : ObjectId("4c637ec8b8642fea02000000"),
"Title" : "Completly fake blogpost number 2", "Message" : "Some fake text to create a database of
blog posts", "Tags" : [ "blog", "post", "even", "tag2" ] }
{ "_id" : ObjectId("4c727cbd91a01b2a14030000"), "author" : ObjectId("4c637ec8b8642fea02000000"),
"Title" : "Completly fake blogpost number 4", "Message" : "Some fake text to create a database of
blog posts", "Tags" : [ "blog", "post", "even", "tag4" ] }
{ "_id" : ObjectId("4c727cbd91a01b2a14050000"), "author" : ObjectId("4c637ec8b8642fea02000000"),
"Title" : "Completly fake blogpost number 6", "Message" : "Some fake text to create a database of
blog posts", "Tags" : [ "blog", "post", "even", "tag6" ] }
...
```

This output should come as no surprise; this query was created for the express purpose of demonstrating how to find and fix a slow query.

The goal is to figure out how to make the query run faster, so use the explain() function to determine how MongoDB is performing this query:

```
> db.posts.find({Tags:"even"}).explain()
{
        "cursor" : "BasicCursor",
        "isMultiKey" : false,
        "n" : 14997,
        "nscannedObjects" : 29997,
        "nscanned" : 29997,
        "nscannedObjectsAllPlans" : 29997,
        "nscannedAllPlans" : 29997,
        "scanAndOrder" : false,
        "indexOnly" : false,
        "nYields" : 0,
        "nChunkSkips" : 0,
        "millis" : 27,
        "indexBounds" : {

        },
        "server" : "Pixl.local:27017"
}
```

You can see from the output here that the query is not using any indexes. The explain() function shows that the query is using a "BasicCursor", which means the query is just performing a simple scan of the collection's records. Specifically, it's scanning all the records in the database one by one to find the tags (all 9999 of them); this process takes 27ms. That may not sound like a long time, but if you were to use this query on a popular page of your website, it would cause additional load to the disk I/O, as well as tremendous stress on the web server. Consequently, this query would cause the connection to the web browser to remain open longer while the page is being created.

■ **Note** If you see a detailed query explanation that shows a significantly larger number of scanned records (nscanned) than it returns (n), then that query is probably a candidate for indexing.

The next step is to determine whether adding an index on the Tags field improves the query's performance:

```
> db.posts.ensureIndex({Tags:1})
```

Now run the explain() function again to see the effect of adding the index:

```
> db.posts.find({Tags:"even"}).explain()
{
    "cursor" : "BtreeCursor Tags_1",
    "isMultiKey" : true,
    "n" : 14997,
    "nscannedObjects" : 14997,
    "nscanned" : 14997,
    "nscannedObjectsAllPlans" : 14997,
    "nscannedAllPlans" : 14997,
    "scanAndOrder" : false,
    "indexOnly" : false,
    "nYields" : 0,
    "nChunkSkips" : 0,
    "millis" : 4,
    "indexBounds" : {
        "Tags" : [
            [
                "even",
                "even"
            ]
        ]
    },
    "server" : "Pixl.local:27017"
}
```

The performance of the query has improved significantly. You can see that the query is now using a BtreeCursor driven by the Tags_1 index. The number of scanned records has been reduced from 29,997 records to the same 14,997 records you expect the query to return, and the execution time has dropped to 4ms.

■ **Note** The most common index type, and the only one used by MongoDB, is the btree (binary-tree). A BtreeCursor is a MongoDB data cursor that uses the binary tree index to navigate from document to document. Btree indexes are very common in database systems because they provide fast inserts and deletes, yet also provide reasonable performance when used to walk or sort data.

Managing Indexes

You've now seen how much impact the introduction of carefully selected indexes can have.

As you learned in Chapter 3, MongoDB's indexes are used for both queries (find, findOne) and sorts. If you intend to use a lot of sorts on your collection, then you should add indexes that correspond to your sort specifications. If you use sort() on a collection where there are no indexes for the fields in the sort specification, then you may get an error message if you exceed the maximum size of the internal sort buffer. So it is a good idea to create indexes for sorts. In the following sections, we'll touch again on the basics, but also add some details that relate to how to manage and manipulate the indexes in your system. We will also cover how such indexes relate to some of the samples.

When you add an index to a collection, MongoDB must maintain it and update it every time you perform any write operation (for example, updates, inserts, or deletes). If you have too many indexes on a collection, it can cause a negative impact on write performance.

Indexes are best used on collections where the majority of access is read access. For write-heavy collections such as those used in logging systems, introducing an index would reduce the peak documents per second that could be streamed into the collection.

■ **Warning**   At this time, you can have a maximum of 64 indexes per collection.

Listing Indexes

MongoDB has a simple helper function, getIndexes(), to list the indexes for a given collection. When executed, it will print a JSON array that contains the details of each index on the given collection, including which fields or elements they refer to and any options you may have set on that index.

```
$mongo
>use blog
>db.posts.getIndexes()
[
        {
                "v" : 1,
                "key" : {
                        "_id" : 1
                },
                "ns" : "blog.posts",
                "name" : "_id_"
        }
]
```

MongoDB maintains a special collection called system.indexes inside each database. This collection keeps track of all the indexes that have been created on all the collections in the databases.

The system.indexes collection is just like any normal collection. You can list its contents, run queries against it, and otherwise perform the usual tasks you can accomplish with a typical collection.

The following example lists the indexes in your simple database:

```
$mongo
>use blog
>db.system.indexes.find()
{ "v" : 1, "key" : { "_id" : 1 }, "ns" : "blog.posts", "name" : "_id_" }
```

```
{ "v" : 1, "key" : { "_id" : 1 }, "ns" : "blog.authors", "name" : "_id_" }
```

The blog database does not have any user-defined indexes, but you can see the two indexes created automatically for the _id field on your two collections: posts and authors. You don't have to do anything to create or delete these *identity indexes*; MongoDB creates and drops them whenever a collection is created or removed.

When you define an index on an element, MongoDB will construct an internal btree index, which it will use to locate documents efficiently. If no suitable index can be found, MongoDB will scan all the documents in the collection to find the records that satisfy the query.

Creating a Simple Index

MongoDB provides the ensureIndex() function for adding new indexes to a collection. This function begins by checking whether an index has already been created with the same specification. If it has, then ensureIndex() just returns that index. This means you can call ensureIndex() as many times as you like, but it won't result in a lot of extra indexes being created for your collection.

The following example defines a simple index:

```
$mongo
>use blog
>db.posts.ensureIndex({Tags:1})
```

This example creates a simple ascending btree index on the Tags field. Creating a descending index instead would require only one small change:

```
>db.posts.ensureIndex({Tags:-1})
```

To index a field in an embedded document, you can use the normal dot notation addressing scheme; that is, if you have a count field that is inside a comments subdocument, you can use the following syntax to index it:

```
>db.posts.ensureIndex({"comments.count":1})
```

If you specify a document field that is an array type, then the index will include all the elements of the array as separate index terms. This is known as a multi-key index, and each document is linked to multiple values in the index. If you look back and examine the explain() output for our queries earlier, you can see mention of this there.

MongoDB has a special operator, all, for performing queries where you wish to select only documents that have all of the terms you supply. In the blog database example, you have a posts collection with an element called Tags. This element has all the tags associated with the posting inside it. The following query finds all articles that have both the sailor and moon tags:

```
>db.posts.find({Tags:{$all: ['sailor', 'moon']}})
```

Without a multi-key index on the Tags field, the query engine would have to scan each document in the collection to see whether either term existed and, if so, to check whether both terms were present.

Creating a Compound Index

It may be tempting to simply create a separate index for each field mentioned in any of your queries. While this may speed up queries without requiring too much thought, it would unfortunately have a significant impact on adding and removing data from your database, as these indexes need to be updated each time. It's also important to note that in MongoDB 2.4 and earlier only one index will ever be used to fulfill the results of a query, so adding a number of small indexes will not normally help query execution.

Compound indexes provide a good way to keep down the number of indexes you have on a collection, allowing you to combine multiple fields into a single index, so you should try to use compound indexes wherever possible.

There are two main types of compound indexes: subdocument indexes and manually defined compound indexes.

MongoDB has some rules that allow it to use compound indexes for queries that do not use all of the component keys. Understanding these rules enables you to construct a set of compound indexes that cover all of the queries you wish to perform against the collection, without having to individually index each element (thereby avoiding the attendant impact on insert/update performance mentioned earlier).

One area where compound indexes may not be useful is when using the index in a sort. Sorting is not good at using the compound index unless the list of terms and sort directions exactly matches the index structure.

When you use a subdocument as an index key, the order of the elements used to build the multi-key index matches the order in which they appear in the subdocument's internal BSON representation. In many cases, this does not give you sufficient control over the process of creating the index.

To get around this limitation while guaranteeing that the query uses an index constructed in the desired fashion, you need to make sure you use the same subdocument structure to create the index that you used when forming the query, as in the following example:

```
>db.articles.find({author:{name: 'joe', email: 'joe@blogger.com'}))
```

You can also create a compound index explicitly by naming all the fields that you wish to combine in the index, and then specifying the order in which to combine them. The following example illustrates how to construct a compound index manually:

```
>db.posts.ensureIndex({"author.name":1, "author.email":1})
```

Specifying Index Options

You can specify several interesting options when creating an index, such as creating unique indexes or enabling background indexing; you'll learn more about these options in the upcoming sections. You specify these options as additional parameters to the ensureIndex() function, as in the following example:

```
>db.posts.ensureIndex({author:1}, {option1:true, option2:true, ..... })
```

Creating an Index in the Background with {background:true}

When you instruct MongoDB to create an index by using the ensureIndex() function for the first time, the server must read all the data in the collection and create the specified index. By default, index builds are done in the foreground, and all operations on the collection's database are blocked until the index operation completes.

MongoDB also includes a feature that allows this initial build of indexes to be performed in the background. Operations by other connections on that database are not blocked while that index is being built. No queries will use the index until it has been built, but the server will allow read and write operations to continue. Once the index operation has been completed, all queries that require the index will immediately start using it. It's worth noting that while an index can be built in the background, it will take longer to complete.

Therefore, you may wish to look at other strategies for building your indexes. Probably the best strategy is to perform the build in rotation within a replica set. To do this, you stop one secondary at a time and start it without its --replSet argument and on a different port, temporarily making it a stand-alone node. You can then perform the index build on this secondary without fear. Once the index build is finished, start the secondary as normal and have it rejoin the replica set and catch up. Repeat this process for all secondary members. Finally, stop the primary and perform the same removal of --replSet and build an index process for it, then have it rejoin the replica set as usual. By rotating through your replica set in this fashion you can build an index without downtime or interruption!

■ **Note**   The index will be built in the background. However, the connection that initiates the request will be blocked, if you issue the command from the MongoDB shell. A command issued on this connection won't return until the indexing operation is complete. At first sight, this appears to contradict the idea that it is a *background* index. However, if you have another MongoDB shell open at the same time, you will find that queries and updates on that collection run unhindered while the index build is in progress. It is only the initiating connection that is blocked. This differs from the behavior you see with a simple ensureIndex() command, which is not run in the background, so that operations on the second MongoDB shell would also be blocked.

KILLING THE INDEXING PROCESS

You can also kill the current indexing process if you think it has hung or is otherwise taking too long. You can do this by invoking the killOp() function:

```
> db.killOp(<operation id>)
```

To run a killOp you need to know the operation ID of the operation. You can get a list of all of the currently running operations on your MongoDB instance by running the db.currentOp() command.

Note that when you invoke the killOp() command, the partial index will also be removed again. This prevents broken or irrelevant data from building up in the database.

Creating an Index with a Unique Key {unique:true}

When you specify the unique option, MongoDB creates an index in which all the keys must be different. This means that MongoDB will return an error if you try to insert a document in which the index key matches the key of an existing document. This is useful for a field where you want to ensure that no two people can have the same identity (that is, the same userid).

However, if you want to add a unique index to an existing collection that is already populated with data, you must make sure that you have *deduped* the key(s). In this case, your attempt to create the index will fail if any two keys are not unique.

The unique option works for simple and compound indexes, but not for multi-key value indexes, where they wouldn't make much sense.

If a document is inserted with a field missing that is specified as a unique key, then MongoDB will automatically insert the field, but will set its value to null. This means that you can only insert one document with a missing key field into such a collection; any additional null values would mean the key is not unique, as required.

Dropping Duplicates Automatically with {dropdups:true}

If you want to create a unique index for a field where you know that duplicate keys exist, you can specify the dropdups option. This option instructs MongoDB to remove documents that would cause the index creation to fail. In this case, MongoDB will retain the first document it finds in its natural ordering of the collection, but then drop any other documents that would result in an index-constraint violation.

■ **Warning**   You need to be very careful when using the `dropdups` option because it *will* result in documents being deleted from your collection.

You should be extremely aware of the data in your collection before using this option; otherwise, you might get unexpected (not to mention unwanted) behavior. It is an extremely good idea to run a group query against a collection for which you intend to make a key unique; this will enable you to determine the number of documents that would be regarded as duplicates *before* you execute this option.

Creating Sparse Indexes with {sparse:true}

Sometimes it can be worthwhile to create an index of only documents that contain an entry for a given field. For example, let's say you want to index emails, and you know that not all emails will have a CC or a BCC field. If you create an index on CC or BCC, then all documents would be added with a "null" value, unless you specify a sparse index. This can be a space-saving mechanism as you only index on valid documents rather than all documents. Of course, this has an impact on any queries that are run and use the sparse index; as there are may be documents that are not evaluated in the query.

TTL Indexes

In computing terms, TTL (Time To Live) is a way of giving a particular piece of data or a request a lifespan by specifying a point at which it becomes invalid. This can be useful for data stored within your MongoDB instance, too, as often it is nice to have old data automatically deleted. In order to create a TTL index you must add the `expireAfterSeconds` flag and a seconds value to a single (noncompound) index. This will indicate that any document that has the indexed field greater than the given TTL value will be deleted when the TTL deletion task next executes. As the deletion task is run once every 60 seconds, there can be some delay before your old documents are removed.

■ **Warning**   The field being indexed must be a BSON date type; otherwise, it will not be evaluated to be deleted. A BSON date will appear as `ISODate` when queried from the shell as in the next example.

Suppose for example that we want to automatically delete anything from the blog's `comments` collection, which has a created timestamp over a certain age. Take this example document from the `comments` collection:

```
>db.comments.find();
{
    "_id" : ObjectId("519859b32fee8059a95eeace"),
    "author" : "david",
    "body" : "foo",
    "ts" : ISODate("2013-05-19T04:48:51.540Z"),
    "tags" : [ ]
}
```

Let's say we want to have any comment older than 28 days deleted. We work out that 28 days is 2,419,200 seconds long. Then we create the index as follows:

```
>db.comments.ensureIndex({ts:1},{ expireAfterSeconds: 2419200})
```

When this document is more than 2,419,200 seconds older than the current system time, it will be deleted. You could test by creating a document more than 2,419,200 seconds old using the following syntax:

```
date = new Date(new Date().getTime()-2419200000);
db.comments.insert({ "author" : test", "body" : "foo", "ts" : date, "tags" : [] });
```

Now simply wait a minute and the document should be deleted.

■ **Note** When you set a TTL index, MongoDB sets the usePowerOf2Sizes flag on the given collection. This will standardize the storage space for each document. This allows the spaces to be reused more effectively by future documents after they have been deleted.

Text Search Indexes

MongoDB 2.4 introduced a new type of index—text indexes, which allow you to perform full text searches! Chapter 8 discussed the text index feature in detail, but it's worth a quick summary here as we look at optimization. Text search has long been a desired feature in MongoDB, as it allows you to search for specific words or text within a large text block. The best example of how text search is relevant is a search feature on the body text of blog posts. This kind of search would allow you to look for words or phrases within one text field (like the body) or more (like body and comments) text fields of a document. So to create a text index we run the following command:

```
>db.posts.ensureIndex( { body: "text" } )
```

■ **Note** A text search is case-insensitive, meaning it will ignore case; "MongoDB" and "mongodb" are considered the same text.

Now we can search using our text index with the text command. To do this, we use the runCommand syntax to use the text command and provide it a value to search:

```
>db.posts.runCommand( "text", { search: "MongoDB" } )
```

The results of your text search will be returned to you in order of relevance.

■ **Warning** MongoDB text search is still relatively new and is undergoing rapid evolution.

Dropping an Index

You can elect to drop all indexes or just one specific index from a collection. Use the following function to remove all indexes from a collection:

```
>db.posts.dropIndexes()
```

To remove a single index from a collection, you use syntax that mirrors the syntax used to create the index with ensureIndex():

```
>db.posts.dropIndex({"author.name":1, "author.email":1});
```

Reindexing a Collection

If you suspect that the indexes in a collection are damaged—for example, if you're getting inconsistent results to your queries—then you can force a reindexing of the affected collection.

This will force MongoDB to drop and re-create all the indexes on the specified collection (see Chapter 9 for more information on how to detect and solve problems with your indexes), as in the following example:

```
> db.posts.reIndex()
{
    "nIndexesWas" : 2,
    "msg" : "indexes dropped for collection",
    "nIndexes" : 2,
    "indexes" : [
        {
            "key" : {
                "_id" : 1
            },
            "ns" : "blog.posts",
            "name" : "_id_"
        },
        {
            "key" : {
                "Tags" : 1
            },
            "ns" : "blog.posts",
            "name" : "Tags_1"
        }
    ],
    "ok" : 1
}
```

The output lists all the indexes the command has rebuilt, including the keys. Also, the nIndexWas: field shows how many indexes existed before running the command, while the nIndex: field gives the total number of indexes after the command has completed. If the two values are not the same, the implication is that there was a problem re-creating some of the indexes in the collection.

How MongoDB Selects Which Indexes It Will Use

When a database system needs to run a query, it has to assemble a *query plan*, which is a list of steps it must run to perform the query. Each query may have multiple query plans that could produce the same result equally well. However, each plan may have elements in it that are more *expensive* to execute than others. For example, a scan of all the records in a collection is an expensive operation, and any plan that incorporates such an approach could be slow. These plans can also include alternative lists of indexes to use for query and sort operations.

Road directions serve as a good illustration of this concept. If you want to get to the diagonally opposite side of a block from one corner, then "take a left, then take a right" and "take a right, then take a left" are equally valid plans for getting to the opposite corner. However, if one of the routes has two stop signs and the other has none, then the former approach is a more expensive plan, while the latter approach is the best plan to use. Collection scans would qualify as potential stop signs when executing your queries.

MongoDB ships with a component called the query analyzer. This component takes a query and the collection the query targets and then produces a set of plans for MongoDB to execute. The explain() function described earlier in this chapter lists both the plan used and the set of alternative plans produced for a given query.

MongoDB also ships with a query optimizer component. The job of this component is to select which execution plan is best suited to run a particular query. In most relational database systems, a query optimizer uses statistics about the distribution of keys in a table, the number of records, the available indexes, the effectiveness of previous choices, and an assortment of weighting factors to calculate the cost of each approach. It then selects the least expensive plan to use.

The query optimizer in MongoDB is simultaneously dumber and smarter than the typical RDBMS query analyzer. For example, it does not use a cost-based method of selecting an execution plan; instead, it runs all of them in parallel and uses the one that returns the results fastest, terminating all the others after the winner crosses the finish line. Thus, the query analyzer in MongoDB uses a simple mechanism (dumb) to ensure that it always gets the fastest result (smart) and the results of these plans are cached and reused for the next 1000 writes, until an explain is executed or any indexes are added, removed, or reindexed on that collection.

Using hint() to Force Using a Specific Index

The query optimizer in MongoDB selects the best index from the set of candidate indexes for a query. It uses the methods just outlined to try to match the best index or set of indexes to a given query. There may be cases, however, where the query optimizer does not make the correct choice, in which case it may be necessary to give the component a helping hand.

You can provide a *hint* to the query optimizer in such cases, nudging the component into making a different choice. For example, if you have used explain() to show which indexes are being used by your query, and you think you would like it to use a different index for a given query, then you can force the query optimizer to do so.

Let's look at an example. Assume that you have an index on a subdocument called author with name and email fields inside it. Also assume that you have the following defined index:

```
>db.posts.ensureIndex({author.name:1, author.email:1})
```

You can use the following hint to force the query optimizer to use the defined index:

```
>db.posts.find({author:{name:'joe', email: 'joe@mongodb.com'}}).hint({author.name:1, author.email:1})
```

If for some reason you want to force a query to use no indexes, that is, if you want to use collection document scanning as the means of selecting records, you can use the following hint to do this:

```
>db.posts.find({author:{name: 'joe', email: 'joe@mongodb.com'}}).hint({$natural:1})
```

Optimizing the Storage of Small Objects

Indexes are the key to speeding up data queries. But another factor that can affect the performance of your application is the size of the data it accesses. Unlike database systems with fixed schemas, MongoDB stores all the schema data for each record inside the record itself. Thus, for large records with large data contents per field, the ratio of schema data to record data is low; however, for small records with small data values, this ratio can grow surprisingly large.

Consider a common problem in one of the application types that MongoDB is well suited for: logging. MongoDB's extraordinary write rate makes streaming events as small documents into a collection very efficient. However, if you want to optimize further the speed at which you can perform this functionality, you can do a couple of things.

First, you can consider *batching* your inserts. MongoDB ships with a multiple-document insert() call. You can use this call to place several events into a collection at the same time. This results in fewer round-trips through the database interface API.

Second (and more importantly), you can reduce the size of your field names. If you have smaller field names, MongoDB can pack more event records into memory before it has to flush them out to disk. This makes the whole system more efficient.

For example, assume you have a collection that is used to log three fields: a time stamp, a counter, and a four-character string used to indicate the source of the data. The total storage size of your data is shown in Table 10-2.

Table 10-2. *The Logging Example Collection Storage Size*

Field	Size
Timestamp	8 bytes
Integer	4 bytes
string	4 bytes
Total	16 bytes

If you use ts, n, and src for the field names, then the total size of the field names is 6 bytes. This is a relatively small value compared to the data size. But now assume you decided to name the fields WhenTheEventHappened, NumberOfEvents, and SourceOfEvents. In this case, the total size of the field names is 48 bytes, or three times the size of the data itself. If you wrote 1TB of data into a collection, then you would be storing 750GB of field names, but only 250GB of actual data.

This does more than waste disk space. It also affects all other aspects of the system's performance, including the index size, data transfer time, and (probably more importantly) the use of precious system RAM to cache the data files.

In logging applications you also need to avoid adding indexes on your collections when writing records; as explained earlier, indexes take time and resources to maintain. Instead, you should add the index immediately before you start analyzing the data.

Finally, you should consider using a schema that splits the event stream into multiple collections. For example, you might write each day's events into a separate collection. Smaller collections take less time to index and analyze.

Summary

In this chapter, we looked at some tools for tracking down slow performance in MongoDB queries, as well as potential solutions for speeding up the slow queries that surface as a result. We also looked at some of the ways to optimize data storage. For example, we looked at ways to ensure that we are making full use of the resources available to the MongoDB server.

The specific techniques described in this chapter enable you to optimize your data and tune the MongoDB system it is stored in. The best approach to take will vary from application to application, and it will depend on many factors, including the application type, data access patterns, read/write ratios, and so on.

## CHAPTER 11

Replication

Like many of its relational cousins, MongoDB supports the replication of a database's contents to another server in real-time or near real-time. MongoDB's replication features are simple to set up and use. They are also among the key features in MongoDB that, along with sharding, bolster the claim that the database is both a Web 2.0 and a cloud-based datastore.

There are many scenarios where you might want to use replication, so the replication support in MongoDB has to be sufficiently flexible that it can cope with all of them. The architects of MongoDB at MongoDB, Inc. have gone to great lengths to make sure that its implementation of replication meets all of today's needs.

In this chapter, we will cover the basics of replication within MongoDB, including the following topics:

- What is replication in MongoDB?

- What is a primary?

- What is a secondary?

- What is the oplog?

■ **Note** Replication is a feature that continues to evolve in MongoDB, and you can expect some changes in how replication works as the product develops. This is particularly true with respect to the clustering of database servers. There have already been a number of changes between the first and second editions of this book. MongoDB, Inc is investing considerable effort in ensuring that MongoDB meets and exceeds everybody's expectations for scalability and availability; replication support is one of the key features that MongoDB. Inc is counting on to help it meet those expectations.

Before looking at replication setup in detail, let's review the goals the various setups are designed to achieve. We'll also outline some of the fundamentals of how replication currently functions in MongoDB and look at the oplog and its role in the replication of data between members of a replica set. These topics form the fundamental basis for understanding replication.

Spelling Out MongoDB's Replication Goals

Among other things, replication can be used to achieve scalability, durability/reliability, and isolation. In the upcoming sections, we'll explore how you can use replication to achieve these goals along the way, while pointing out potential traps and mistakes to avoid.

Improving Scalability

For web applications in particular, scalability is a critical design requirement, especially those that rely heavily on backend databases. Replication can help you create more scalable applications in two ways:

- *Improve redundancy*: Replication can help you improve redundancy by enabling you to host an application in several data centers. In this approach, you ensure that there is a local copy of the data in each data center, so that the application can have high-speed access to it. Users can then be connected to the data center that is closest to them, minimizing latency.

- *Improve performance*: Replication can under certain circumstances, help you improve an application's raw performance. This is particularly true for cases where you have a large web application with a predominantly read-based dataset, and you want to distribute queries to multiple database servers to increase parallelism. Or with query loads that have widely different working sets such as reporting or aggregation.

■ **Note**   MongoDB also supports a feature called *sharding*, which is designed to assist you in creating more scalable applications with or without replication for truly high scalability. See Chapter 12 for more information about using sharding and replication together in MongoDB.

Improving Durability/Reliability

Replication is commonly used to help guard against hardware failure or database corruption and allows flexibility when performing backups or other potentially high-impact maintenance activity with little or no impact – as these tasks can be performed individually on members of the set without impacting the set as a whole. Some specific examples where people use replication in this manner include the following:

- *When you want to have a duplicate of your database that is running at a delay.* You may want to protect yourself against flaws in your application or provide a simple mechanism to provide *trend* information by highlighting the differences between the results of queries against both datasets. This can also provide a safety buffer for human errors and avoids the need to fully restore from backup.

- *When you want a backup system in case of a failure.* You may want to run a replica as a backup in cases where normal backup schemes would take too long to restore in the event of a system failure.

- *When you want a redundant system for administrative purposes.* You may want to run a replica so you can rotate between nodes for administrative tasks such as backups or upgrades.

Providing Isolation

There are some processes that, if run against the production database, would significantly impact that database's performance or availability. You can use replication to create synchronized copies that isolate processes from the production database, for example:

- *When you want to run reports or backups without impacting the performance of your production system*: Maintaining a hidden secondary replica enables you to isolate queries from your reporting system and make sure that the end-of-month reports don't delay or otherwise impact your normal operations.

Replication Fundamentals

As you have seen, a replica set (or replSet) is a way to set up multiple MongoDB instances to contain the same data for redundancy and other related measures. In addition to knowing this, you should also understand how MongoDB accomplishes its replication, so you'll know how best to administer your own replica set.

You are already aware of the goals of replication in MongoDB, and if you have read the first edition of this book or have been using MongoDB since its early days, you will know that there have been a number of different ways that one could accomplish replication, including these:

- Master/Slave Replication

- Master/Master Replication

- Replica Pairs

These methods of replication have all been superseded by the concept of the *replica set*. In MongoDB a replica set is made up of a *primary* node and a number of *secondary* or *arbiter* nodes. A replica set should be made up of an odd number of members, meaning a minimum of three. This requirement arises because MongoDB replica sets have a rule that the primary must be able to see a majority of other nodes in order to allow it to continue being primary. This rule is enforced to avoid a "split brain" situation, where you have two primaries because of a potential fault in networking, as illustrated in Figure 11-1.

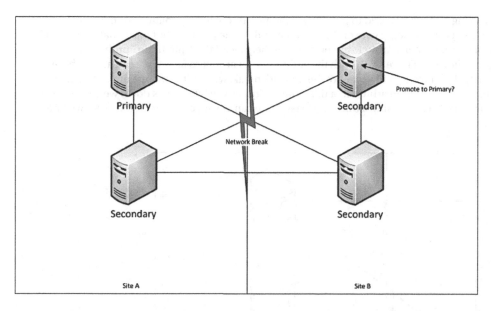

Figure 11-1. *The Split-brain problem*

What Is a Primary?

In replica set terms, a primary is the source of truth at a given moment for your replica set. It is the only node in the set to which data can be written and from which all other nodes replicate their data. A primary is elected by agreement of a majority of all voting members, known as a *quorum*.

Once a primary is elected, all secondaries will use it as the source of truth for their replication, and as such all writes must be directed to this member.

What Is a Secondary?

A secondary member is a data-carrying nonprimary member, which can (barring a few exceptions) theoretically become a primary. It is a node, which can be read from and which replicates its data from the primary of its set in as close to real-time as possible. By default, if you directly connect to a secondary without any read preference, you cannot perform read operations. This is done to reinforce that with any read to a nonprimary, if there is a delay in replication, you may be reading from older data. You can use the command rs.slaveOk() to set the current connection you are on to read from secondaries. Or, if you are using a driver, you can set a read preference, as we will discuss later in this chapter.

■ **Note** The concept of a primary is and should be ephemeral. That is, ideally you should have no "fixed" concept of which node is primary. In a replica set, all of the secondaries are writing the same data as the primary in order to keep up with replication. Therefore, if the secondaries are substantially less capable, they may not be able to cope in the event they are promoted to primary.

What Is an Arbiter?

An *arbiter* is a non–data-bearing node that is used to provide an additional vote to help maintain a majority for replica set elections. It does not cast a deciding vote or direct which node is the primary, but participates and can be a member of a quorum to decide a primary. Arbiters are best used to help avoid the "split brain" problem described earlier. Consider the diagram shown in Figure 11-2. With the addition of an arbiter to Site A, we can always have one side that can create a majority. This means in the event of the network break, we don't wind up with two primaries! We can add further redundancy by having an arbiter in a third Site C. This way, if Site A goes down we can still form a majority from the nodes in Sites B and C. Using a third site like this we can always continue in the event we lose connectivity to any one site.

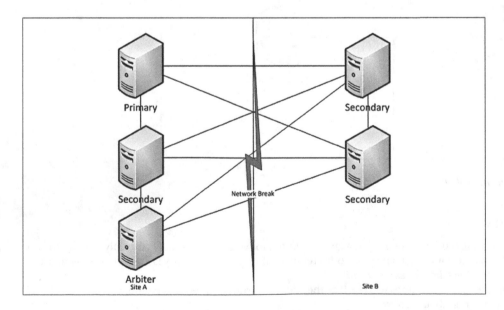

Figure 11-2. *Split Brain Problem Solved*

Drilling Down on the Oplog

In simple terms, the oplog (operation log) is a capped collection with a rolling record of the changes that a primary instance makes to its databases for the purpose of replaying those changes to a secondary to ensure that the databases are identical. Each member of a replica set maintains its own oplog, and the secondaries query the primary's (or other more up-to-date secondary's) oplog for new entries to apply to their own copies of all databases.

The oplog creates a timestamp for each entry. This enables a secondary to track how far it has read from the oplog during a previous read, and what entries it needs to transfer to catch up. If you stop a secondary and restart it a relatively short later time, it will use the primary's oplog to retrieve all the changes it has missed while offline.

Because it is not practical to have an infinitely large oplog, the oplog is limited or *capped* at a particular size.

You can think of the oplog as a window on the recent activity of your primary instance; if that window is too small, then operations will be lost from the oplog before they can be applied to the secondaries. If an oplog has not yet been created on the current instance, the --oplogSize startup option allows you to set the size of your oplog in MB By default for a Linux or Windows 64-bit system, the oplogSize will be set to five percent of the free disk space available for data storage. If your system is write/update intensive, then you may need to increase this size to ensure that slaves can be offline for a reasonable amount of time without losing data.

For example, if you have a daily backup from the slave that takes an hour to complete, the size of the oplog will have to be set to allow the slave to stay offline for that hour plus an additional amount of time to provide a safety margin.

It's critical that you take into account the update rate on all the databases present on the master when calculating a suitable size for the oplog.

You can get some idea about a suitable size for your oplog by using the db.printReplicationInfo() command, which runs on the master instance:

```
$mongo
>db.printReplicationInfo()
configured oplog size: 15000MB
log length start to end: 6456672secs (1793.52hrs)
oplog first event time:  Wed Mar 20 2013 17:00:43 GMT+1100 (EST)
oplog last event time:   Mon Jun 03 2013 09:31:55 GMT+1000 (EST)
now:                     Mon Jun 03 2013 20:22:20 GMT+1000 (EST)
```

This command shows the current size of your oplog, as well as the amount of time it will take to fill up at the current update rate. From this information, you can estimate whether you need to increase or decrease the size of your oplog. You can also look at how far behind a given member of your replica set is from the primary by reviewing the repl lag section in MongoDB Monitoring Service (MMS). If you have not installed MMS already, I truly suggest you do now, as the larger and more scaled your MongoDB cluster becomes, the more important stats like those MMS provides become. For more background, you should review the MMS section of Chapter 9.

Implementing a Replica Set

In this section, you will learn how to set up a simple replica set configuration. You will also learn how to add and remove members from the cluster. As discussed earlier, replica sets are based on the concept of a single primary server and a number of secondary or arbiter servers that will replicate writes from the primary (see Figure 11-3).

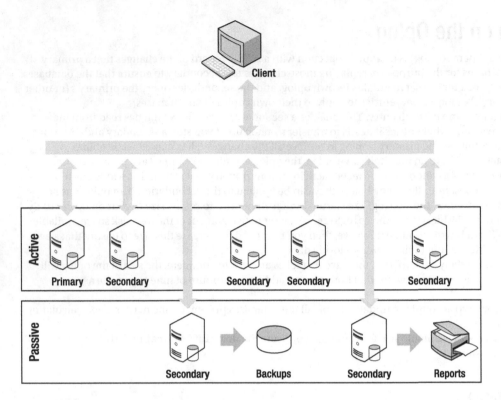

Figure 11-3. *A cluster implemented with a replica set*

Replica sets also feature the concept of *active* and *passive* members. Passive secondary servers don't participate in elections for a new primary when the current primary becomes unavailable; instead, they serve the same purpose as *hidden* members, and they can be used as reporting or backup datasets.

Member servers of replica sets do not need to be designated as set members on startup. Instead, configuration is done through server-level commands that are sent through the normal server interface. This makes it easier to create configuration management tools that allow dynamic configuration and management of clusters of machines.

In the upcoming sections, you will learn how to accomplish the following:

1. Create a replica set.

2. Add a server to a replica set.

3. Add an arbiter to a replica set.

4. Inspect and perform operations on a replica set.

5. Configure individual members of a replica set.

6. Connect to a replica set from your application.

7. Set Read Preference from within your application

8. Set Write Concern from within your application

9. Use Replica Set tags with Read Preference and Write Concern

10. Use the web interface to inspect the status of your replica set

Creating a Replica Set

The best way to learn how to create a replica set is by looking at an example. In the example that follows, you will create a replica set called testset. This set will have three members (two active and one passive). Table 11-1 lists the members of this set.

Table 11-1. *Configuring the Replica Set*

Service	Daemon	Address	Dbpath
Active Member 1	mongod	[hostname]:27021	/db/active1/data
Active Member 2	mongod	[hostname]:27022	/db/active2/data
Passive Member 1	mongod	[hostname]:27023	/db/passive1/data

Replica sets will allow you to use localhost as an identifier, but only when all machines are co-located on one server. This occurs as each member of a replica set must be able to contact all other MongoDB instances via hostname for replication to function.

Normally when working with replica sets we use hostnames; you can find the current hostname by using the hostname command, as in the following example:

$hostname
```
Pixl.local
```

In the examples that follow, replace the term [hostname] with whatever value is returned by running the hostname command on your own system.

Getting a Replica Set Member Up and Running

The first step is to get the first active member up and running. To do so, open a terminal window and type the following:

```
$ mkdir -p /db/active1/data
$ mongod --dbpath /db/active1/data --port 27021 --replSet testset
```

The --replSet option tells the instance the name of the replica set it is joining. This is the first member of the replica set, so you can give it the address of any other member, even if that member has not been started up yet. Only one member address is required, but you can also provide the names of other members by separating their addresses with commas, as shown in the following example:

```
$ mongod --dbpath /db/active1/data --port 27021 --replSet testset
```

■ **Note**   If you don't wish to run each of these MongoDB instances in its own shell instance, you can add the --fork and --logpath *<file>* options to tell this instance to open itself in the background and direct its logging to the specified file.

To keep things simple, this example will rely on only one address. The next step is to get the other members up and running. Do so by opening two more terminal windows, and then type the following into the first window to get the second member up and running:

```
$ mkdir -p /db/active2/data
$ mongod --dbpath /db/active2/data --port 27022  --replSet testset
```

Next, type this into the second window to get the final (passive) member up and running:

```
$ mkdir -p /db/passive1/data
$ mongod --dbpath /db/passive1/data --port 27023 --replSet testset
```

At this point, you have three server instances running and communicating with each other; however, you do not quite have your replica set running, because you haven't yet initialized the replica set and instructed each member about its role and responsibilities.

To do that, you need to attach to one of the servers and initialize the replica set. The following code selects the first server to attach to:

```
$mongo [hostname]:27021
```

Next, you need to initialize the first member of this set to create its oplog and a default configuration document. You can see the MongoD instance suggesting that you need to do this in your logfiles:

```
Mon Jun  3 21:25:23.712 [rsStart] replSet can't get local.system.replset config from self or any
seed (EMPTYCONFIG)
Mon Jun  3 21:25:23.712 [rsStart] replSet info you may need to run replSetInitiate --
rs.initiate() in the shell -- if that is not already done
```

So run the rs.initiate command:

```
> rs.initiate()
{
    "info2" : "no configuration explicitly specified -- making one",
    "me" : "[hostname]:27021",
    "info" : "Config now saved locally. Should come online in about a minute.",
    "ok" : 1
}
```

Finally, you should check the status of the replica set to determine whether it has been set up correctly:

```
>rs.status()
{
    "set" : "testset",
    "date" : ISODate("2013-06-03T11:28:58Z"),
    "myState" : 1,
    "members" : [
        {
            "_id" : 0,
            "name" : "[hostname]:27021",
            "health" : 1,
            "state" : 1,
            "stateStr" : "PRIMARY",
```

```
                "uptime" : 264,
                "optime" : {
                        "t" : 1370258919,
                        "i" : 1
                },
                "optimeDate" : ISODate("2013-06-03T11:28:39Z"),
                "self" : true
            }
        ],
        "ok" : 1
}
```

The output here indicates that all is OK: you've successfully configured, set up, and initialized a new replica set. Remember that you should use the name of your own machine in place of *[hostname]* because neither "localhost" nor "127.0.0.1" will work.

Adding a Server to a Replica Set

Now that you have started your new replica set, you need to start adding members to it. Let's start by adding your first secondary. You can do this by simply adding the rs.add() command and providing the hostname and port of this instance. To add that, connect to your primary and run the following:

```
$ mongo [hostname]:27021
> rs.add("[hostname]:27021")
{ "ok" : 1 }
```

You will need to wait a minute or two as this node brings itself online, creates its own oplog, and readies itself. You can monitor the progress with rs.status() while waiting till this node comes online as a secondary:

```
>use admin
>rs.status() {
    "set" : "testset",
    "date" : ISODate("2013-06-03T11:36:37Z"),
    "myState" : 1,
    "members" : [
        {
            "_id" : 0,
            "name" : "[hostname]:27021",
            "health" : 1,
            "state" : 1,
            "stateStr" : "PRIMARY",
            "uptime" : 723,
            "optime" : {
                "t" : 1370259331,
                "i" : 1
            },
            "optimeDate" : ISODate("2013-06-03T11:35:31Z"),
            "self" : true
        },
```

```
            {
                "_id" : 1,
                "name" : "[hostname]:27022",
                "health" : 1,
                "state" : 2,
                "stateStr" : "SECONDARY",
                "uptime" : 66,
                "optime" : {
                        "t" : 1370259331,
                        "i" : 1
                },
                "optimeDate" : ISODate("2013-06-03T11:35:31Z"),
                "lastHeartbeat" : ISODate("2013-06-03T11:36:35Z"),
                "lastHeartbeatRecv" : ISODate("2013-06-03T11:36:36Z"),
                "pingMs" : 0,
                "syncingTo" : "[hostname]:27021"
            }
        ],
        "ok" : 1
}
```

Now let's make use of that third passive member. First add the member as usual with rs.add():

```
$ mongo [hostname]:27022
> rs.add("[hostname]:27022")
{ "ok" : 1 }
```

Now we need to make a copy of the config document and modify it. Run the following command to create a document called conf, which contains your current replica set configuration.

```
> conf = rs.conf()
{
    "_id" : "testset",
    "version" : 3,
    "members" : [
        {
            "_id" : 0,
            "host" : "[hostname]:27021"
        },
        {
            "_id" : 1,
            "host" : "[hostname]:27022"
        },
        {
            "_id" : 2,
            "host" : "[hostname]:27023"
        }
    ]
}
```

Now that your configuration document is loaded you need to modify it. We want to set the node to be *hidden* and have a priority of 0, so it will not be elected to be the primary. Notice that the document has a members array, which contains a document for each member of the replica set. You need to pick the member you wish to access using the array operator []. So to create a value of hidden : true for the third member, we need to update the array element at 2 (remember, arrays start at 0). Run the following:

```
> conf.members[2].hidden = true
true
```

Now we can set a *priority* value of 0 using the same commands:

```
> conf.members[2].priority = 0
0
```

You can output this config document by simply executing the name of the variable you placed the config document into:

```
> conf
{
    "_id" : "testset",
    "version" : 3,
    "members" : [
        {
            "_id" : 0,
            "host" : "[hostname]:27021"
        },
        {
            "_id" : 1,
            "host" : "[hostname]:27022"
        },
        {
            "_id" : 2,
            "host" : "[hostname]:27023",
            "hidden" : true,
            "priority" : 0
        }
    ]
}
```

As you can see, this member now has the hidden value set and a priority of 0. Now all we need to do is update the replica set configuration to use this document. We do this by issuing the rs.reconfig() command with our new config document as an argument.

```
> rs.reconfig(conf)
Tue Jun  4 20:01:45.234 DBClientCursor::init call() failed
Tue Jun  4 20:01:45.235 trying reconnect to 127.0.0.1:27021
Tue Jun  4 20:01:45.235 reconnect 127.0.0.1:27021 ok
reconnected to server after rs command (which is normal)
```

Your whole replica set lost connectivity and then reconnected! This happens because of the reconfiguration. Any changes to a replica set will potentially cause a replica set to reconfigure itself and have a new election, which under most circumstances has the previous primary step back into its role. Now if we re-run the rs.conf() command you can see your new replica set configuration in action.

```
> rs.conf()
{
        "_id" : "testset",
        "version" : 4,
        "members" : [
                {
                        "_id" : 0,
                        "host" : "[hostname]:27021"
                },
                {
                        "_id" : 1,
                        "host" : "[hostname]:27022"
                },
                {
                        "_id" : 2,
                        "host" : "[hostname]:27023",
                        "priority" : 0,
                        "hidden" : true
                }
        ]
}
```

Notice that this replica set configuration's version number has now increased. This happens automatically as part of the reconfiguration to ensure that any replica set members don't have the wrong configuration document.

You should now have a fully configured and working three-member replica set with an active primary and a hidden "passive."

Adding an Arbiter

Adding an arbiter to be a voting member of your replica set is an easy process. Let's start by spinning up a new member.

```
$ mkdir -p /db/arbiter1/data
$ mongod --dbpath /db/ arbiter1/data --port 27024  --replSet testset -rest
```

Now that you have a new member created, it's just a matter of adding the new arbiter with the rs.addArb() command:

```
>rs.addArb("[hostname]:27024")
{ "ok" : 1 }
```

And if you now run rs.status(), you will see your arbiter in the output:

```
{
        "_id" : 3,
        "name" : "Pixl.local:27024",
        "health" : 1,
        "state" : 7,
```

```
        "stateStr" : "ARBITER",
        "uptime" : 721,
        "lastHeartbeat" : ISODate("2013-06-07T11:21:01Z"),
        "lastHeartbeatRecv" : ISODate("2013-06-07T11:21:00Z"),
        "pingMs" : 0
}
```

You may have recognized a problem here; we have four nodes now. That's an even number, and even is bad! If we continue to run like this, your MongoDB nodes will start logging the following:

```
[rsMgr] replSet total number of votes is even - add arbiter or give one member an extra vote
```

To fix that, we know that we need to have an odd number of members; so one potential solution is to add another arbiter as the log message suggests, but that's not strictly elegant as we add extra complexity that isn't required. The best solution is to stop one of the existing nodes from voting and being viewed as a member of the quorum. We can do this by setting votes to zero for our hidden secondary. We do this in the same manner as we did to set the hidden and priority values.

```
conf = rs.conf()
conf.members[2].votes = 0
rs.reconfig(conf)
```

And that's it. We have now set our passive node to be truly passive: it will never become primary; it is viewed as part of the replica set by clients; and it cannot participate in elections or be counted toward a majority. To test this, you can try shutting down the passive node, and the arbiter and your other two nodes will continue on primary unchanged; whereas before, the primary would have stepped down, citing that it could not see a majority of nodes.

Replica Set Chaining

You have seen that normally a member of a replica set will attempt to sync data from the primary of that set. But that is not the only place replica set secondaries can sync from; they can also sync-from other secondaries. In this manner your secondaries can form a "sync-chain," in which each one syncs the latest data from other secondaries in your replica set.

Managing Replica Sets

MongoDB provides a number of commands for managing the configuration and status of a replica set. Table 11-2 shows the available commands that you can use to create, manipulate, and inspect the state of a cluster in a replica set.

Table 11-2. Commands for Manipulating and Inspecting Replica Sets

Command	Description
rs.help()	Returns the list of the commands in this table.
rs.status()	Returns information about the current state of the replica set. This command lists each member server, along with information about its status, including the last time it was contacted. This call can be used to provide a simple health check of the entire cluster.
rs.initiate()	Initializes a replica set using default parameters.
rs.initiate(*replSetcfg*)	Initializes a replica set using a configuration description.
rs.add("*host:port*")	Adds a member server to the replica set with a simple string that provides hostname and (optionally) a specific port.
rs.add(*membercfg*)	Adds a member server to the replica set using a configuration description. You must use this method if you want to specify specific attributes (for example, a priority for the new member server).
rs.addArb("host:port")	Adds a new member server to operate as an arbiter. The member does not need to have been started with a --replSet option; any mongod instance running on any reachable machine can perform this task. Take care that this server is reachable by all members of the replica set.
rs.stepDown()	Makes the primary server relinquish its role and forces the election of a new primary server in the cluster when you run this command against the primary member of a replica set. Note that only active secondary servers are available as candidates for becoming the new primary server and the original primary may be re-elected if no other candidate member is available after 60 seconds of waiting.
rs.syncFrom("host:port")	Make a secondary sync from a given member. Can be used to form a sync chain.
rs.freeze(secs)	Freeze a given member and make it ineligible from becoming a primary for the specified number of seconds.
rs.remove("host:port")	Remove a given member from a replica set.
rs.slaveOk()	Set this connection so that it will allow reads from secondaries.
rs.conf()	Redisplays the configuration structure of the current replica set. This command is useful for obtaining a configuration structure for a replica set. This configuration structure can be modified and then supplied to rs.initiate() again to change the structure's configuration. This technique provides the only supported way to remove a member server from a replica set; there is currently no direct method available for doing that.
db.isMaster()	This function is not specific to replica sets; rather, it is a general replication support function that allows an application or driver to determine whether a particular connected instance is the master/primary server in a replication topology.

The following sections take a closer look at some of the more commonly used commands listed in Table 11-2, providing additional details about what they do and how to use them.

Inspecting an Instance's Status with rs.status()

As you should be aware to from our earlier adventures in adding members to a replica set, rs.status()is probably the command that you will use most often when working with replica sets. It allows you to inspect the status of the instance you are currently attached to, including its role in the replica set:

>rs.status()
```
> rs.status();
{
        "set" : "testset",
        "date" : ISODate("2013-06-04T10:57:24Z"),
        "myState" : 1,
        "members" : [
                {
                        "_id" : 0,
                        "name" : "[hostname]:27021",
                        "health" : 1,
                        "state" : 1,
                        "stateStr" : "PRIMARY",
                        "uptime" : 4131,
                        "optime" : Timestamp(1370340105, 1),
                        "optimeDate" : ISODate("2013-06-04T10:01:45Z"),
                        "self" : true
                },
                {
                        "_id" : 1,
                        "name" : "[hostname]:27022",
                        "health" : 1,
                        "state" : 2,
                        "stateStr" : "SECONDARY",
                        "uptime" : 3339,
                        "optime" : Timestamp(1370340105, 1),
                        "optimeDate" : ISODate("2013-06-04T10:01:45Z"),
                        "lastHeartbeat" : ISODate("2013-06-04T10:57:23Z"),
                        "lastHeartbeatRecv" : ISODate("2013-06-04T10:57:23Z"),
                        "pingMs" : 0,
                        "syncingTo" : "[hostname]:27021"
                },
                {
                        "_id" : 2,
                        "name" : "[hostname]:27023",
                        "health" : 1,
                        "state" : 2,
                        "stateStr" : "SECONDARY",
                        "uptime" : 3339,
                        "optime" : Timestamp(1370340105, 1),
                        "optimeDate" : ISODate("2013-06-04T10:01:45Z"),
                        "lastHeartbeat" : ISODate("2013-06-04T10:57:22Z"),
                        "lastHeartbeatRecv" : ISODate("2013-06-04T10:57:23Z"),
```

```
            "pingMs" : 0,
            "syncingTo" : "[hostname]:27021"
        }
    ],
    "ok" : 1
}
```

Each field shown in the example has a meaning, as described in Table 11-3. These values can be used to understand the status of current members of the replica set.

Table 11-3. *Values for the rs.status Fields*

Value	Description
_id	The ID of this member as part of the replica set
Name	The member's hostname
Health	The health value of the replSet
State	The numeric value of the state
StateStr	The string representation of this replica set member's state
Uptime	How long this member has been up
optime	The time of the last operation applied on this member, in the format of a timestamp and an integer value
optimeDate	The date of the last applied operation
lastHeartbeat	The date of the last heartbeat sent
lastHeartbeatRecv	The date of the last heartbeat received
pingMs	The ping time between the member on whom rs.status() was run and each remote member
syncingTo	The member of the replica set to which this given node is syncing to match

In the preceding example, the rs.status() command was run against the primary server member. The information returned for this command shows that the primary server is operating with a myState value of 1; in other words, the "Member is operating as a primary (master)."

Forcing a New Election with rs.stepDown()

You can use the rs.stepDown() command to force a primary server to stand down for 60 seconds; the command also forces the election of a new primary server. This command is useful in the following situations:

- When you need to take the server hosting the primary instance offline, whether to investigate the server or to implement hardware upgrades or maintenance.

- When you want to run a diagnostic process against the data structures.

- When you want to simulate the effect of a primary failure and force your cluster to fail over, so you can test how your application responds to such an event.

The following example shows the output returned if you run the `rs.stepDown()` command against the `testset` replica set:

```
> rs.stepDown()
> rs.status()
{
     "set" : "testset",
     "date" : ISODate("2013-06-04T11:19:01Z"),
     "myState" : 2,
     "members" : [
          {
               "_id" : 0,
               "name" : "[hostname]:27021",
               "health" : 1,
               "state" : 2,
               "stateStr" : "SECONDARY",
               "uptime" : 5428,
               "optime" : Timestamp(1370340105, 1),
               "optimeDate" : ISODate("2013-06-04T10:01:45Z"),
               "self" : true
          },
          {
               "_id" : 1,
               "name" : "[hostname]:27022",
               "health" : 1,
               "state" : 2,
               "stateStr" : "SECONDARY",
               "uptime" : 4636,
               "optime" : Timestamp(1370340105, 1),
               "optimeDate" : ISODate("2013-06-04T10:01:45Z"),
               "lastHeartbeat" : ISODate("2013-06-04T11:19:00Z"),
               "lastHeartbeatRecv" : ISODate("2013-06-04T11:19:00Z"),
               "pingMs" : 0,
               "syncingTo" : "[hostname]:27021"
          },
          {
               "_id" : 2,
               "name" : "[hostname]:27023",
               "health" : 1,
               "state" : 2,
               "stateStr" : "SECONDARY",
               "uptime" : 4636,
               "optime" : Timestamp(1370340105, 1),
               "optimeDate" : ISODate("2013-06-04T10:01:45Z"),
               "lastHeartbeat" : ISODate("2013-06-04T11:19:01Z"),
               "lastHeartbeatRecv" : ISODate("2013-06-04T11:19:00Z"),
               "pingMs" : 0,
```

```
                "lastHeartbeatMessage" : "db exception in producer: 10278 dbclient error
communicating with server: [hostname]:27021",
                "syncingTo" : "[hostname]:27021"
            }
    ],
    "ok" : 1
}
```

In this example, you ran the rs.stepDown() command against the primary server. The output of the rs.status() command shows that all members of the replica set are now secondaries. If you run rs.status() subsequently, you should see that another member has stepped up to be primary (assuming one is eligible).

Determining If a Member Is the Primary Server

The db.isMaster() command isn't strictly for replica sets. Nevertheless, this command is extremely useful because it allows an application to test whether a current connection is to a primary server:

```
>db.isMaster()
{
    "setName" : "testset",
    "ismaster" : true,
    "secondary" : false,
    "hosts" : [
        "[hostname]:27022",
        "[hostname]:27021"
    ],
    "primary" : "[hostname]:27022",
    "me" : "[hostname]:27022",
    "maxBsonObjectSize" : 16777216,
    "maxMessageSizeBytes" : 48000000,
    "localTime" : ISODate("2013-06-04T11:22:28.771Z"),
    "ok" : 1
}
```

If you run isMaster() against your testset replica set cluster at this point, it shows that the server you have run it against is not a master/primary server ("ismaster" == false). If the server instance you run this command against is a member of a replica set, the command will also return a map of the known server instances in the set, including the roles of the individual servers in that set.

Configuring the Options for Replica Set Members

The replica set functionality includes a number of options you can use to control the behavior of a replica set's members. When you run the rs.initiate(*replSetcfg*) or rs.add(*membercfg*) options, you have to supply a configuration structure that describes the characteristics of a replica set's members:

```
{
  _id : <setname>,

  members: [
    {
      _id : <ordinal>,
      host : <hostname[:port]>,
```

```
        [ priority: <priority>, ]
        [arbiterOnly : true, ]
        [ votes : <n>, ]
        [ hidden: true, ]
        [ tags: { document }, ]
        [ slaveDelay: <seconds>, ]
        [ buildIndexes: true, ]
      }
      , ...
  ],

  settings: {
    [ chainingAllowed : <boolean>, ]
    [ getLastErrorModes: <modes>, ]
    [ getLastErrorDefaults: <lasterrdefaults>, ]
  }
}
```

For rs.initiate(), you should supply the full configuration structure, as shown here. The topmost level of the configuration structure itself includes three levels: _id, members, and settings. The _id is the name of the replica set, as supplied with the --replSet command-line option when you create the replica set members. The members array consists of a set of structures that describe each member of the set; this is the member structure that you supply to the rs.add() command when adding an individual server to the set. Finally, the settings array contains options that apply to the entire replica set.

Organization of the members Structure

The members structure contains all the entries required to configure each of the member instances of the replica set; you can see all of these entries listed in Table 11-4.

Table 11-4. *Configuring Member Server Properties*

Option	Description
members.$._id	(Mandatory) Integer: This element specifies the ordinal position of the member structure in the member array. Possible values for this element include integers greater than or equal to 0. This value enables you to address specific member structures, so you can perform add, remove, and overwrite operations.
members.$.host	(Mandatory) String: This element specifies the name of the server in the form host:port; note that the host portion *cannot* be localhost or 127.0.0.1.
members.$.priority	(Optional) Float: The element represents the *weight* assigned to the server when elections for a new primary server are conducted. If the primary server becomes unavailable, then a secondary server will be promoted based on this value. Any secondary server with a nonzero value is considered to be active and eligible to become a primary server. Thus, setting this value to zero forces the secondary to become passive. If multiple secondary servers share equal priority, then a vote will be taken, and an arbiter (if configured) may be called upon to resolve any deadlocks. The default value for this element is 1.0.

(*continued*)

Table 11-4. (*continued*)

Option	Description
members.$.arbiterOnly	(Optional) Boolean: This member operates as an arbiter for electing new primary servers. It is not involved in any other function of the replica set, and it does not need to have been started with a --replSet command-line option. Any running mongod process in your system can perform this task. The default value of this element is false.
members.$.votes	(Optional) Integer: This element specifies the number of votes the instance can cast to elect other instances as a primary server; the default value of this element is 1.
members.$. hidden	(Optional) Boolean: This hides the node from the output of db.isMaster() and so prevents read operations from occurring on the node, even with a secondary read preference.
members.$.tags	(Optional) Document: This allows you to set the tags for replica set tagged read preferences.
members.$.slaveDelay	(Optional) Integer: This allows you to set the slave to be "delayed" a specified number of seconds behind the primary.
members.$.buildIndexes	(Optional) Boolean: This option is used to disable the building of indexes. It should never bet set on a node that can theoretically become primary. This capability can be useful for backup nodes and the like when indexes are unimportant and you wish to save space.

Exploring the Options Available in the Settings Structure

Table 11-5 lists the replica set properties available in the Settings structure. These settings are applied globally to the entire replica set; you use these properties to configure how replica set members communicate with each other.

Table 11-5. *Inter-server Communication Properties for the Settings Structure*

Option	Description
settings.chainingAllowed	(Optional) Boolean: Allows you to specify if the member is allowed to replicate from other secondaries. Defaults to true
settings.getLastErrorModes	(Optional) Modes: Used in setting custom write concerns, as described later in this chapter.
Settings.getLastErrorDefaults	(Optional) Defaults: Used in setting custom write concerns

Connecting to a Replica Set from Your Application

Connecting to a replica set from PHP is similar to connecting to a single MongoDB instance. The only difference is that it can provide either a single replica set instance address or a list of replica set members; the connection library will work out which server is the primary server and direct queries to that machine, even if the primary server is not one of the members that you provide. For this reason it is often best to specify multiple members in your connection string regardless; this way, you remove the risk associated with trying to discover from only one member which may be offline. The following example shows how to connect to a replica set from a PHP application:

```php
<?php

$m = new MongoClient("mongodb://localhost:27021,
        localhost:27022", array("replicaSet" => "testSet"));
...
?>
```

Setting Read Preference from within Your Application

A read preference in MongoDB is a way to select which members of a replica set you wish to read from. By specifying a read preference to your driver you tell it to run queries against a particular member (or members) of a replica set. Currently there are five modes that you can set as read preference on your driver, as listed in Table 11-6.

Table 11-6. *Read Preference Options*

Option	Description
Primary	Reads will only be directed at the primary. This read preference is blocked if used explicitly in conjunction with tagged read preferences. This is also the default read preference.
PrimaryPreferred	Reads will be directed at the primary, unless there is no primary available; then reads will be directed at a secondary.
Secondary	Reads will only be directed at secondary nodes. If no secondary is available, this option will generate an exception.
SecondaryPreferred	Reads will be directed at a secondary unless none is available; then reads will be directed at a primary. This corresponds to the behavior of the old "slaveOk" secondary read method.
Nearest	Reads from the nearest node regardless of whether that is a primary or secondary. Nearest uses network latency to determine which node to use.

■ **Note** If you set a read preference that means your reads may come from a secondary, you must be aware that this data may not be fully up to date; certain operations may not have been replicated from your primary.

You can set a read preference in PHP using the setReadPreference() command on a connection object as follows:

```php
<?php
$m = new MongoClient("mongodb://localhost:27021,
        localhost:27022", array("replicaSet" => "testSet"));
$m->setReadPreference(MongoClient::RP_SECONDARY_PREFERRED, array());
...
?>
```

And from now, any queries you make on that connection will be run against secondary nodes in your cluster. You can also set read preference by adding a read preference tag to your URI. A URI with a read preference of nearest specified would look like this:

```
mongodb://localhost:27021,localhost:27022?readPreference=nearest
```

Setting Write Concern from within Your Application

Write concern is a similar concept to read preference. You use write concern to specify how many nodes this data needs to have been safely committed to before it is considered to be "complete. "This test is done using MongoDB's Get Last Error (GLE) mechanism to check the last error that occurred on the connection. You can set several write concern modes, which allow you to configure how certain you are that a write will be persisted when it is executed. Each is listed in Table 11-7.

Table 11-7. MongoDB Write Concern Levels

Option	Description
W=0 or Unacknowledged	A fire-and-forget write. The write will be sent, but no attempt to acknowledge if it was committed will be made.
W=1 or Acknowledged	A write must be confirmed by the primary. This is the default.
W=N or Replica Set Acknowledged	The primary must confirm the write, and N–1 members must replicate this write from the primary. This option is more robust but can cause delays if there is replication lag on members in your replica set, or if not enough members are up at the time the write is committed because of an outage or the like.
W=Majority	A write must be written to the primary and replicated by enough members that a majority of members in the set have confirmed the write. As with w=n, this can cause problems during outages or if there is replication lag.
J=true or Journaled	Can be used with w= write concerns to specify that the write must be persisted to the journal to be considered confirmed.

In order to use a write concern with an insert, you simply add the w option to the given insert() function, as shown here:

```
$col->insert($document, array("w" => 1));
```

This attempts to insert a document into our collection with a w=1 value for an acknowledged write.

Using Tags for Read Preference and Write Concern

In addition to the read preference and write concern options just discussed, there is another way you can proceed—tags. This mechanism allows you to set custom tags on members of your replica sets and then use these tags with your read preference and write concern settings to direct operations in a more granular fashion. So, without further ado, let's get started. You can set tags on your replica set by adding them to the tags section of your replica set config file. Let's start by adding tags for sites of a and b to our replica set config:

```
conf=rs.conf()
conf.members[0].tags = {site : "a"}
conf.members[1].tags = {site : "b"}
conf.members[2].tags = {site : "a"}
rs.reconfigure(conf)
```

Now we can check out our new config and you can see that we have set our two sites in place; they are defined in the tags section of each configuration document.

```
rs.conf()
{
     "_id" : "testset",
     "version" : 8,
     "members" : [
          {
               "_id" : 0,
               "host" : "Pixl.local:27021",
               "tags" : {
                    "site" : "a"
               }
          },
          {
               "_id" : 1,
               "host" : "Pixl.local:27022",
               "tags" : {
                    "site" : "b"
               }
          },
          {
               "_id" : 2,
               "host" : "Pixl.local:27023",
               "priority" : 0,
               "hidden" : true,
               "tags" : {
                    "site" : "a"
               }
          },
          {
               "_id" : 3,
               "host" : "Pixl.local:27024",
               "arbiterOnly" : true
          }
     ]
}
```

Now let's start making use of our new tags! We can set a read preference of the nearest member of our replica set in site a.

```
$m->setReadPreference(MongoClient::RP_NEAREST, array(    array('site' => 'a'),));
```

Now that we have tackled read preference, let's start on write concern. Write concern is slightly more complex, as we first need to modify our replica set configuration to add the extra getLastErrorModes. In this case we want to create a write concern stating that a given write must be committed to enough nodes to have been written to two different sites. This means a write must at minimum be committed to site a and site b. To do this we need to set the getLastErrorModes variable to be a document that contains the name of our new write concern and a rule that says we want it written to two different "site" tags. This is done as follows:

```
conf = rs.conf()
conf.settings. getLastErrorModes = { bothSites : { "site": 2 } } }
rs.reconfig(conf)
```

Now we need to insert our document and specify our new write concern.

```
$col->insert($document, array("w" => "bothSites"));
```

It's as easy as that. Now we can guarantee that our writes are committed to both sites! Now, let's say we want to make this the default write concern for any write made to our cluster.

```
conf = rs.conf()
conf.settings.getLastErrorDefaults = { bothSites : 1 } }
rs.reconfig(conf)
```

Now any writes we make will be made using the default write concern of bothSites. So if we just perform a vanilla insert!

Summary

MongoDB provides a rich set of tools for implementing redundant and robust replication topologies. In this chapter, you learned about many of these tools, including some of the reasons and motivations for using them. You also learned how to set up many different replica set topologies. Additionally, you learned how to inspect the status of replication systems using both the command-line tools and the built-in web interface. And finally, you learned how to set up and configure read preferences and write concerns to ensure that you are reading from and writing to the correct places.

Please take the time required to evaluate each of the options and functions described in this chapter to make sure you build a replica set best suited to your particular needs before attempting to use one in a production environment. It is incredibly easy to use MongoDB to create test beds on a single machine; just as we have done in this chapter. Therefore you are strongly encouraged to experiment with each method to make sure that you fully understand the benefits and limitations of each approach, including how it will perform with your particular data and application.

■ ■ ■

## CHAPTER 12

Sharding

Whether you're building the next Facebook or just a simple database application, you will probably need to scale your app up at some point if it's successful. If you don't want to be continually replacing your hardware (or you begin approaching the limits of what you can do on just one piece of hardware), then you will want to use a technique that allows you to add capacity incrementally to your system, as you need it. *Sharding* is a technique that allows you to spread your data across multiple machines, yet does so in a way that mimics an app hitting a single database.

Ideally suited for cloud-based computing platforms, sharding as implemented by MongoDB is perfect for dynamic, load-sensitive automatic scaling, where you ramp up your capacity as you need it and turn it down when you don't.

This chapter will walk you through implementing sharding in MongoDB and will look at some of the advanced functionality provided within MongoDB's sharding implementation, such as tag sharding and hashed shard keys.

Exploring the Need for Sharding

When the World Wide Web was just getting under way, the number of sites, users, and the amount of information available online was low. The Web consisted of a few thousand sites and a population of only tens or perhaps hundreds of thousands of users predominantly centered on the academic and research communities. In those early days, data tended to be simple: hand-maintained HTML documents connected together by hyperlinks. The original design objective of the protocols that make up the Web was to provide a means of creating navigable references to documents stored on different servers around the Internet.

Even a current big brand name such as Yahoo! had only a minuscule presence on the Web compared to its offerings today. The original product around which the company was formed was the Yahoo directory, little more than a network of hand-edited links to popular sites. These links were maintained by a small but enthusiastic band of people called *the surfers*. Each page in the Yahoo directory was a simple HTML document stored in a tree of filesystem directories and maintained using a simple text editor.

But as the size of the net started to explode—and the number of sites and visitors started its near-vertical climb upwards—the sheer volume of resources available forced the early Web pioneers to move away from simple documents to more complex dynamic page generation from separate data stores.

Search engines started to spider the Web and pull together databases of links that today number in the hundreds of billions of links and tens of billions of stored pages.

These developments prompted the movement to datasets managed and maintained by evolving content management systems that were stored mainly in databases for easier access.

At the same time, new kinds of services evolved that stored more than just documents and link sets. For example, audio, video, events, and all kinds of other data started to make their way into these huge datastores. This process is often described as the "industrialization of data"—and in many ways it shares parallels with the industrial revolution centered on manufacturing during the 19th century.

Eventually, every successful company on the Web faces the problem of how to access the data stored in these mammoth databases. They find that there are only so many queries per second that can be handled with a single database server, and network interfaces and disk drives can only transfer so many megabytes per second to and from the web servers. Companies that provide web-based services can quickly find themselves exceeding the performance of a single server, network, or drive array. In such cases, they are compelled to divide and distribute their massive collections of data. The usual solution is to *partition* these mammoth chunks of data into smaller pieces that can be managed more reliably and quickly. At the same time, these companies need to maintain the ability to perform operations across the entire breadth of the data held in their large clusters of machines.

Replication, which you learned about in some detail in Chapter 11, can be an effective tool for overcoming some of these scaling issues, enabling you to create multiple identical copies of your data in multiple servers. This enables you (in the correct circumstances) to spread out your server load across more machines.

Before long, however, you run headlong into another problem, where the individual tables or collections that make up your dataset grow so large that their size exceeds the capacity of a single database system to manage them effectively. For example, Facebook has let it be known that it receives over *300 million* photos per day! And the site has been operating for almost 10 years.

Over a year that's 109.5 billion photos, and that amount of data in one table is not feasible. So Facebook, like many companies before them, looked at ways of distributing that set of records across a large number of database servers. The solution adopted by Facebook serves as one of the better-documented (and publicized) implementations of sharding in the real world.

Partitioning Horizontal and Vertical Data

Data partitioning is the mechanism of splitting data across multiple independent datastores. Those datastores can be coresident (on the same system) or remote (on separate systems). The motivation for coresident partitioning is to reduce the size of individual indexes and reduce the amount of I/O that is needed to update records. The motivation for remote partitioning is to increase the bandwidth of access to data, by having more RAM in which to store data, by avoiding disk access, or by having more network interfaces and disk I/O channels available.

Partitioning Data Vertically

In the traditional view of databases, data is stored in rows and columns. Vertical partitioning consists of breaking up a record on column boundaries and storing the parts in separate tables or collections. It can be argued that a relational database design that uses joined tables with a one-to-one relationship is a form of coresident vertical data partitioning.

MongoDB, however, does not lend itself to this form of partitioning, because the structure of its records (documents) does not fit the nice and tidy row-and-column model. Therefore, there are few opportunities to cleanly separate a row based on its column boundaries. MongoDB also promotes the use of *embedded* documents, and it does not directly support the ability to *join* associated collections together on the server (these can be done in your application).

Partitioning Data Horizontally

Horizontal partitioning is the only alternative when using MongoDB, and *sharding* is the common term for a popular form of horizontal partitioning. Sharding allows you to split a collection across multiple servers to improve performance in a collection that contains a large number of documents.

A simple example of sharding occurs when a collection of user records is divided across a set of servers, so that all the records for people with last names that begin with the letters A–G are on one server, H–M are on another, and so on. The rule that splits the data is known as the *shard key*.

In simple terms, sharding allows you to treat the *cloud* of shards as through it were a single collection, and an application does not need to be aware that the data is distributed across multiple machines. Traditional sharding implementations require the application to be actively involved in determining which server a particular document is stored on, so it can route its requests properly. Traditionally, there is a library bound to the application, and this library is responsible for storing and querying data in sharded data sets.

MongoDB has a unique method for sharding, where a MongoS routing process manages the splitting of the data and the routing of requests to the required shard server. If a query requires data from multiple shards, then the MongoS will manage the process of merging the data obtained from each shard back into a single cursor.

This feature, more than any other, is what earns MongoDB its stripes as a *cloud* or web-oriented database.

Analyzing a Simple Sharding Scenario

Let's assume you want to implement a simple sharding solution for a fictitious Gaelic social network. Figure 12-1 shows a simplified representation of how this application could be sharded.

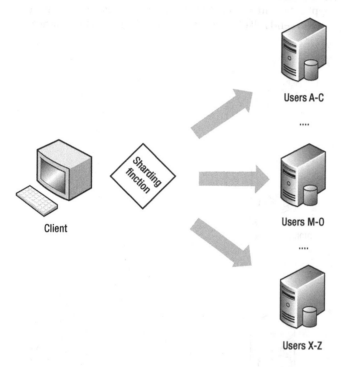

Figure 12-1. *Simple sharding of a User collection*

There are a number of problems with this simplified view of our application. Let's look at the most obvious ones.

First, if your Gaelic network is targeted at the Irish and Scottish communities around the world, then the database will have a large number of names that start with *Mac* and *Mc* (MacDonald, McDougal, and so on) for the Scottish population and *O'* (O'Reilly, O'Conner, and so on) for the Irish population. Thus, using the simple sharding key based on the first letter of the last name will place an undue number of user records on the shard that supports the letter range "M–O." Similarly, the shard that supports the letter range "X–Z" will perform very little work at all.

An important characteristic of a sharding system is that it must ensure that the data is spread evenly across the available set of shard servers. This prevents *hotspots* that can affect the overall performance of the cluster from developing. Let's call this *Requirement 1: The ability to distribute data evenly across all shards.*

Another thing to keep in mind: when you split your dataset across multiple servers, you effectively increase your dataset's vulnerability to hardware failure. That is, you increase the chance that a single server failure will affect the availability of your data as you add servers. Again, an important characteristic of a reliable sharding system is that— like a RAID system commonly used with disk drives—it stores each piece of data on more than one server, and it can tolerate individual shard servers becoming unavailable. Let's call this *Requirement 2: The ability to store shard data in a fault-tolerant fashion.*

Finally, you want to make sure that you can add or remove servers from the set of shards without having to back up and restore the data and *redistribute* it across a smaller or larger set of shards. Further, you need to be able to do this without causing any down time on the cluster. Let's call this *Requirement 3: The ability to add or remove shards while the system is running.*

The upcoming sections will cover how to address these requirements.

Implementing Sharding with MongoDB

MongoDB uses a *proxy* mechanism to support sharding (see Figure 12-2); the provided mongos daemon acts as a *controller* for multiple mongod-based shard servers. Your application attaches to the mongos process as though it were a single MongoDB database server; thereafter, your application sends all of its commands (such as updates, queries, and deletes) to that mongos process.

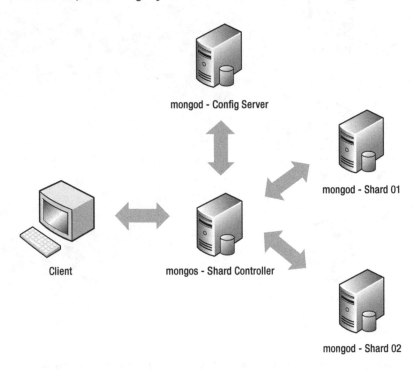

Figure 12-2. *A simple sharding setup without redundancy*

The mongos process is responsible for managing which MongoDB server is sent the commands from your application, and this daemon will reissue queries that cross multiple shards to multiple servers and aggregate the results together.

MongoDB implements sharding at the collection level, not the database level. In many systems, only one or two collections may grow to the point where sharding is required. Thus, sharding should be used judiciously; you don't want to impose the overhead of managing the distribution of data for smaller collections if you don't need to.

Let's return to the fictitious Gaelic social network example. In this application, the user collection contains details about its users and their profiles. This collection is likely to grow to the point where it needs to be sharded. However, other collections, such as events, countries, and states, are unlikely to ever become so large that sharding would provide any benefit.

The sharding system uses the shard key to map data into *chunks*, which are logical contiguous ranges of document keys (see Chapter 5 for more information on chunks). Each chunk identifies a number of documents with a particular continuous range of sharding key values; these values enable the mongos controller to quickly find a chunk that contains a document it needs to work on. MongoDB's sharding system then stores this chunk on an available shard store; the config servers keep track of which chunk is stored on which shard server. This is an important feature of the implementation because it allows you to add and remove shards from a cluster without having to back up and restore the data.

When you add a new shard to the cluster, the system will migrate a number of chunks across the new set of servers in order to distribute them evenly. Similarly, when you remove a shard, the sharding controller will *drain* the chunks out of the shard being taken offline and redistribute them to the remaining shard servers.

A sharding setup for MongoDB also needs a place to store the configuration of its shards, as well as a place to store information about each shard server in the cluster. To support this, a MongoDB server called a *config server* is required; this server instance is a mongod server running in a special role. As explained earlier, the config servers also act as directories that allow the location of each chunk to be determined. You can have either one (development) or three (production) config servers in your cluster. It is always recommended to run with three config servers in production, as the loss of your config server will mean you can no longer determine which parts of your sharded data are on which shards!

At first glance, it appears that implementing a solution that relies on sharding requires a lot of servers! However, you can co-host multiple instances of each of the different services required to create a sharding setup on a relatively small number of physical servers (similar to what you saw in Chapter 11's coverage of replication), but you will need to implement strict resource management to avoid having MongoDB processes compete with each other for things like RAM. Figure 12-3 shows a fully redundant sharding system that uses replica sets for the shard storage and the config servers, as well as a set of mongos to manage the cluster. It also shows how those services can be condensed to run on just three physical servers.

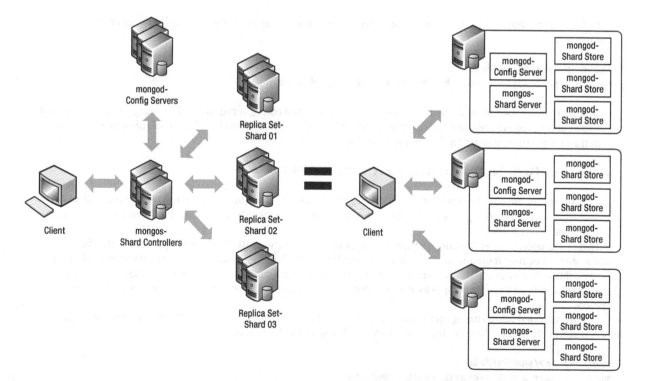

Figure 12-3. *A redundant sharding configuration*

Carefully placing the shard storage instances so that they are correctly distributed among the physical servers enables you to ensure that your system can tolerate the failure of one or more servers in your cluster. This mirrors the approach used by RAID disk controllers to distribute data across multiple drives in stripes, enabling RAID configurations to recover from a failed drive.

Setting Up a Sharding Configuration

To use sharding effectively, it's important that you understand how it works. The next example will walk you through setting up a test configuration on a single machine. You will configure this example like the simple sharding system shown in Figure 12-2, with two differences: this example will keep things simple by using only two shards, and these shards will be single mongods rather than full replica sets. Finally, you will learn how to create a sharded collection and a simple PHP test program that demonstrates how to use this collection.

In this test configuration, you will use the services listed in Table 12-1.

Table 12-1. *Server Instances in the Test Configuration*

Service	Daemon	Port	Dbpath
Shard Controller	mongos	27021	N/A
Config Server	mongod	27022	/db/config/data
Shard0	mongod	27023	/db/shard1/data
Shard1	mongod	27024	/db/shard2/data

Let's begin by setting up the configuration server. Do so by opening a new terminal window and typing the following code:

```
$ mkdir -p /db/config/data
$ mongod --port 27022 --dbpath /db/config/data --configsvr
```

Be sure to leave your terminal window open once you have the config server up and running, or feel free to add the --fork and --logpath options to your commands. Next, you need to set up the shard controller (mongos). To do so, open a new terminal window and type the following:

```
$ mongos --configdb localhost:27022 --port 27021 --chunkSize 1
```

This brings up the shard controller, which should announce that it's listening on port 27021. If you look at the terminal window for the config server, you should see that the shard server has connected to its config server and registered itself with it.

In this example, you set the chunk size to its smallest possible size, 1MB. This is not a practical value for real-world systems, because it means that the chunk storage is smaller than the maximum size of a document (16MB). However, this is just a demonstration, and the small chunk size allows you to create a lot of chunks to exercise the sharding setup without also having to load a lot of data. By default, chunkSize is set to 64MB unless otherwise specified.

Finally, you're ready to bring up the two shard servers. To do so, you will need two fresh terminal windows, one for each server. Type the following into one window to bring up the first server:

```
$ mkdir -p /db/shard0/data
$ mongod --port 27023 --dbpath /db/shard0/data
```

And type the following into the second window to bring up the second server:

```
$ mkdir -p /db/shard1/data
$ mongod --port 27024 --dbpath /db/shard1/data
```

You have your servers up and running. Next, you need to tell the sharding system where the shard servers are located. To do this, you need to connect to your shard controller (mongos) using your server's hostname. You could use localhost, but that limits the scalability of your cluster to this machine alone. You should replace the *<hostname>* tags with your own hostname when running the examples that follow. It's important to remember that, even though mongos is not a full MongoDB instance, it appears to be a full instance to your application. Therefore, you can just use the mongo command shell to attach to the shard controller and add your two shards, as shown here:

```
$ mongo <hostname>:27021
> sh.addShard("<hostname>:27023")
{ "shardAdded" : "shard0000", "ok" : 1 }
> sh.addShard( "<hostname>:27024")
{ "shardAdded" : "shard0001", "ok" : 1 }
```

Your two shard servers are now activated; next, you need to check the shards using the listshards command:

```
> db.printShardingStatus();
--- Sharding Status ---
  sharding version: {
      "_id" : 1,
      "version" : 3,
      "minCompatibleVersion" : 3,
      "currentVersion" : 4,
      "clusterId" : ObjectId("5240282df4ee9323185c70b2")
}
  shards:
      {  "_id" : "shard0000",  "host" : "<hostname>:27023" }
      {  "_id" : "shard0001",  "host" : "<hostname>:27024" }
  databases:
      {  "_id" : "admin",  "partitioned" : false,  "primary" : "config" }
      {  "_id" : "test",  "partitioned" : false,  "primary" : "shard0000" }
```

You now have a working sharded environment, but no sharded data; next, you will create a new database called testdb, and then activate a collection called testcollection inside this database. You will shard this collection, so you will give this collection an entry called testkey that you will use as the sharding function:

```
> sh.enableSharding("testdb")
{ "ok" : 1 }
> sh.shardCollection("testdb.testcollection", {testkey : 1})
{ "collectionsharded" : "testdb.testcollection", "ok" : 1 }
```

Thus far, you have created a sharded cluster with two shard storage servers. You have also created a database on it with a sharded collection. A server without any data in it is of no use to anybody, so it's time to get some data into this collection, so you can see how the shards are distributed.

To do this, you will use a small PHP program to load the sharded collection with some data. The data you will load consists of a single field called testkey. This field contains a random number and a second field with a fixed chunk of text inside it (the purpose of this second field is to make sure you can create a reasonable number of chunks to shard). This collection serves as the main data table for a fictitious website called TextAndARandomNumber.com. The following code creates a PHP program that inserts data into your sharded server:

```php
<?php
// Open a database connection to the mongos daemon
$mongo = new MongoClient("localhost:27021");
// Select the test database
$db = $mongo->selectDB('testdb');
// Select the TestIndex collection
$collection = $db->testcollection;

for($i=0; $i < 100000 ; $i++){
        $data=array();
        $data['testkey'] = rand(1,100000);
        $data['testtext'] = "Because of the nature of MongoDB, many of the more "
                . "traditional functions that a DB Administrator "
                . "would perform are not required.  Creating new databases, "
                . "collections and new fields on the server are no longer necessary, "
                . "as MongoDB will create these elements on-the-fly as you access them."
                . "Therefore, for the vast majority of cases managing databases and "
                . "schemas is not required.";
        $collection->insert($data);
}
```

This small program will connect to the shard controller (mongos) and insert 100,000 records with random testkeys and some testtext to pad out the documents. As mentioned previously, this sample text causes these documents to occupy a sufficient number of chunks to make using the sharding mechanism feasible.

The following command runs the test program:

$php testshard.php

Once the program has finished running, you can connect to the mongos instance with the command shell and verify that the data has been stored:

$mongo localhost:27021
>use testdb
>db.testcollection.count()
100000

At this point, you can see that your server has stored 100,000 records. Now you need to connect to each shard and see how many items have been stored in testdb.testcollection for each shard. The following code enables you to connect to the first shard and see how many records are stored in it from the testcollection collection:

$mongo localhost:27023
>use testdb
>db.testcollection.count()
48875

And this code enables you to connect to the second shard and see how many records are stored in it from the testcollection collection:

```
$mongo localhost:27024
>use testdb
>db.testcollection.count()
51125
```

■ **Note**   You may see different values for the number of documents in each shard, depending on when exactly you look at the individual shards. The mongos instance may initially place all the chunks on one shard, but over time it will *rebalance* the shard set to evenly distribute data among all the shards by moving chunks around. Thus, the number of records stored in a given shard may change from moment to moment. This satisfies "Requirement 1: The ability to distribute data evenly across all shards."

Adding a New Shard to the Cluster

Let's assume business is really jumping at TextAndARandomNumber.com. To keep up with the demand, you decide to add a new shard server to the cluster to spread out the load a little more.

Adding a new shard is easy; all it requires is that you repeat the steps described previously. Begin by creating the new shard storage server and place it on port 27025, so it does not clash with your existing servers:

```
$ sudo mkdir -p /db/shard2/data
$ sudo mongod --port 27025 --dbpath /db/shard2/data
```

Next, you need to add the new shard server to the cluster. You do this by logging into the sharding controller (mongos), and then using the admin command addshard:

```
$mongo localhost:27021
>sh.addShard("localhost:27025")
{ "shardAdded" : "shard0002", "ok" : 1 }
```

At this point, you can run the listshards command to verify that the shard has been added to the cluster. Doing so reveals that a new shard server (shard2) is now present in the shards array:

```
> db.printShardingStatus();
--- Sharding Status ---
  sharding version: {
    "_id" : 1,
    "version" : 3,
    "minCompatibleVersion" : 3,
    "currentVersion" : 4,
    "clusterId" : ObjectId("5240282df4ee9323185c70b2")
}
  shards:
    {  "_id" : "shard0000",  "host" : "<hostname>:27023" }
    {  "_id" : "shard0001",  "host" : "<hostname>:27024" }
    {  "_id" : "shard0002",  "host" : "<hostname>:27025" }
```

```
databases:
    { "_id" : "admin",  "partitioned" : false,  "primary" : "config" }
    { "_id" : "test",   "partitioned" : false,  "primary" : "shard0000" }
```

If you log in to the new shard storage server you have created on port 27025 and look at testcollection, you will see something interesting:

```
$mongo localhost:27025
> use testdb
switched to db testdb
> show collections
system.indexes
testcollection
> db.testcollection.count()
4657
> db.testcollection.count()
4758
> db.testcollection.count()
6268
```

This shows that the number of items in the testcollection on your new shard2 storage server is slowly going up. What you are seeing is proof that the sharding system is rebalancing the data across the expanded cluster. Over time, the sharding system will migrate chunks from the shard0 and shard1 storage servers to create an even distribution of data across the three servers that make up the cluster. This process is automatic, and it will happen even if there is no new data being inserted into the testcollection collection. In this case, the mongos shard controller is moving chunks to the new server, and then registering them with the config server.

This is one of the factors to consider when choosing a chunk size. If your chunkSize value is very large, you will get a less even distribution of data across your shards; conversely, the smaller your chunkSize value, the more even the distribution of your data will be.

Removing a Shard from the Cluster

It was great while it lasted, but now assume that TextAndARandomNumber.com was a flash in the pan and its sizzle has fizzled. After a few weeks of frenzied activity, the site's traffic started to fall off, so you had to start to look for ways to cut your running costs—in other words, that new shard server had to go!

In the next example, you will remove the shard server you added previously. To initiate this process, log in to the shard controller (mongos) and issue the removeShard command:

```
$ mongo localhost:27021
> use admin
switched to db admin
> db.runCommand({removeShard : "localhost:27025"})
{
    "msg" : "draining started successfully",
    "state" : "started",
    "shard" : "shard0002",
    "ok" : 1
}
```

The removeShard command responds with a message indicating that the removal process has started. It also indicates that mongos has begun relocating the chunks on the target shard server to the other shard servers in the cluster. This process is known as *draining* the shard.

You can check the progress of the draining process by reissuing the removeShard command. The response will tell you how many chunks and databases still need to be drained from the shard:

```
> db.runCommand({removeShard : "localhost:27025"})
{
    "msg" : "draining ongoing",
    "state" : "ongoing",
    "remaining" : {
        "chunks" : NumberLong( 12 ),
        "dbs" : NumberLong( 0 )
    },
    "ok" : 1
}
```

Finally, the removeShard process will terminate, and you will get a message indicating that the removal process is complete:

```
> db.runCommand({removeShard : "localhost:27025"})
{
    "msg" : "removeshard completed successfully",
    "state" : "completed",
    "shard" : "shard0002",
    "ok" : 1
}
```

To verify that the removeShard command was successful, you can run listshards to confirm that the desired shard server has been removed from the cluster. For example, the following output shows that the shard2 server that you created previously is no longer listed in the shards array:

```
>db.runCommand({listshards:1})
{
    "shards" : [
        {
            "_id" : "shard0000",
            "host" : "localhost:27023"
        },
        {
            "_id" : "shard0001",
            "host" : "localhost:27024"
        }
    ],
    "ok" : 1
}
```

At this point, you can terminate the Shard2 mongod process and delete its storage files because its data has been migrated back to the other servers.

■ **Note** The ability to add and remove shards to and from your cluster without having to take it offline is a critical component of MongoDB's ability to support highly scalable, highly available, large-capacity datastores. This satisfies the final requirement: "Requirement 3: The ability to add or remove shards while the system is running."

Determining How You're Connected

Your application can be connected either to a standard nonsharded database (mongod) or to a shard controller (mongos). MongoDB makes both of these processes; for all but a few use cases, the database and shard controller look and behave exactly the same way. However, sometimes it may be important to determine what type of system you are connected to.

MongoDB provides the isdbgrid command, which you can use to interrogate the connected data system to determine whether it is sharded. The following snippet shows how to use this command, as well as what its output looks like:

```
$mongo
>use testdb
>db.runCommand({ isdbgrid : 1});
{ "isdbgrid" : 1, "hostname" : "Pixl.local", "ok" : 1 }
```

The response includes the isdbgrid:1 field, which tells you that the database you are connected to is enabled for sharding. A response of isdbgrid:0 would indicate that you are connected to a nonsharded database.

Listing the Status of a Sharded Cluster

MongoDB also includes a simple command for dumping the status of a sharding cluster: printShardingStatus().

This command can give you a lot of insight into the internals of the sharding system. The following snippet shows how to invoke the printShardingStatus() command, but strips out some of the output returned to make it easier to read:

```
 $mongo localhost:27021
>sh.status();
--- Sharding Status ---
  sharding version: {
      "_id" : 1,
      "version" : 3,
      "minCompatibleVersion" : 3,
      "currentVersion" : 4,
      "clusterId" : ObjectId("51c699a7dd9fc53b6cdc4718")
}
  shards:
      {  "_id" : "shard0000",  "host" : "localhost:27023" }
      {  "_id" : "shard0001",  "host" : "localhost:27024" }
  databases:
      {  "_id" : "admin",  "partitioned" : false,  "primary" : "config" }
      {  "_id" : "test",  "partitioned" : false,  "primary" : "shard0000" }
      {  "_id" : "testdb",  "partitioned" : true,  "primary" : "shard0000" }
          testdb.testcollection
                shard key: { "testkey" : 1 }
```

```
chunks:
        shard0000    2
        shard0001    3
    { "testkey" : { "$minKey" : 1 } } -->> { "testkey" : 0 } on : shard0000 Timestamp(4, 0)
    { "testkey" : 0 } -->> { "testkey" : 14860 } on : shard0000 Timestamp(3, 1)
    { "testkey" : 14860 } -->> { "testkey" : 45477 } on : shard0001 Timestamp(4, 1)
    { "testkey" : 45477 } -->> { "testkey" : 76041 } on : shard0001 Timestamp(3, 4)
    { "testkey" : 76041 } -->> { "testkey" : { "$maxKey" : 1 } } on : shard0001
Timestamp(3, 5)
```

This output lists the shard servers, the configuration of each sharded database/collection, and each chunk in the sharded dataset. Because you used a small chunkSize value to simulate a larger sharding setup, this report lists a lot of chunks. An important piece of information that can be obtained from this listing is the range of *sharding keys* associated with each chunk. The output also shows which shard server the specific chunks are stored on. You can use the output returned by this command as the basis for a tool to analyze the distribution of a shard server's keys and chunks. For example, you might use this data to determine whether there is any *clumping* of data in the dataset.

Using Replica Sets to Implement Shards

The examples you have seen so far rely on a single mongod instance to implement each shard. In Chapter 11, you learned how to create replica sets, which are clusters of mongod instances working together to provide redundant and fail-safe storage.

When adding shards to the sharded cluster, you can provide the name of a replica set and the address of a member of that replica set, and that shard will be instanced on each of the replica set members. Mongos will track which instance is the primary server for the replica set; it will also make sure that all shard writes are made to that instance.

Combining sharding and replica sets enables you to create high-performance, highly reliable clusters that can tolerate multi-machine failure. It also enables you to maximize the performance and availability of cheap, commodity-class hardware.

■ **Note**   The ability to use replica sets as a storage mechanism for shards satisfies "Requirement 2: The ability to store shard data in a fault-tolerant fashion."

The Balancer

We've previously discussed how MongoDB can automatically keep your workload distributed among all the shards in your cluster. While you may think that this is done via some form of patented MongoDB-Magic, that's not the case. Your MongoS process has an element within it called the *balancer*, which moves the logical chunks of data around within your cluster to ensure that they are evenly distributed among all your shards. The balancer speaks to the shards and tells them to migrate data from one shard to another. You can see the distribution of chunks within the sh. status() output in the following example. You can see that my data is partitioned with two chunks on shard0000 and three on shard0001.

```
{  "_id" : "testdb",  "partitioned" : true,  "primary" : "shard0000" }
    testdb.testcollection
        shard key: { "testkey" : 1 }
        chunks:
            shard0000    2
            shard0001    3
```

While the balancer does all this work automatically on your behalf, you do have some say in when it operates. You can stop and start the balancer on demand and set a window in which it can operate. To stop the balancer, you connect to the MongoS and issue the sh.stopBalancer() command:

```
> sh.stopBalancer();
Waiting for active hosts...
Waiting for the balancer lock...
Waiting again for active hosts after balancer is off...
```

As you can see, the balancer is now off; the command has set the balancer state to off and waited and confirmed that the balancer has completed any migrations that were running. To start the balancer is the same process; we run the sh.startBalancer() command:

```
> sh.startBalancer();
```

Now, both of these commands can take a few moments to complete and return, as they both wait to confirm that the balancer is up and actually moving. If you are having trouble or wish to confirm the state for yourself manually, you can perform the following checks. First, you can check what the balancer flag is set to. This is the document that acts as the on/off switch for the balancer and it is located in the config database.

```
> use config
switched to db config
db.settings.find({_id:"balancer"})
{ "_id" : "balancer", "stopped" : true }
```

Now you can see that the document here with an _id value of balancer is set to stopped : true, which means that the balancer is not running (stopped). This, however, does not mean that there aren't already migrations running; to confirm that, we need to check out the "balancer lock."

The balancer lock exists to ensure that only one balancer can perform balancing actions at a given time. You can find the balancer lock with the following command:

```
> use config
switched to db config
> db.locks.find({_id:"balancer"});
{ "_id" : "balancer", "process" : "Pixl.local:40000:1372325678:16807", "state" : 0, "ts" :
ObjectId("51cc11c57ce3f0ee9684caff"), "when" : ISODate("2013-06-27T10:19:49.820Z"), "who" :
"Pixl.local:40000:1372325678:16807:Balancer:282475249", "why" : "doing balance round" }
```

You can see that this is a significantly more complex document than the settings document. The most important things, however, are the state entry, which says whether the lock is taken, with 0 meaning "free" or "not taken," and anything else meaning "in use." You should also pay attention to the timestamp, which says when the lock was taken out. Compare the "free" lock just shown with the "taken" lock next, which shows the balancer was active.

```
> db.locks.find({_id:"balancer"});
{ "_id" : "balancer", "process" : "Pixl.local:40000:1372325678:16807", "state" : 1, "ts" :
ObjectId("51cc11cc7ce3f0ee9684cb00"), "when" : ISODate("2013-06-27T10:19:56.307Z"), "who" :
"Pixl.local:40000:1372325678:16807:Balancer:282475249", "why" : "doing balance round" }
```

Now you know how to start and stop the balancer, and how to check what the balancer is doing at a given point. You will also want to be able to set a window when the balancer will be active. As an example, let's set our balancer to run between 8PM and 6AM, which lets it run overnight when our cluster is (hypothetically) less active. To do this, we update the balancer settings document from before, as it controls whether the balancer is running. The exchange looks like this:

```
> use config
switched to db config
>db.settings.update({_id:"balancer"}, { $set : { activeWindow : { start : "20:00", stop : "6:00" } }
}
```

And that will do it; your balancer document will now have an activeWindow that will start it at 8PM and stop it at 6AM. You should now be able to start and stop the balancer, confirm its state and when it was last running, and finally set a time window in which the balancer is active.

Hashed Shard Keys

Earlier we discussed how important it is to pick the correct shard key. If you pick the wrong shard key, you can cause all kinds of performance problems. Take, for example, sharding on _id, which is an ever-increasing value. Each insert you make will be sent to the shard in your set that currently holds the highest _id value. As each new insert is the "largest" value that has been inserted, you will always be inserting data to the same place. This means you will have one "hot" shard in your cluster that is receiving all inserts and has all documents being migrated from it to the other shards—not very efficient.

To people solve this problem, MongoDB 2.4 introduced a new feature—hashed shard keys! A hashed shard key will create a hash for each of the values on a given field and then use these hashes to perform the chunking and sharding operations. This allows you to take an increasing value such as an _id field and generate a hash for each given _id value, which will give randomness to values. Adding this level of randomness should normally allow you to distribute writes evenly to all shards. The cost, however, is that you'll have random reads as well, which can be a performance penalty if you wish to perform operations over a range of documents. For this reason hashed sharding may be inefficient when compared with a user-selected shard key under certain workloads.

■ **Note**   Because of the way hashing is implemented, there are some limitations when you shard on floating-point (decimal) numbers, which mean that values such as 2.3, 2.4, and 2.9 will become the same hashed value.

So, to create a hashed shard we simply run the shardCollection and create a "hashed" index!

```
sh.shardCollection( " testdb.testhashed", { _id: "hashed" } )
```

And that's it! You have now created a hashed shard key, which will hash the incoming _id values in order to distribute your data in a more "random" nature. Now, with all this in mind, some of you may be saying – why not always use a hashed shard key?

Good question; and the answer is that sharding is just one of "those" dark arts. The optimum shard key is one that allows your writes to be distributed well over a number of shards, so that the writes are effectively parallel. It is also a key that allows you to group so that writes go to only one or a limited number of shards, and it must allow you to make more effective use of the indexes held on the individual shards. All of those factors will be determined by your use case, what you are storing, and how you are retrieving it.

Tag Sharding

Sometimes, under certain circumstances it makes sense to say "I wish I could have all of that data on this shard". This is where MongoDB's tag sharding can shine. You can set up tags so that given values of your shard key are directed at specific shards within your cluster! The first step in this process is to work out what you want to achieve with your tag setup. In the next example we will work through a simple setup where we want to have our data distributed based on geography, with one location in the US and another in the EU.

The first step in this process is to add some new tags to our existing shards. We do this with the sh.addShardTag function, simply adding the name of our shard and a tag we wish to give it. In the example I have made shard0000 the US shard and shard0001 the EU shard:

```
> sh.addShardTag("shard0000","US");
> sh.addShardTag("shard0001","EU");
```

Now, in order to view these changes we can run the sh.status() command and review the output:

```
> sh.status();
--- Sharding Status ---
  sharding version: {
        "_id" : 1,
        "version" : 3,
        "minCompatibleVersion" : 3,
        "currentVersion" : 4,
        "clusterId" : ObjectId("51c699a7dd9fc53b6cdc4718")
}
  shards:
        {  "_id" : "shard0000",  "host" : "localhost:27023",  "tags" : [        "US" ] }
        {  "_id" : "shard0001",  "host" : "localhost:27024",  "tags" : [        "EU" ] }
...
```

As you can see, our shards now have the US and EU tags against their names, but these alone will do nothing; we need to tell the MongoS to route data for our given collection to those shards based on some rules. This is where the tricky part comes in; we need to configure our sharding so that the data we are sharding on contains something we can perform the rule evaluations against in order to route them correctly. In addition to this, we still want to maintain the same distribution logic as before. If you recall from the earlier discussion how chunks are broken down, you can see that for the most part we just need to have this breakdown by region occur "before."

The solution here is to add to our shard key an extra key that represents the region the data belongs in and have this as the first element of our shard key. So, now we need to shard a new collection in order to get these tags added:

```
> sh.shardCollection("testdb.testtagsharding", {region:1, testkey:1})
{ "collectionsharded" : "testdb.testtagsharding", "ok" : 1 }
```

■ **Note**   While the tag portion of a key does not need to be the first element, it is often best that it is; this way, chunks are first broken down by tag.

At this point we have our tags set up, we have our shard key, which will break our chunks up into nice regional pieces, and now all we need is the rules! To add these we use the sh.addTagRange command. This command takes the namespace of our collection, along with minimum and maximum range values, and the tag to which that data should be sent. MongoDB's tag ranges are minimum-inclusive and maximum-exclusive. Thus if we want anything that has a value of EU to be sent to the tag EU, we need to have a range from EU to EV. And for US we want a range from US to UT. This gives us the following commands:

```
> sh.addTagRange("testdb.testtagsharding", {region:"EU"}, {region:"EV"}, "EU")
> sh.addTagRange("testdb.testtagsharding", {region:"US"}, {region:"UT"}, "US")
```

From now on any documents that match these criteria will be sent to those shards. So let's introduce a few documents in order to test things. I've written a short loop to introduce 10,000 documents that match our shard key into the cluster.

```
for(i=0;i<10000;i++){db.getSiblingDB("testdb").testtagsharding.insert({region:"EU",testkey:i})}
```

Now we run sh.status() and can see the shard chunking breakdown:

```
testdb.testtagsharding
        shard key: { "region" : 1, "testkey" : 1 }
        chunks:
                shard0000       3
                { "region" : { "$minKey" : 1 }, "testkey" : { "$minKey" : 1 } } -->> { "region" :
"EU", "testkey" : { "$minKey" : 1 } } on : shard0000 Timestamp(1, 3)
                { "region" : "EU", "testkey" : { "$minKey" : 1 } } -->> { "region" : "EU", "testkey"
: 0 } on : shard0000 Timestamp(1, 4)
                { "region" : "EU", "testkey" : 0 } -->> { "region" : { "$maxKey" : 1 }, "testkey" :
{ "$maxKey" : 1 } } on : shard0000 Timestamp(1, 2)
                tag: EU  { "region" : "EU" } -->> { "region" : "EV" }
                tag: US  { "region" : "US" } -->> { "region" : "UT" }
```

From this we can see the breakdown of which chunks are where; there are three chunks on the EU shard and none on the US shard. From the ranges we can see that two of those chunks should be empty. If you go onto each of the individual shard servers, you will find that all of the 10,000 documents we inserted are on only one shard. You may have noticed the following message in your logfile:

```
Sun Jun 30 12:11:16.549 [Balancer] chunk { _id: "testdb.testtagsharding-region_"EU"testkey_MinKey",
lastmod: Timestamp 1000|2, lastmodEpoch: ObjectId('51cf7c240a2cd2040f766e38'), ns: "testdb.
testtagsharding", min: { region: "EU", testkey: MinKey }, max: { region: MaxKey, testkey: MaxKey },
shard: "shard0000" } is not on a shard with the right tag: EU
Sun Jun 30 12:11:16.549 [Balancer]  going to move to: shard0001
```

This message appears because we have set up our tag ranges to work only on the EU and US values. We can rework them slightly, given what we now know, to cover all tag ranges. Let's remove those tag ranges and add new ranges; we can remove the old documents with the following commands:

```
> use config
> db.tags.remove({ns:"testdb.testtagsharding"});
```

Now we can add the tags back, but this time we can run from minKey to US and from US to maxKey, just like the chunk ranges in the previous example! To do this, use the special MinKey and MaxKey operators, which represent the least and the greatest possible values for the shard key range.

```
> sh.addTagRange("testdb.testtagsharding", {region:MinKey}, {region:"US"}, "EU")
> sh.addTagRange("testdb.testtagsharding", {region:"US"}, {region:MaxKey}, "US")
```

Now if we run sh.status() again, you can see the ranges; this time, things look to be running better:

```
testdb.testtagsharding
        shard key: { "region" : 1, "testkey" : 1 }
        chunks:
                shard0001       3
                shard0000       1
            { "region" : { "$minKey" : 1 }, "testkey" : { "$minKey" : 1 } } -->> { "region" :
"EU", "testkey" : { "$minKey" : 1 } } on : shard0001 Timestamp(4, 0)
            { "region" : "EU", "testkey" : { "$minKey" : 1 } } -->> { "region" : "EU", "testkey"
: 0 } on : shard0001 Timestamp(2, 0)
            { "region" : "EU", "testkey" : 0 } -->> { "region" : "US", "testkey" : { "$minKey" :
1 } } on : shard0001 Timestamp(3, 0)
            { "region" : "US", "testkey" : { "$minKey" : 1 } } -->> { "region" : { "$maxKey" : 1 },
"testkey" : { "$maxKey" : 1 } } on : shard0000 Timestamp(4, 1)
                tag: EU  { "region" : { "$minKey" : 1 } } -->> { "region" : "US" }
                tag: US  { "region" : "US" } -->> { "region" : { "$maxKey" : 1 } }
```

Our data is better distributed, and the ranges involved cover the whole range of shard keys from the minimum value to the maximum value. If we further insert entries into the collection, their data will be correctly routed to our desired shards. No mess and no fuss.

Summary

Sharding enables you to scale your datastores to handle extremely large datasets. It also enables you to grow the cluster to match the growth in your system. MongoDB provides a simple automatic sharding configuration that works well for most requirements. Even though this process is automated, you can still fine-tune its characteristics to support your specific needs. Sharding is one of the key features of MongoDB that set it apart from other data-storage technologies. Following this chapter you should understand how to shard your data over a number of MongoDB instances, manage and maintain a sharded cluster, and how to take advantage of tag sharding and hashed shard keys. We hope this book has helped you see the many ways that MongoDB is designed to cope better with the rigorous demands of modern web-based applications than is possible using more traditional database tools.

Topics you have learned about in this book include the following:

- How to install and configure MongoDB on a variety of platforms.

- How to access MongoDB from various development languages.

- How to connect with the community surrounding the product, including how to obtain help and advice.

- How to design and build applications that take advantage of MongoDB's unique strengths.

- How to optimize, administer, and troubleshoot MongoDB-based datastores.

- How to create scalable fault-tolerant installations that span multiple servers.

You are strongly encouraged to explore the many samples and examples provided in this book. Other PHP examples can be found in the PHP MongoDB driver documentation located at www.php.net/manual/en/book.mongo.php. MongoDB is an extremely approachable tool, and its ease of installation and operation encourage experimentation. So don't hold back: crank it up and start playing with it! And remarkably soon you, too, will begin to appreciate all the possibilities that this intriguing product opens up for your applications.

Index

Get the eBook for only $10!

Now you can take the weightless companion with you anywhere, anytime. Your purchase of this book entitles you to 3 electronic versions for only $10.

This Apress title will prove so indispensible that you'll want to carry it with you everywhere, which is why we are offering the eBook in 3 formats for only $10 if you have already purchased the print book.

Convenient and fully searchable, the PDF version enables you to easily find and copy code—or perform examples by quickly toggling between instructions and applications. The MOBI format is ideal for your Kindle, while the ePUB can be utilized on a variety of mobile devices.

Go to www.apress.com/promo/tendollars to purchase your companion eBook.

All Apress eBooks are subject to copyright. All rights are reserved by the Publisher, whether the whole or part of the material is concerned, specifically the rights of translation, reprinting, reuse of illustrations, recitation, broadcasting, reproduction on microfilms or in any other physical way, and transmission or information storage and retrieval, electronic adaptation, computer software, or by similar or dissimilar methodology now known or hereafter developed. Exempted from this legal reservation are brief excerpts in connection with reviews or scholarly analysis or material supplied specifically for the purpose of being entered and executed on a computer system, for exclusive use by the purchaser of the work. Duplication of this publication or parts thereof is permitted only under the provisions of the Copyright Law of the Publisher's location, in its current version, and permission for use must always be obtained from Springer. Permissions for use may be obtained through RightsLink at the Copyright Clearance Center. Violations are liable to prosecution under the respective Copyright Law.

Get the eBook for only $10!

Now you can have the weightless companion with you anywhere anytime. Your purchase of this book allows you to the electronic versions for only $10.

This Apress title will prove so indispensible that you'll want to carry it with you everywhere, and this why we are offering the eBook in 5 formats for only $10 if you have already purchased the print book.

Convenient and fully searchable, the PDF version enables you to easily find and copy code—or perform examples by quickly toggling between instructions and applications. The MOBI format is ideal for your Kindle, while the ePUB can be utilized by a variety of mobile devices.

Go to www.apress.com/promo/tendollars/ to purchase your companion eBook.

All Apress eBooks subject to copyright. All rights reserved. No part of this work may be reproduced or transmitted in any form or by any means, electronic or mechanical, including photocopying, recording, or by any information storage or retrieval system, without the prior written permission of the copyright owner and the publisher.